Ethnicity and Nationalism in Africa

Constructivist Reflections and Contemporary Politics

Edited by

Paris Yeros
Department of International Relations
London School of Economics

First published in Great Britain 1999 by
MACMILLAN PRESS LTD
Houndmills, Basingstoke, Hampshire RG21 6XS and London
Companies and representatives throughout the world

A catalogue record for this book is available from the British Library.

ISBN 0–333–71213–7

 First published in the United States of America 1999 by
ST. MARTIN'S PRESS, INC.,
Scholarly and Reference Division,
175 Fifth Avenue, New York, N.Y. 10010

ISBN 0–312–21837–0

Library of Congress Cataloging-in-Publication Data
Ethnicity and nationalism in Africa : constructivist reflections and
contemporary politics / edited by Paris Yeros.
  p. cm.
Includes bibliographical references and index.
ISBN 0–312–21837–0 (cloth)
1. Ethnicity—Africa. 2. Nationalism—Africa. 3. Ethnology-
-Africa—Methodology. 4. Political science—Africa—Methodology.
5. Africa—Historiography—Methodology. I. Yeros, Paris, 1968- .
GN645.E833 1998
305.8'0096—dc21   98–28306
                                                                                    CIP

Selection, editorial matter and Chapters 1 and 6 © Paris Yeros 1999
Other chapters © Macmillan Press Ltd 1999

All rights reserved. No reproduction, copy or transmission of this publication may be made without written permission.

No paragraph of this publication may be reproduced, copied or transmitted save with written permission or in accordance with the provisions of the Copyright, Designs and Patents Act 1988, or under the terms of any licence permitting limited copying issued by the Copyright Licensing Agency, 90 Tottenham Court Road, London W1P 9HE.

Any person who does any unauthorised act in relation to this publication may be liable to criminal prosecution and civil claims for damages.

The authors have asserted their rights to be identified as the authors of this work in accordance with the Copyright, Designs and Patents Act 1988.

This book is printed on paper suitable for recycling and made from fully managed and sustained forest sources.

10 9 8 7 6 5 4 3 2 1
08 07 06 05 04 03 02 01 00 99

Printed and bound in Great Britain by
Antony Rowe Ltd, Chippenham, Wiltshire

Contents

Notes on Contributors   vii

Preface   ix

1. Introduction: On the Uses and Implications of Constructivism   1
   Paris Yeros

2. The (Re)Construction of Ethnicity in Africa: Extending the Chronology, Conceptualisation and Discourse   15
   Ronald R. Atkinson

3. A Non-ethnic State for Africa? A Life-world Approach to the Imagining of Communities   45
   Thomas Hylland Eriksen

4. Nationalism and Ethnicity in the Horn of Africa   65
   John Markakis

5. Rethinking Ethnicity: Identification, Hybridity and Democracy   81
   Aletta J. Norval

6. Towards a Normative Theory of Ethnicity: Reflections on the Politics of Constructivism   101
   Paris Yeros

7. Concluding Comments   133
   Terence Ranger

Index   145

Notes on Contributors

Ronald R. Atkinson is Associate Professor in the Department of History at the University of South Carolina. He has published *The Roots of Ethnicity: The Origins of the Acholi of Uganda before 1800* (1994), and numerous other works on the Acholi. He has also written on early Buganda history, on early Akyem in present-day Ghana, and on the effective teaching and learning of African history. In addition, from 1990 to 1996 he was the US co-editor of a joint US-South Africa project to develop programmes and materials in educational management and leadership for black school leaders in South Africa. He has written extensively in this area and is co-editor, with Judy L. Wyatt and Zeph A. Senkhane, of *The Effective Principal: School Management and Leadership for a New South Africa*.

Thomas Hylland Eriksen is Professor of Social Anthropology at the University of Oslo. He has published widely on ethnicity and nationalism, identity politics, globalisation, minorities, and other anthropological topics. His books in English include *Communicating Cultural Difference and Identity* (1988), *Us and Them in Modern Societies* (1992), *Ethnicity and Nationalism* (1993), *Small Places, Large Issues* (1995), and *Common Denominators* (1998).

John Markakis has a long teaching career in universities in the United States, Africa, Britain, and Greece. He has done extensive research in social and political developments in the countries of the Horn of Africa, and has published several books and many articles on the region, including entries in the *Encyclopaedia Britannica* (1995). Among his publications are *National and Class Conflict in the Horn of Africa* (1987) and *Resource Conflict in the Horn of Africa* (1998). He also edited *The Decline of Pastoralism and Political Conflict in the Horn of Africa* (1992), and co-edited *Ethnicity and Conflict in the Horn of Africa* (1994) and *Ethnicity and State in Eastern Africa* (1998).

Aletta J. Norval is Lecturer in Political Theory in the Department of Government, University of Essex. She is Director of the Graduate Programme in Ideology and Discourse Analysis. She has published widely on post-structuralist political theory as well as on South African politics, including *Deconstructing Apartheid Discourse* (1996), and she has co-edited, with David Howarth, *South Africa in Transition: New Theoretical Perspectives* (forthcoming).

Terence Ranger is currently Visiting Professor at the University of Zimbabwe, after holding Chairs in Dar es Salaam, Los Angeles, Manchester, and Oxford. He is the author of many books and articles on African history, and is editor, with Eric Hobsbawm, of *The Invention of Tradition* (1983).

Paris Yeros is a PhD student in the Department of International Relations at the London School of Economics, writing a dissertation on citizenship and social movements in Southern Africa. He has been an active member of the Association for the Study of Ethnicity and Nationalism (ASEN). He is former editor of *Millennium: Journal of International Studies*, and is also co-editor, with Sarah Owen, of *Poverty in World Politics: Whose Global Era?* (forthcoming).

Preface

This volume is the outcome of the conference on 'Ethnicity and Nationalism in Africa', held at the London School of Economics in May 1996, under the auspices of the Association for the Study of Ethnicity and Nationalism (ASEN). Its focus at the time was much broader; it was not intended as a 'constructivist reflection' of any sort. Rather, the idea was to bring together scholars from diverse disciplines to discuss the current issues, concepts, and methods in the study of ethnicity and nationalism. It was in the course of the conference that it became clear that all the contributors emphasised their 'constructivist' understanding of ethnicity and nationhood. What was less clear, however, was the meaning of constructivism itself. Less clear even was the relevance and implications of constructivist research in an era marked by the proliferation of ethnic conflict, 'democratisation', and the 'retreat' of the state in terms of both capacity and legitimacy. In this volume we have sought to focus on these issues and connections and to take the debate a step further. We have sought, first, to clarify the similarities and differences among those who have come to be known as constructivists; and second, to address the political implications of constructivist research.

Many thanks are due to a number of persons who contributed to the success of the conference. I would first like to thank Bruce Cauthen for his contribution to the organisation of the conference in the capacity of co-chair. I would also like to thank the panelists who, together with the present authors, contributed to the vitality of the discussion. They include Martin Dent, Obi Igwara, Shula Marks, Stanley Trapido, and James Mayall. Many thanks are due also to the conference participants.

Finally, I am grateful to the sponsor of the conference, ASEN, for supporting this initiative. I also wish to thank the London School of Economics for its ongoing support for the study of ethnicity and nationalism.

Paris Yeros

1. Introduction: On the Uses and Implications of Constructivism

Paris Yeros

There is less agreement than one might expect on what is 'constructivism', whence it emerged, and what are its implications. In this volume, we have proceeded under the assumption that we share something basic in our approaches to ethnicity and nationalism, both in Africa and in the contemporary world more generally. Basic among the contributors is an understanding of ethnicity and nationhood as phenomena that are socially constructed, that is, as products of human thought and action. The emphasis on social construction is, above all, an ontological one, and one that stands opposed to primordialist imaginings of the world.

Yet, to say that the contributors share this emphasis is not to say that they cohere neatly into a homogeneous 'school'. Indeed, as we begin to give our own particular accounts, it becomes immediately apparent that those who label *themselves* as constructivists, and hold true to the constructivist ontology, go on to draw on diverse conceptualisations of society and politics in spelling out what 'construction' actually consists in. Thus, constructivists disagree on what should be properly considered constructivist, what should be its precise theoretical point of reference, and what is its political significance. If an ironic analogy may be allowed, constructivism today resembles a nation-in-formation, busily invoking traditions, and preoccupying itself with its origins, purpose, and destiny.

In this context, the present collective exercise is concerned to reveal the diversity among those who label themselves as constructivists, and to critically assess the usefulness and implications of their concepts. The book thus revolves around two questions: What is constructivism? What are its political implications? The first question has entailed a retrospective inquiry into the emergence and 'soul(s)' of constructivism. The second question has entailed a critical inquiry into the usefulness of constructivist approaches with regard to contemporary politics.

By way of introduction, I will offer an account of the multifarious origins of constructivist thought as it relates to the study of ethnicity and nationalism in Africa. I will begin with a common conceptual reference point, the concept of the 'imagined community', and then look back and seek out other interpretive frameworks that could reasonably be considered 'constructivist' in the sense that I have noted above. These interpretive frameworks are variously represented in this volume, and I will locate the six contributions, however tentatively, within these frameworks. Along the way, I will also address previous attempts to define constructivism; these have resorted to the creation of typologies, distinguishing a 'model' constructivism from a primordialism and an instrumentalism. I will argue that such a typology is problematic, and I will suggest, instead, that there is a wide range of approaches that can claim to be constructivist (including a form of instrumentalism), such that it is best to speak of constructivisms of different sorts, with differing methods and politics.

On The Uses of Constructivism

In the development of the study of ethnicity and nationalism, the concepts of 'ethnicity' and 'nationhood' are often considered to be distinct.[1] They have had, consequently, a different set of theories aiming to explain their emergence and functions. Conventionally, ethnicity has been conceptualised within a continuum between primordialism and instrumentalism.[2] Meanwhile, nationhood and nationalism have been understood as phenomena that either owe their existence to various dimensions of 'modernity' – that is, the Enlightenment, industrialisation, capitalist social relations, print-capitalism, or the state – or to the determinate resilience of ethnicity in conjunction with modern socio-political circumstances.[3] Constructivists have not necessarily refuted this conceptual distinction. They have, however, produced conceptual tools that have been applied to both ethnicity and nationhood – and which also offer the possibility of transcending the distinction itself.[4]

One such concept that has been applied to both is 'imagined community', developed by Benedict Anderson in the early 1980s. In his own work, Anderson employed this concept mainly to demonstrate the emergence of nationhood at the historical conjunction of capitalism and print technology. However, by no means did Anderson limit 'imagining' to nationhood, as his account of religious communities makes clear. Indeed, he argued that all communities are imagined – differing only 'by the style in which they are imagined' – thus allowing for the possibility of employing the concept of 'imagining' for ethnicity as well.[5]

In this volume, Thomas Hylland Eriksen uses the concept of imagined community and pursues this line of argument further. He employs the concept of 'imagining' for the analysis of both ethnicity and nationhood, while maintaining the distinction between the two. He justifies this distinction on the basis of differences in the sociological underpinnings and symbolic referents of each, noting that nations, at the state level, need not be imagined and organised on the basis of the shared collective memories, territorial attachments, customs, and values of ethnic groups. With this conceptual distinction in mind, Eriksen sets out a 'life-world' approach through which to gain better understanding of the particular instances and structures of relevance through which each type of identity, whether ethnic or national (or gender or class, for that matter), is socially activated and invested with meaning. Eriksen attributes the activation and heightened politicisation of ethnicity to the failure of states to deliver social goods and to remain meaningful foci of allegiance.

Anderson's concept of 'imagining' has proved to be very versatile in this sense, and has been widely used. Notwithstanding criticisms leveled against it, it remains highly influential.[6] Moreover, it is often referred to as the 'departure' for constructivism in the study of ethnicity and nationalism. Undoubtedly, the ontological primacy that Anderson attributes to 'imagining' in the constitution of community locates him in the forefront of constructivist thought.

To refer to his work as *the* departure for constructivism, however, is also problematic. In the study of ethnicity in Africa, the constructivist departure has been traced further back to the 1970s. Ronald Atkinson gives an extensive account of this theoretical movement. Using Crawford Young's three-part typology of theories of ethnicity, which identifies the 'three ways' as primordialism, instrumentalism, and constructivism, Atkinson notes that the constructivist era of the 1980s was preceded by a number of 'early' constructivist approaches, the most influential of which were those of John Iliffe and Terence Ranger.[7] Both Iliffe and Ranger sought to demonstrate the novelty of ethnic consciousness and social organisation: their 'creation' or 'invention' during the colonial period by colonial administrators, missionaries, and African political entrepreneurs.[8]

These constructivist developments in the study of ethnicity in Africa cross-fertilised in the 1980s with the approaches of Anderson, Eric Hobsbawm, and Ernest Gellner which were concerned to demonstrate the novelty and modernity of nationhood, in Europe and elsewhere. The constructivist movement thus gained a more generalised and broader-based character. One important attempt to capture and make sense of this movement within African Studies in the late 1980s was the publication of the collection of essays edited and introduced by Leroy Vail, and entitled *The Creation of Tribalism in Southern Africa*.[9] This was an attempt to distill the essence, as it were, of constructivism as practiced by historians of Africa. It has often been referred to as the 'quintessential' constructivist statement, represented specifically by Vail's 'model' for the study of ethnicity. Young refers to Vail's model as one that contrasts instrumentalism and primordialism in that it does not 'take ethnicity for granted', and he proceeds to define constructivism as follows:

> [t]he constructivist inverts the logic of the instrumentalist and primordialist, both of whom presume the existence of communal consciousness, either as a weapon in pursuit of collective advantage

or as inner essence. The constructivist sees ethnicity as the product of human agency, a creative social act through which such commonalities as speech code, cultural practice, ecological adaptation, and political organization become woven into a consciousness of shared identity. Once a threshold is reached, the consciousness may become to a degree self-reproducing at a group level but continue to be contingent for the individual, who remains engaged in an ongoing process of transacting and redefining identity. The constructivist thus places higher stress on contingency, flux, and change of identity that the other two major approaches would concede.[10]

The attempt, however, to integrate constructivism into a single model in the above manner encounters the problem of reconciling several quite disparate approaches. For the significance of Vail's model lies mainly in its historisation of ethnicity, the long-term historical analysis that he and his collaborators employ, and not in its internal coherence. Vail's model draws on the insights of a number of interpretive frameworks, discernable among which are inventionism, Andersonian 'imagining', and instrumentalism.[11] The combination of these does not produce a new and sufficiently lucid conceptualisation of society and politics on the basis of which one can approach, select, and interpret historical events. The constituent frameworks are irreconcilable mainly because they are founded on dissimilar normative assumptions, and indeed give conflicting guidance as to the way in which one should conceptualise society, what to look for in the social process and how to interpret it. The significance of such normativity was made amply clear by Terence Ranger a decade after the publication of *The Invention of Tradition*, when he revisited and reassessed critically the 'invention of tradition' approach precisely on its normative assumptions. He compared this approach with that of 'imagined community', and showed the latter to be free of the politically disempowering assumptions of a top-down, once-and-for-all understanding of social change that are inherent in inventionism.[12] Combining any of these approaches requires, above all, a critical assessment of their normative assumptions.[13]

Vail's other contribution, nonetheless, should be emphasised. The long-term historical analysis that he proposes has given fresh impetus to the historisation of ethnicity. In this volume, both Atkinson and Ranger take this a step further, by extending their inquiry to the pre-colonial period. Specifically, central to Atkinson's argument is that current conceptualisations of ethnicity in Africa are restrictive insofar as they presume the 'modernity' of ethnicity, falsely requiring the presence of Europeans, colonialism, capitalism, and the modern state. Such a conceptualisation, he argues, grants too much power to colonial rule in Africa, denies African agency in social change, and implies the establishment of colonial rule in a political vacuum.

Atkinson proposes instead the extension of both the chronology and the conceptualisation of ethnicity, by investigating forms of collective identity and their construction prior to colonial rule. He refers to the case of a common Acholi consciousness in pre-colonial East Africa, constructed through a socio-political order based on chiefly institutions, a system of redistributive tribute, and symbols of sovereignty. From the late seventeenth century onwards, argues Atkinson, Acholi identity was dynamic and ever-changing; nonetheless, it provided an ethnic basis from which British colonisers could select in order to administer the Acholi as a 'tribe'.

Ranger responds to Atkinson on both methodological and empirical grounds. While agreeing that pre-colonial history should not be ignored, he inquires into a larger range of pre-colonial identities. He questions whether these should be interpreted as 'ethnic', and, furthermore, he cautions against interpreting pre-colonial African societies *only* in 'ethnic' terms. This line of inquiry, Ranger notes, is similar to the inventionist one in its polemical intentions, insofar as it aims 'not to deny identity to Africans, but to liberate them from the assumption that African identities always have and still are 'tribal'". Ranger argues that reading 'ethnicity' into kinship or language is not a straightforward matter, as languages co-existed, interacted, and syncretised, and as kinship was based on an idea of assimilation rather than one of descent. While ethnicity was one possible form of identity, Ranger argues that there is no reason to privilege this over other forms, such as those of citizen, townsman, subject, or believer. Nor is the project of inquiring into ethnic roots or 'latent ethnicity' on firm ground, for 'latent ethnicity' is a retrospective concept. It is useful only in bringing to light the variety of identities – based on belief, 'type of life', or place, for example – from which African political entrepreneurs and colonial administrators could choose, privilege, and reify as 'tribal' and as the basis for social organisation.

Interest in pre-colonial identities is of more recent historiographical vintage, as Atkinson indicates, and as a topic of research it is likely to receive increasing attention. Having said this, however, we are still left with the question as to whether the historisation of ethnicity – which, as I claim, has been the main contribution of Vail's model – merits differentiation as a 'third way'. Ultimately, such a claim would stand or fall depending specifically on the way in which one identifies the 'second way', instrumentalism. In his typology, Young clearly has in mind an instrumentalism that 'takes ethnicity for granted', and which can be contrasted, on that basis, to a constructivism that does not. Instrumentalism itself, however, is a very broad church, comprising theorists from traditions as different as functionalism, Marxism, and rational-choice, to name only three.[14] These have produced their own peculiar instrumentalisms, some of which cannot be usefully distinguished from a constructivism that 'does not take ethnicity for granted', and all of which, furthermore, are employable in long-term historical analysis.

John Comaroff, in his own assessment of constructivist approaches, has included instrumentalism as a form of constructivism, ultimately distinguishing only between a primordialism and a broadly defined constructivism.[15] I concur with such a categorisation, for the reason that there is no *necessary* connection between instrumentalism and essentialism. Instrumentalists need not take ethnicity for granted; nor are they incapable of adopting a long-term historical perspective. In this volume, John Markakis' instrumentalism is a case in point. While interpreting ethnic mobilisation as deriving from objective material interests, Markakis goes on to historicise the emergence of ethnic consciousness and nationalism. Importantly, he assumes neither the fixity, nor the homogeneity, nor the boundedness of the ethnic or national 'unit', while also drawing on Fredrik Barth's transactionalist insights to argue that ethnic boundaries and solidarity may be reinforced, as in the case of contemporary Ethiopia, where political competition and interaction is institutionalised precisely on the basis of ethnicity. Nonetheless, he argues that ethnic-constitutional solutions as that of Ethiopia should be viewed with caution, as one cannot take it for granted that such a settlement will deliver equitable distribution of resources, especially since it cannot be assumed that ethnic groups are internally integrated, with common interests, and one given unproblematic culture.

Once we allow for the inclusion of a non-essentialist instrumentalism in a broader category of constructivism, it would not be inappropriate to trace constructivism back to a further theoretical antecedent. I would argue that Fredrik Barth's transactionalist model was one of the earliest attempts to break away from a primordialist ontology (albeit not entirely successfully), and for this reason should be entertained as an early form of constructivism.[16] One should at least acknowledge that, while synthesising many of the insights produced by the Manchester School anthropologists, Barth concerted a new 'ethnicity paradigm' that became an important point of reference for Africanists and non-Africanists alike who sought to investigate the dynamic character of ethnic identity.

Given the breadth of our resulting constructivism, it is more useful to try to make sense of it and to assess it critically by distinguishing between types of constructivism. Comaroff, for example, has identified four constructivisms, namely a realist (*i.e.*, instrumentalist), a cultural, a political, and a radical historicist.[17] I offer a different typology, distinguishing between a empiricist/positivist form of constructivist theory and a 'normative' one. In the former, I include and distinguish between transactionalist, instrumentalist, inventionist, and moral ethnicity approaches – a distinction which has more to do with the underlying normative assumptions of each approach. These distinctions serve my purpose of critiquing positivist constructivisms precisely on the basis of their normativity, which, significantly, remains largely obscured by their positivist methods. Informed mainly by the work of Charles

Taylor, the 'normative' alternative to ethnicity that I put forth is concerned not with explaining an 'emergence' of ethnicity, but, ultimately, with engaging ethically and practically with the diverse political claims made in the name of ethnicity. Thus, I come to understand ethnicity as an array of political idioms, mainly those that refer to 'history', 'tradition', 'descent', and 'virtue', through which moral debate is made relevant and meaningful – much like the 'moral ethnicity' approach of John Lonsdale.[18] This is a debate in which we are all politically involved not least through the 'scientific' conceptions of ethnicity that we propagate. I argue that empirical constructivisms not only under-theorise this involvement; in the face of diverse political claims made in ethnic terms, they are equipped only with 'general' theories and 'empirically proven' images of ethnicity, through which they can only make summary moral pronouncements about ethnicity as a form of identity and politics that is either wholly legitimate or illegitimate.

This normative constructivism shares an affinity with Aletta Norval's approach, inasmuch as she also takes issue with positivist constructivisms. Norval argues that these interpret 'constructedness' via a conception of the social that is based on the objective/subjective dichotomy. Such a dichotomy enables the type of inquiry that separates out 'objective' interests from 'subjective' identity, and deems the former to be a more fundamental and a more proper realm of inquiry than identity itself. Drawing specifically on Judith Butler's post-structuralism, Norval understands the 'givens' of ethnicity neither as non-material nor as merely epiphenomenal, but conceives their materiality as a process that becomes stabilised over time. By this account, inquiry shifts to the process of identification itself: the process through which identities come to be seen as meaningful places of belonging and through which 'objective' interests themselves may be constructed.

Norval goes on to reserve the 'constructivist' label mainly for post-positivist approaches that do not rely on the objective/subjective dichotomy. Thus, whereas Young would identify a model constructivism that does not take ethnicity for granted, Norval identifies a model constructivism that does not take *objectivity* for granted. In Norval's category one could include Andersonian 'imagining', but more importantly, the full range of 'practice theories' whose ontology is not only constructivist in the minimal way in which I have defined it, but go further to give priority to, and theorise more extensively, 'social practice' as the fundamental social phenomenon by reference to which all social entities, structures, and identities are to be understood.[19] Norval's understanding of constructivism in the study of nationalism, with its emphasis on the symbolic, imaginary constitution of society, is increasingly becoming the most common one, and this probably owes much to the influence of Anderson's work.

It is important, however, to keep in mind the diversity of approaches that claim the constructivist label for themselves, on the basis of different criteria.

In this sense, writing the history of constructivist thought largely depends on the 'model' constructivism that one has in mind. If we take Norval's model, we would keep the primordialist and instrumentalist types in place, but the constructivist story would begin with post-positivist social practice theorists. If we take Young's model, we would again maintain the primordialist and instrumentalist types, but constructivism would begin with the early inventionists. If we take the broader, more inclusive understanding of constructivism that I follow here, then the constructivist story would begin with non-essentialist instrumentalisms and transactionalisms. This latter proposal, however, would further require the distinguishing between types of constructivisms, as many would differ in important ways in both their methods and politics.

The six constructivisms that are represented in this volume span the range from instrumentalism, to 'life-world' and other interpretations of 'imagining', and to a 'normative' and a post-structuralist approach. While these do not exhaust the possibilities, they provide a sample of the forms that constructivism may take and a focus for the assessment of the usefulness and political implications of constructivism.

On The Political Implications of Constructivisms

Besides trying to make sense of the origins of constructivisms, more important even is the question as to their usefulness and political implications. For the project of defining oneself in a constructivist tradition, and of developing concepts within it, is not an end in itself. Indeed, it is a futile exercise unless it enables us to make better sense of, and to act in, the world in which we live. If one accepts that our actions are informed by the way in which we make sense of our world, then we must be concerned with the political implications of the concepts that we develop and the methods that we use. This is no less important in the study of ethnicity and nationalism, where often 'social theory reappears as ideology', as Comaroff has keenly observed; 'each of the dominant approaches, dressed in local language and borne by "organic intellectuals", serves as both charter and alibi for one kind of identity politics'.[20] These concerns are more urgent still in a 'post-national' era marked by erosions in the capacity and legitimacy of states and by the intensification of ethnic politics. Thus, whether we are writing about identities in post-colonial, colonial, or pre-colonial Africa, or we are conceptualising ethnicity and how it works, we are participating in the political present, however diffusely.

The contributors address themselves in one way or another to this problematic. Hence, one concern that runs through the volume has to do with the question of 'whom theory is for' and 'for what purpose'. Alongside this, there is a concern with understanding the contexts and meanings of ethnic and nationalist politics; and, finally, there is a concern with expanding citizenship and deepening democracy. These three sets of questions are intimately related to each other.

The political nature of concepts and methods in the historiography of ethnicity and nationalism in Africa is addressed mainly by Ranger and Atkinson. Ranger has long been concerned with this, as his 'revisitings' of inventionism testify. In his original formulation of inventionism, Ranger posited the process of ethnification in a way that de-emphasised the agency of African societies.[21] As he later noted, the implication of a top-down concept of 'invention', combined with a static concept of 'tradition', was largely to remove Africans from the realm of politics. The removal was a double one, in the sense that it did not only efface the political agency of those who were 'ethnified', but it also undermined their capacity even to have a 'proper' (*i.e.*, non-ethnic) consciousness. The normative intentions of this formulation, however, were to demonstrate that Africans, not unlike anyone else, were not 'naturally' tribal, and could participate in other identities, particularly that of the nation-state. In his second thoughts on inventionism, Ranger sought to reconcile the novelty of ethnicity with his long-standing commitment to writing about African agency and resistance under European domination. Inevitably, the question that arose once again was which history should one be writing, for whom, how, and for what purpose. In his second formulation, Ranger sought to place more emphasis on the imaginative investment in ethnicity – to 'take ethnicity seriously', as it were – but at the same time to show the dynamism of ethnic identity and its contested nature. As such, Ranger's intention was to endorse an adaptable, inclusive ethnicity that could interact with a pluralist nation-state.[22]

Atkinson's response to this politico-historiographic question regarding agency has differed markedly from Ranger's second formulation, as well as his third in this volume. By writing about pre-colonial ethnicity, Atkinson seeks to disentangle the historiography of African ethnicity from a restrictive 'modernist' imagination whose furniture consists only of capitalism, colonialism, and the modern state. He thus also seeks to come to terms with the perenniality and intensity of ethnic consciousness in the post-colonial period. But his normative intention can be said to involve a 'reclaiming' of ethnicity, and thereby also African agency, by valorising autochthonous forms of *ethnic* consciousness. As such, Atkinson not only 'takes ethnicity seriously', but seeks to demonstrate African agency via ethnicity. It is here that the differences in the implications between Atkinson's and Ranger's formulations become clearer. In his third thoughts, Ranger focuses on conceptual difficulties pertaining to the use of the term 'ethnicity' when writing about pre-colonial identities. More importantly, however, on a methodological level, he warns against obscuring other identities when writing about ethnicity. In particular, Ranger warns against the dangers of privileging ethnicity in historiography at the expense of other identities, especially at a time when ethnic polarisation seems ubiquitous. He argues that other identities in the past were no less 'latent' than ethnicity. According to Ranger, these should be elicited and should register in our historical imagination.

What I would call the 'Africanising' of ethnicity by Atkinson and the 'going beyond' ethnicity by Ranger are two forms of politico-historiographic engagement with ethnicity. I would contend, however, that it is not necessary to judge ethnicity in such an 'either/or' manner, and that Ranger's second thoughts are still pertinent and useful. I argue that, if we reconceptualise ethnicity and agree that ethnicity and 'tradition' are dynamic as opposed to static, that they are not bounded but capable of syncretising universalist and particularist political languages, and that they do not serve a *singular* socio-political function, then we can also give ethnicity the benefit of the doubt: we do not need to assume that it has a *constant* moral standing, such that it must either be endorsed or rejected in its entirety. Political claims expressed in ethnic terminology may be of a counter-exclusionary nature, just as they may be of an exclusionary one. Lonsdale's concept of 'moral ethnicity' goes far in redefining ethnicity in a way which allows, and does not foreclose, the possibility of ethical debate *vis-à-vis* ethnicity. In this light, and in answer to the politico-methodological question posed above, if we consider ethnic discourse as entailing a moral debate, then we can also engage ethically with the ethnic process, and endorse the moral claims that contest exclusion. I would argue that such a possibility of an ethical engagement with the diversity of claims made in ethnic language is not possible within the interpretive frameworks of various functionalisms, rational-choice, and inventionism, all of which prejudge and predetermine our moral response to ethnic identification.

Engaging with ethnicity in such a manner necessarily presupposes what Eriksen calls a 'life-world' approach, one which seeks to understand the contexts within which ethnic identity becomes meaningful to the social actors themselves. In his chapter, Eriksen warns against developing concepts of ethnicity and nationhood that are incommensurable with the experienced life-worlds of the people in question, especially because policy recommendations flow from these concepts. The predominant paradigms of ethnicity and nationalism tend to 'caricature', in Eriksen's own words, 'those life-worlds, often creating contrasts between a (benign, liberal) cosmopolitan attitude and a (totalitarian, irrational) localist or ethnicist attitude; a kind of contrast which is less marked in ongoing social life than in social science models, and which is both inaccurate and potentially politically harmful'. Eriksen thus emphasises the profound differences in the structures of relevance on which theorists, on the one hand, and the people they study, on the other, draw in their constructions of identity. He argues that the symbolic, economic, and political investment in an imagined community occurs when this community offers in return something valuable, meaningful, and useful within the context of experience. In this light, the ethnification of societies occurs when the nation-state fails to retain its relevance and legitimacy as an imagined community which delivers these goods and when people activate other sub-state communities to provide for themselves. Our concepts of ethnicity and nationhood must reconcile themselves with these realities, without dismissing them as 'essentialistic'. Eriksen argues that we must meet this challenge by offering realistic conceptual possibilities for envisioning supra-ethnic nations. If our models of nationhood are to be relevant, they must give up the idea of homogeneity and extricate the concept of nationality from 'ethnic' types of imaginaries, mythologies, and symbolisms, whose conflation with nationality in the past gave rise to the post-colonial social engineering projects of 'nation-building'. Models of nationhood, argues Eriksen, must seek out pluricultural or civic/political possibilities.

These concerns send our inquiry down a parallel path. Concepts and methods in historiography and ethnography, as Eriksen suggests, ought not to be developed in a politically detached manner. That is, we ought also to be critically aware of the concepts of citizenship and democracy within which we are undertaking any ethnography or historiography, and how our understanding of ethnicity and nationality can be reconciled with these concepts. Conventional understandings of citizenship and democracy, and particularly their conceptual association with cultural/ethnic homogeneity, are being increasingly challenged and redefined.[23] In this volume, Markakis and Norval address further these conceptual problems and transformations; they offer a materialist and a radical pluralist account, with reference to Horn of Africa and South Africa, respectively.

Markakis addresses the constitutional changes presided over by the TPLF (Tigray Peoples Liberation Front) in post-war Ethiopia, and, specifically, the novelty and problems of a federal system whose constituent units are ethnic groups. Importantly, such a system legally uncouples citizenship in the Ethiopian state from nationality ('nationality' here meaning cultural/ethnic identity). Markakis argues, however, that, although the choice of ethnicity as the building block for democracy has been a realistic one in Ethiopia, its success is not guaranteed. 'If ethnicity was all about culture', he maintains, 'the Ethiopian formula could be a recipe for success. However, ethnicity is mainly about state power, and success or failure hinges upon whether or not the new arrangement will make power accessible to the larger groups on an equitable basis'. In this regard, the new order will be challenged by the long process of economic recovery and the distributive problems that are inherent in it. Markakis argues further that the efficacy of ethnicity as the basis of government will also be tested by the soundness of the assumptions relating to the internal homogeneity of ethnic groups and the use of linguistic criteria for their demarcation.

At the crux of this debate is the nature and moral status of culture and identity. Norval offers a contrasting account of the connections between identity and democracy. She problematises not only identity conceived as prior to culture, but also identity as culturally 'hybrid' when hybridity is assumed to be a feature only of marginalised groups, and when this in itself is assumed to be disruptive of exclusionary political orders. With reference to 'coloured' South Africans in the post-apartheid era, Norval argues that democratic politics do not directly follow from hybridity. Counter-exclusionary politics arising from the legitimacy of difference need to be intentionally articulated, in order to contest both coercive separateness, such as that of apartheid, and coercive unity, such as that inherent in the homogenising tendencies of liberal democracies. Radical democracy thus requires the active cultivation of difference. Norval emphasises that this is as important in relation to ethnic identification as it is in relation to the politics that contest the gendered exclusions within ethnic discourse.

Regardless of the merits of one interpretation or the other, the important point to draw out here is that there are a number of alternatives for reconceptualising citizenship and democracy in the process of abandoning the static and isolate 'cultural island' imageries of ethnicity and nationhood which are closely associated with conventional understandings of citizenship and democracy. Theories of ethnicity and nationalism, especially those with functionalist and primordialist ontologies, have in the past greatly contributed to such imageries. As such, they have also hampered our thinking about how dynamic and syncretic (or hybrid) understandings of ethnicity and nationhood can be reconciled with more dynamic and contextual concepts of citizenship and democracy.

This brings us back to our starting point, the concern with the political implications of constructivisms. Whether one is concerned with such historiographic and ethnographic questions as whose history to be writing and how to understand and evaluate the contexts and meanings of ethnicity and nationhood, one is already engaging with concepts of citizenship and democracy. The contributors to this volume – each with his or her own methods and politics, and all sharing the broad constructivist ontology – offer their own answers to various aspects of these questions. That which 'constructivism' appears to lose in its lack of homogeneity, it gains in its diversity and innovativeness.

NOTES

I am grateful to Dominique Jacquin-Berdal and Sarah Owen for their helpful comments on this chapter.

Introduction 13

1. See, for example, Anthony D. Smith, *National Identity* (London: Penguin Books, 1991).
2. For early primordialist and instrumentalist accounts, see Clifford Geertz, 'The Integrative Revolution: Primordial Sentiment and Civil Politics in the New States', in Clifford Geertz (ed.), *Old Societies and New States: The Quest for Modernity in Asia and Africa* (New York, NY: The Free Press, 1963), pp. 105–57, and Abner Cohen, *Custom and Politics in Urban Africa: A Study of Migrants in Yoruba Towns* (London: Routledge and Kegan Paul, 1969), respectively.
3. On the centrality of Enlightenment thought, see Elie Kedourie, *Nationalism*, Fourth Edition (Oxford and Cambridge, MA: Blackwell Publishers, 1993); on industrialisation, see Ernest Gellner, *Nations and Nationalism* (Oxford: Blackwell Publishers, 1983); on capitalist social relations, see Eric Hobsbawm, *Nations and Nationalism Since 1780* (Cambridge: Cambridge University Press, 1990); on print-capitalism, see Benedict Anderson, *Imagined Communities: Reflections on the Origin and Spread of Nationalism* (London and New York, NY: Verso, 1983); on the state, see John Breuilly, *Nationalism and the State* (Manchester: Manchester University Press, 1982); and on the ethnic origins of nations, see Anthony D. Smith, *The Ethnic Origins of Nations* (Oxford and New York, NY: Basil Blackwell, 1986).
4. Aletta Norval, for example, has argued elsewhere against the project of developing a theory of ethnicity as such, suggesting instead the need to theorise the processes through which all political identities are symbolically constructed; see Aletta Norval, 'Thinking Identities: Against a Theory of Ethnicity', in Edwin N. Wilmsen and Patrick McAllister (eds.), *The Politics of Difference: Ethnic Premises in a World of Power* (Chicago, IL, and London: The University of Chicago Press, 1996), pp. 59–70.
5. Anderson, *op. cit.*, in note 3, p. 6.
6. For critiques of Anderson, see Partha Chaterjee, 'Whose Imagined Community?', *Millennium: Journal of International Studies* (Vol. 20, No. 3, 1991), pp. 521–5; Christopher J. Ullock, 'Imagining Community: A Metaphysics of Being or Becoming?', *Millennium* (Vol. 25, No. 2, 1996), pp. 425–40; and Norval, *op. cit.*, in note 4.
7. See Crawford Young, 'Evolving Modes of Consciousness and Ideology: Nationalism and Ethnicity', in David E. Apter and Carl G. Rosberg (eds.), *Political Development and the New Realism in Sub-Saharan Africa* (London and Charlottesville, VA: University Press of Virginia, 1994), pp. 61–86.
8. John Iliffe, 'The Creation of Tribes', in *A Modern History of Tanganyika* (Cambridge: Cambridge University Press, 1979), pp. 318–41, and Terence Ranger, 'European Attitudes and African Realities: The Rise and Fall of the Matola Chiefs of South-East Tanzania', *Journal of African History* (Vol. 20, No. 1, 1979), pp. 63–82.
9. Leroy Vail (ed.), *The Creation of Tribalism in Southern Africa* (London: James Currey/Berkeley and Los Angeles, CA: University of California Press, 1989).
10. Young, *op. cit.*, in note 7, pp. 79–80.
11. See Leroy Vail, 'Introduction: Ethnicity in Southern African History', *op. cit.*, in note 9, pp. 1–19.
12. Terence Ranger, 'The Invention of Tradition in Colonial Africa', in Eric Hobsbawm and Terence Ranger (eds.), *The Invention of Tradition* (Cambridge: Cambridge University Press, 1983), pp. 211–262, and 'The Invention of Tradition Revisited: The Case of Colonial Africa', in Terence Ranger and Olufemi Vaughan (eds.), *Legitimacy and the State in Twentieth-century Africa* (Basingstoke: Macmillan

Press, in association with St. Antony's College, Oxford, 1993), pp. 62–111.
13. I take up these normative issues at more length in Chapter 6 of the present volume, where I compare and contrast the normative assumptions underpinning transactionalist, instrumentalist, inventionist, and moral ethnicity approaches.
14. For a comparison of functionalist and rational-choice instrumentalisms, see my discussion of the work of Abner Cohen and Robert Bates in Chapter 6.
15. John Comaroff, 'Ethnicity, Nationalism, and the Politics of Difference in an Age of Revolution', in Wilmsen and McAllister (eds.), *op. cit.*, in note 4, pp. 162–85.
16. Fredrik Barth, 'Introduction', in Fredrik Barth (ed.), *Ethnic Groups and Boundaries: The Social Organization of Cultural Difference* (Oslo: Scandinavian University Press, 1969). I address Barth's not entirely successful departure from primordialism in Chapter 6 of the present volume.
17. See Comaroff, *op. cit.*, in note 15, pp. 164–5.
18. See John Lonsdale, 'The Moral Economy of Mau Mau: The Problem' and 'The Moral Economy of Mau Mau: Wealth, Poverty and Civic Virtue in Kikuyu Political Thought', in Bruce Berman and John Lonsdale, *Unhappy Valley: Conflict in Kenya and Africa, Book II: Violence and Ethnicity* (London: James Currey/Nairobi: Heinemann Kenya/Athens, OH: Ohio University Press, 1992), Chapters 11 and 12, respectively.
19. For an overview of 'practice theories', and a Witgensteinian critique, see Theodore Schatski, *Social Practices* (Cambridge: Cambridge University Press, 1996); see also Judith Butler, *Bodies That Matter* (New York, NY: Routledge, 1993); Anthony Giddens, *The Constitution of Society* (Cambridge: Polity Press, 1984); and Charles Taylor, *Sources of the Self* (Cambridge: Cambridge University Press, 1989).
20. Comaroff, *op. cit.*, in note 15, p. 180.
21. Ranger, 'The Invention of Tradition in Colonial Africa', *op. cit.*, in note 12.
22. Ranger, 'The Invention of Tradition Revisited', *op. cit.*, in note 12.
23. Redefinitions of citizenship and democracy are being pursued from a number of perspectives. For a liberal account, see Will Kymlicka, *Multicultural Citizenship: A Liberal Theory of Minority Rights* (Oxford: Oxford University Press, 1995); for a critical-theory account, see Andrew Linklater, *The Transformation of Political Community: Ethical Foundations of the Post-Westphalian Era* (Cambridge: Polity Press, 1998); for a communitarian account, see David Miller, *On Nationality* (Oxford: Oxford University Press, 1995); and for a feminist account, see Nira Yuval-Davis, *Gender and Nation* (London: Sage Publications, 1997). See also the exchange between Charles Taylor and William Connolly: Charles Taylor, 'The Politics of Recognition', in Amy Gutman (ed.), *Multiculturalism: Examining the Politics of Recognition* (Princeton, NJ: Princeton University Press, 1994), pp. 25–73, and William E. Connolly, 'Pluralism, Multiculturalism and the Nation-state: Rethinking the Connections', *Journal of Political Ideologies* (Vol. 1, No. 1, 1996), pp. 53–73.

2. The (Re)Construction of Ethnicity in Africa: Extending the Chronology, Conceptualisation and Discourse

Ronald R. Atkinson

As the end of the twentieth century nears, ethnicity seems entrenched as a commanding presence in the world – as a powerful political idiom and mobilising ideology, as a significant component of popular consciousness, and as a major focus of academic discourse. This was not apparent just a few decades ago. Crawford Young notes that the years from the end of World War II through the 1980s 'witnessed the apotheosis of the nation-state...when this form of polity appeared astonishingly ascendant', or even 'a natural culmination of human progress and fulfillment of historic destiny'.[1] These, however, were transient impressions, fostered by a specific set of historical conjunctures in the post-War period and shattered by the end of the Cold War, the collapse of the Soviet Union, and the particular ferocity of 'ethnic cleansing', or 'ethnocide', marking civil wars in the former Yugoslavia and Rwanda.

By the mid-1990s, the 'vision of a nationalism triumphant' had also passed in Africa, as alternative identities and ideologies, often seemingly ethnic in nature, could no longer be suppressed, dismissed, or denied. In Young's words,

> [r]eality has progressively intruded into the reflections of political activist and academic analyst alike. Nationalism has vanished as a paradigm and bears more subdued hues as ideology. Ethnicity – as ideology and consciousness – acquires a deference as intellectual object which corresponds to its transparent impact in the real world of empirical events.[2]

This assessment of the importance of ethnicity in Africa as both a phenomenon in the real world (however imaginary it might also be) and as a subject for analysis and debate provides the beginning point for this paper. Such a stance is not meant to deny that ethnicity is a fluid, complex, and contested category – as both concept and phenomenon.[3] What this stance does challenge are arguments or assertions that disavow ethnicity as an appropriate or meaningful subject for academic discourse. One form of such disavowal contends essentially that ethnicity should not 'be taken too seriously' as a concept for analysis because 'the term proves to be of interestingly limited value'.[4] Anthropologist Philip Burnham adds two additional, often related arguments:

> [i]n some current anthropological circles, even to mention the words 'ethnic group' is to stand accused of siding with a colonialist anthropology that employed a highly reified and ideological notion of 'tribe' to serve its particular ends....Often linked with such theoretical positions is the view that to focus on ethnic conflicts in the recently independent states of Africa is an anti-progressive position, one that is inappropriate for social scientists working in these countries.[5]

In addition to recalling that both the practical and theoretical value or validity of such concepts as class and gender have been challenged in similar ways (if from different directions), Burnham's response seems right on target:

> I can only reply that to call a goat a sheep is no more an aid to understanding animal classification than is calling ethnicity by another name an aid to understanding political process. Such linguistic subtleties will not make the problem disappear.[6]

Nor will failing to address at all the conceptual and political issues associated with ethnicity.[7]

This paper address issues surrounding ethnicity in Africa in three parts. The first two trace the ways in which ethnicity has been represented and reconstructed over the last fifty years in the study of Africa, first within the disciplines of anthropology, sociology, and political science, and then in history. For reasons explored below, this half-century of scholarship has had an overwhelming twentieth-century focus, consequently privileging colonial (and post-colonial) ethnicity in Africa, with its 'modern' and often European components. The third part challenges this focus. Colonial rule in Africa was, undoubtedly, marked by powerful new forces that played a major role in shaping the particular manifestations of modern ethnicity all across the continent. At the same time, it seems at least as incontrovertible that African colonial rule did not occur in an historical vacuum, nor erase or totally overwhelm all that had gone before. Thus, I will argue, to ignore pre-colonial collective identities, fail to explore the dynamics involved in their construction and representation, or deny their relevance or resonance in the twentieth century – as does most of the literature – is an unwarranted and unnecessary limitation of both concept and chronology in the (re)construction of ethnicity in Africa.

Ethnicity in the Study of Africa

The academic study of ethnicity in Africa was pioneered by a group of anthropologists working out of the Rhodes-Livingston Institute in then Northern Rhodesia over the 1940s and 1950s. Their work explored the dynamics of urban inter-ethnic relations among African workers on the Copperbelt of Central Africa, dynamics that tended to heighten ethnic identities through ethnic-based competition and to produce standardised attitudes and interactions among such groups.[8]

Important as these studies were, they were necessarily products of their time. This meant, among other things, that the language in which they were couched was predominantly the language of 'tribe' (even if their approach did not fit many common perceptions associated with the term). Tribe, after all, was the typical characterisation of ethnic groups in Africa in both academic and popular thinking until the 1970s, and remains common in non-academic representations of African identity even now, including the media. What makes this point significant is the power of three widely-held stereotypes that accompany the notion of tribe, stereotypes that continue to resonate in popular consciousness today, even when the newer terms 'ethnicity' or 'ethnic group' are used rather than the older 'tribal' or 'tribe'.

The first of these is that people can be divided into two, virtually universal categories: those who are tribal and those who are not. Implicit in this view, writes Peter Skalnik, 'is the idea that the former...represent an earlier stage in human social evolution when people belonged to "tribes" rather than modern nations'.[9] That Africans 'naturally' belonged to tribes – unlike Europeans – was a cardinal tenet in the belief systems of almost all involved in colonial rule in Africa, and remains so for most Europeans (and Americans) today. Second, even though all Africans supposedly are members of entities called tribes, the criteria defining these tribes have proven elusive. One common idea is that tribes are politically defined units, although, as Skalnik notes, the concept and term persists in much popular thought 'precisely because it implies significant additional dimensions such as culture, language, territory and even race'.[10] Third, tribal identities are 'regarded as ancient and powerful, and not open to amelioration, so that animosity and tension arise whenever and wherever members of different "tribes" come into contact with each other'.[11]

By the later 1960s, the notion of 'tribe' began to be debated and criticised within anthropology.[12] Apart from such challenges, however, along with the earlier Copperbelt studies already noted and Abner Cohen's work on Hausa migrants in Ibadan, little in anthropology over the 1950s and 1960s dealt with ethnicity in ways that moved beyond a tribal paradigm or stereotypes.[13]

Outside of anthropology, the study of Africa during the 1950s and 1960s focused on politics and nationalism, as the forces of decolonisation swept across the continent. James Coleman and C.R.D. Halisi's survey of Africanist political science notes that the 1950s were dominated by studies of nationalism, political parties, elections, and ideology; during the 1960s, political modernisation also 'had an evanescent appeal'. Across the political spectrum, most political scientists (along with anthropologists and other observers) regarded ethnicity – or 'tribalism' as it was still usually called – as a parochial remnant of a 'traditional' past that was fated to be transformed or overcome by modernisation, nationalism, and nation-building. If ethnicity was dealt with at all, it tended to be treated reluctantly and with limited analytical emphasis.[14]

Historians were similarly influenced by the central political dynamic of decolonisation. Martin Klein has noted that Africanist history into the 1970s was 'political in focus…occupied with chronology, and…concerned to refute those who sold Africa short'.[15] These characteristics were part of an emphasis in this period on pre-colonial history, within which there was a focus on political history in general, and, in particular, on 'state-building' among African states or the 'enlargement of scale' in societies with state-like structures.[16]

By the end of the 1960s, then, the attention of most political scientists and historians working in Africa was directed to issues of politics and political developments. And even as some anthropologists (and others) were beginning to question the tribal paradigm, most academics, political pundits, and African political leaders – of all political stripes – either decried or ignored ethnic/'tribal' consciousness as a fading and unfortunate relic of Africa's 'pre-modern' past. It was at this juncture that Fredrik Barth's *Ethnic Groups and Boundaries* was published.[17] While Thomas Hylland Eriksen notes some 'clear predecessors' to this work – particularly the Copperbelt studies – this edited volume, and particularly Barth's introduction, marks a fairly sharp dividing line in the study of ethnic groups and ethnicity.[18]

Barth challenged conventional views about ethnicity, many based on ideas about tribes in Africa. For Barth, an ethnic group consists of 'a membership which identifies itself, and is identified by others, as constituting a category distinguishable from other categories of the same order'; namely a category that 'classifies a person in terms of his basic, most general identity, presumptively determined by his origin and background'.[19] Such *presumptive* origins do not mean that an ethnic group or identity results from some primordial cultural unity or can be equated with a cultural unit. Barth rejected these notions, along with the idea of closed and virtually impermeable boundaries between ethnic groups that developed distinctive features in at least relative isolation from one other. Ethnic boundaries, argued Barth, result from social *interaction*, not isolation.[20] John Sharp continues Barth's argument (while adding a more clearly delineated political power component):

[e]thnic boundaries are not sustained, moreover, because of traditional *cultural* differences, but because of political differences. Ethnicity is a political process by which people seek to form groups, and to differentiate one set of people from another, by appealing to the *idea* of ineluctable cultural difference....[In fact] people can readily invent cultural differences if it is in their political interests to do so. Ethnicity is the pursuit of political goals – the acquisition or maintenance of power, the mobilisation of a following – through the idiom of cultural commonness and difference.[21]

Thus, ethnic groups and identities are not a necessary or natural outcome of cultural beliefs and practices, but a creation of socio-historical dynamics, politics, and ideology. Conceptualising ethnicity in this way was much more powerful analytically than earlier approaches, and contributed to the crucial idea that such terms as tribe, ethnic group, and nation are 'fundamentally constructs of the human imagination rather than entities with a concrete, practical existence in the real world'.[22]

The publication of Barth's work in 1969 was both an indication of, and stimulus to, the increasing importance of ethnicity as an area for academic study, in Africa and elsewhere. During the decade of the 1970s, six comparative, cross-disciplinary journals devoted extensively to the study of ethnicity were founded (although none were African-focused): *Plural Societies* (1970), *Canadian Review of Studies in Nationalism* (1973), *Ethnicity* (1974), *Ethnic Groups* (1976), *Ethnic and Racial Studies* (1978), and *Research in Race and Ethnic Relations* (1979).

Within anthropology, the 1970s saw a shift away from 'tribe' as both term and paradigm (even if stereotypes about tribe persisted in many contexts). As Ronald Cohen wrote in reviewing anthropology during the decade, '[q]uite suddenly, with little comment or ceremony, ethnicity is an ubiquitous presence'.[23] Indeed, the 1970s saw numerous studies by anthropologists on various aspects of ethnicity, including at least seven book-length studies with a significant or even exclusive African focus.[24]

In Africanist political science, the virtual silence of the 1950s and 1960s was followed in the 1970s by a number of book-length works that helped shape new conceptions of ethnicity.[25] Cynthia Enloe, Nathan Glazer and Daniel Patrick Moynihan, and Africanist Crawford Young all contributed broadly comparative studies during the decade as well.[26] In addition, ethnicity became a focus in sociology and sociolinguistics, and in Soviet, South Asian, European, and American studies.[27] As we shall see in the next section, however, Africanist historians during the 1970s only rarely dealt explicitly or extensively with ethnicity.

The 1980s saw the publication of a number of comparative and theoretical works focusing on ethnicity, from a wide range of perspectives and approaches.[28] Studies in related fields also provided significant comparative material, especially books on nationalism by John Breuilly, Benedict Anderson, and Ernest Gellner, plus Eric Hobsbawm and Terence Ranger's book on the invention of tradition.[29]

Even with all of this broad theoretical and comparative work, studies of ethnicity in Africa during the 1980s seem not to have held at 1970s levels. Eriksen's survey of anthropology, though not claiming exhaustive bibliographic coverage, is instructive: it lists no book-length studies in Africanist anthropology with ethnicity as a major focus, and only three articles and one occasional paper.[30] In a series of review articles, meanwhile, Crawford Young cites only three books in Africanist political science over the 1980s that focused extensively on ethnicity.[31] Only Africanist historians, as we shall see in the next section, increased their attention to ethnicity during the decade.

In sum, ethnicity received much more attention as a topic of study in Africa during the 1970s and 1980s than before. This, however, should not be exaggerated. In all disciplines, in and outside Africa, other concerns and emphases took precedence. For scholars to the Centre or Right, the accent of the 1950s and 1960s on politics, political history, the state, and modernisation continued (including limited consideration of ethnicity), even if such work was no longer at centre stage. The dominant voices in academic discourse over the 1970s and 1980s were those asserting structuralist and materialist – usually Marxist or Marxian – interpretations of African society, economy, and polity. Coleman and Halisi's assessment of Africanist political science applied to much other scholarly work in Africa: 'issues of class, dependency, and "political economy", the emerging omnibus code words of the new epoch, asserted their primacy'.[32] Within these contexts, ethnicity was often viewed as a particularly regrettable 'false consciousness', to be trivialised, dismissed, or disparaged.

The inclination to minimise ethnicity in Africanist scholarship persisted despite the surge of ethnic consciousness across Africa in the wake of the failed political and economic promises of the anti-colonial nationalist struggle. Within a few short years of independence, early hopes gave way to the political entrenchment and material enrichment of dominant political classes, most often in the form of one-party states or military rule. Looking back from the perspective of the late 1980s, Leroy Vail writes that

> [i]n effect the revitalization of 'tribalism' was structured into the one-party system by the very fact of that system's existence. Ethnicity became the home of the opposition in states where class consciousness was largely undeveloped. Ethnic particularism has consequently continued to bedevil efforts to 'build nations' to the specifications of the ruling party for the past two decades or more....With its power to

By the mid to late 1980s, argues Young, both earlier positions were being largely superseded by or incorporated into a broadly (and variously) delineated third approach to ethnicity: 'constructivism'. Influenced by post-structuralist theoretical discourse in general and more specifically by Anderson's conceptualisation of the nation as an 'imagined community', most constructivists incorporated and built upon insights of the two earlier perspectives while also turning them on their heads. For constructivists, writes Young, 'the essence of the problematic is the creation of ethnicity':

> [t]he constructivist inverts the logic of the instrumentalist and primordialist, both of whom presume the existence of communal consciousness, either as weapon in pursuit of collective advantage or as inner essence. The constructivist sees ethnicity as the product of human agency, a creative social act through which such commonalities as speech code, cultural practice, ecological adaptation, and political organization become woven into a consciousness of shared identity....The constructivist thus places higher stress on contingency, flux, and change of identity than the other two approaches would concede.[49]

Constructivist approaches move beyond taking the ethnic unit, ethnic identity, or ethnicity for granted or accepting these as givens. Instead, ethnic groups and ethnicity need to be explained and accounted for in dynamic terms. This allows for theorising and reconstructing ethnicity as it evolves, redefines itself, and is redefined by others over time, and invites the consideration of complexity and fluidity, of the multiple (and ever-changing) forces that shape notions of collective identity, from both within and without, and by both the powerful and the subaltern or dominated. In short, constructivist notions are – or can certainly be construed to be – fundamentally historical. It is thus hardly surprising that while a wide range of scholars across disciplines have contributed to the constructivist approach to ethnicity, historians – including, perhaps especially, historians of Africa – have been influential in this endeavour.

History and the Study of Ethnicity in Africa

Through the 1970s, in scholarship on Africa as well as on other parts of the world, most contributions to the study of ethnicity came from anthropologists, political scientists, and sociologists, *not* historians. I have found only six works by Africanist historians before 1980 that deal explicitly and at some length with ethnicity. All date from the mid- to late-1970s, focus regionally on East Africa, and present early constructivist analyses of ethnicity.

The first is a 1975 article by Margaret Jean Hay that explicitly utilises insights from Fredrik Barth's work on ethnic boundaries and boundary maintenance in a study of local trade and markets in Western Kenya.[50] The second is a review essay by John Lonsdale that challenges a pre-colonial history of the Gusii of Kenya for its largely unquestioned acceptance of an ancient Gusii ethnic identity, suggesting instead a series of constructivist arguments for how that identity (and Gusii beliefs about it) might have changed over time.[51]

Next, in one of two relevant 1978 articles, Carole Buchanan articulates and argues against standard colonial stereotypes and manipulations of ethnicity in Africa, before presenting evidence for the existence of kinship ties that cross-cut ethnic (and political) boundaries in pre-colonial western Uganda, promoting significant inter-ethnic contact.[52] Catharine Newbury's article is a thoroughly constructivist analysis of ethnic identity in Rwanda during both the later pre-colonial and colonial periods; she argues against a 'primordialist' Hutu-Tutsi cleavage and for fluid and changing degrees of stratification and notions of ethnicity in Rwanda over time, depending on political, social, and economic changes.[53]

Then, in 1979, John Iliffe and Terence Ranger both published work on the colonial creation of tribes in Tanganyika.[54] Both are classic, if very early, examples of constructivist ideas about ethnicity as outlined above. Each critically discusses colonial stereotypes about tribes, and then acknowledges and explores the role of both Europeans and Africans in the construction of new African identities in the colonial context of indirect rule. This included colonial administrators and missionaries, on one side, and Africans of all sorts, on the other: colonial chiefs and commoners, Western educated elite and the non-literate majority, and those living in both town and countryside. As Iliffe wrote, 'Europeans believed Africans belonged to tribes; Africans built tribes to belong to'.[55]

To conclude this summary of early treatments of ethnicity by Africanist historians, I would like to make two final points. First, all take a constructivist approach. Indeed, they are among the earliest (if typically unacknowledged) examples of such in the literature. Second, the ways in which Iliffe and Ranger deal with the colonial construction of ethnic identities (and boundaries) would become central in much of the constructivist work on ethnicity in Africa that came after; conversely, the example of Newbury's insightful analysis of the construction of ethnicity across the pre-colonial/colonial divide was not, unfortunately, as often followed. The centrality of the Iliffe/Ranger view is illustrated in a generalised model of ethnicity advanced by Leroy Vail in 1989 and cited by Young as a quintessential statement of the constructivist position:

[t]he creation of ethnicity as an ideological statement of popular appeal in the context of profound social, economic and political change in southern Africa was the result of the differential conjunction of various historical forces and phenomena....One may discern three such variables in the creation and implanting of the ethnic message. First, as was the case in the creation of such ideologies elsewhere, for example in nineteenth century European nationalism, it was essential to have a group of intellectuals involved in formulating it – a group of culture brokers [local and expatriate]. Second, there was the widespread use of African intermediaries to administer the subordinate peoples, a system usually summed up in the phrase 'indirect rule', and this served to define the boundaries and texture of the new ideologies. Third, ordinary people had a real need for so-called 'traditional values' at a time of rapid social change, thus opening the way for the wide acceptance of the new ideologies.[56]

However insightful this early historical work is, it was certainly rare through the 1970s. Indeed, by the 1980s, many in the social science disciplines that had been dominant in the academic discourse on ethnicity began to criticise the fundamental ahistorical nature of this work, and to call for more – and more serious – attention to history.[57] Africanists, and especially historians of Africa, began to respond. From 1980 to 1988, at least eighteen published sources provided substantive historical analyses of ethnicity in Africa (and even though this list is not exhaustive, it is worth noting that it represents a three-fold increase over the 1970s).

All eighteen of these sources fit into Young's constructivist category. Three are by anthropologists who responded in a significant way to the call for more historically-minded work on ethnicity previously noted; historians produced the remainder. Twelve have a primary, or sole, emphasis on the colonial period and fit into Vail's generalised model of colonially-constructed ethnicity quoted just above. Four others, including the only two book-length studies, examine ethnicity during both the pre-colonial (mainly late pre-colonial) and colonial periods. Just two focus mainly on pre-colonial manifestations of ethnic identity. In terms of geographical coverage, eleven deal with Southern Africa (three with South Africa specifically), five with East Africa, only one with West Africa, and one with Africa in general.

Of the Southern African sources, all but two focus on colonial topics, including all three dealing expressly with South Africa. The first of these three is John Wright's careful historical investigation of the shifting meanings of the term 'Nguni' in colonial South Africa.[58] The other two are in the 1987 volume edited by Shula Marks and Stanley Trapido. Here, Isabel Hofmeyer examines the role of early twentieth-century Afrikaans language and literature in fostering an Afrikaner ethnic identity, and William Beinart uses interviews with a single migrant labourer to trace the impact on his life of worker, ethnic, and nationalist identities and ideologies – as defined by both self and others.[59] These three essays mark the beginnings of an important shift in progressive South African scholarship, in which ethnicity is seen as a relevant and significant topic for exploration.[60]

Southern African regional sources dealing with colonial creations of ethnicity began with Leroy Vail's 1981 article on ways in which missionary language policies and enthusiastic African responses to mission-provided educational opportunities created new ethnic identities in northern colonial Malawi.[61] Next was Terence Ranger's 1982 survey of the role of both Europeans and Africans in creating racial and ethnic identities in colonial Southern Africa (following up on themes that he and Iliffe presented a few years earlier).[62] In 1984 Landeg White discussed a colonially-created 'tribalism from above' in southern Malawi, when Yao chiefs were strengthened following the 1915 Chilembwe uprising.[63] Two 1985 sources examined the colonial creation of ethnicity in neighbouring Zambia: one by anthropologist Wim van Binsbergen in the western part of the colony, the other by historian Robert Papstein in the northwest.[64] Finally, Patrick Harries' 1988 work explored ways in which missionary language policy in late-nineteenth-century colonial southern Mozambique and parts of neighbouring Transvaal helped create new ethnic identities there.[65]

The two Southern African sources that focus on pre-colonial (or, in the case of nineteenth-century southern Mozambique, effectively pre-colonial) ethnicity were Patrick Harries' article emphasising the ethnic and linguistic fluidity that characterised nineteenth-century southern Mozambique and surrounding areas, and Carolyn Hamilton and John Wright's essay challenging an exclusive emphasis on the colonial creation of 'tribes' and 'tribalism'.[66] Instead, the latter contend that 'modern "tribalism" is a creation of the impact of colonialism on forms of ethnic consciousness whose roots lie deep in the pre-colonial past' – an argument pursued further in the third part of this paper.[67]

East African sources included four of the five studies that bridge the pre-colonial and colonial periods, including the only two book-length studies identified for this period. Richard Waller contributed two essays examining both pre-colonial and colonial Maasai ethnic identity and boundaries, which he convincingly reconstructs as complex, contested, and fluid.[68] Catharine Newbury's monograph followed up her earlier article, expanding her analysis of the complicated and changing nature of stratification, clientship, and ethnicity in Rwanda over both the late pre-colonial and colonial periods.[69] Charles Ambler's book looks at the central Kenya past from a regional perspective, and shows how late-nineteenth-century people in this region interacted within and across relatively permeable ethnic boundaries in intricate and dynamic ways, and how ideas of identity evolved and shifted over time.[70] Finally, in the only East African example focusing exclusively on ethnicity in a colonial context, anthropologist Jay O'Brien's article reconstructs the emergence of new ethnic identities in the Sudan accompanying migrant labour and capitalist production on the Gezira cotton scheme.[71]

Lastly in this period, Terence Ranger explored in a wide-ranging and well-known essay the multi-faceted ways in which both Europeans and Africans contributed to 'invented tradition' in colonial Africa, including the effect of such tradition on the development of new identities.[72] And in the only West African source identified, anthropologist Richard Fardon provides a relatively brief, but increasingly familiar, analysis of the colonial creation of a new kind of Chamba ethnic identity among people living along the Nigeria-Cameroon border, especially as a result of colonial education; he also criticises over-generalised uses of ethnicity as a term and concept.[73]

The years since 1989, as already noted, have been marked by an outpouring of work on ethnicity. The remainder of this section provides a brief overview of book-length Africanist studies that deal extensively with ethnicity.

The first, and most broadly applicable, observation on the thirty books under review, representing a thorough mix of disciplines, is that all of them are marked by essentially constructivist approaches in their representations and analyses of ethnicity. Second, as with the historical studies of the 1970s and 1980s reviewed above, the geographical focus of these more recent sources is predominantly on Southern and East Africa. The extent to which these two regions dominate, however, is considerably less than before (seventeen of thirty, as opposed to sixteen of eighteen), with correspondingly more attention paid to West Africa (five books, all since 1994), general Africa (five books), and Central Africa (three books).[74]

Third, over one-third of these recent sources (twelve of thirty) have a predominantly or even exclusively post-colonial or contemporary focus. Given the clear significance in Africa's present and recent past of politics – and even political violence – cast in ethnic terms, this is hardly surprising. Seven of these twelve are authored or edited by political scientists.[75] Three others are by anthropologists/sociologists;[76] two are volumes co-edited by an anthropologist and an historian;[77] and one is a monograph by postmodernist literary and culture critic Rob Nixon.[78]

Fourth, at the same time that this set of books deals as much as it does with recent or contemporary manifestations of ethnicity, it has an even more pronounced emphasis on history, an emphasis that extends well beyond the contributions of historians *per se*. Indeed, twenty-one of the thirty titles have a significant, or even predominant, historical focus. Nine of these twenty-one are single-authored, explicitly historical works by historians.[79] Two single-authored books by anthropologists are also thoroughly historical.[80] So are both co-authored works (one by two historians, the other by a political scientist and an historian),[81] and three of the seven edited volumes.[82] Moreover, three additional edited volumes and two more anthropological monographs, while focusing primarily on contemporary issues or the very recent past, also devote considerable attention to history.[83] Clearly, the call by social scientists in the 1980s for more attention to history in studies of ethnicity has been answered, and not just by historians.

Finally, however, even with the prominent place of historians and the accent on historically-oriented constructivist analysis, the history typically considered relevant is limited to the colonial and post-colonial periods. Only four of the thirty books focus primarily on the pre-colonial period.[84] Six other volumes deal extensively with both the pre-colonial and colonial eras, though only three of the six extend their discussion farther back in time than the mid- to late-nineteenth century.[85]

Extending the Chronology, Conceptualisation, and Discourse

From the very beginnings of academic research on ethnicity, Africa has had an important place. Anthropologists working on the Copperbelt of Central Africa are usually credited as founders of the modern study of ethnicity; Africanist James Coleman pioneered the examination of ethnicity within the discipline of political science; Africanist scholars, including historians, have played a leading role in developing a constructivist approach to understanding and reconstructing ethnicity, and establishing this approach as dominant in academic discourse. The primary role that historians of Africa have played in this process has been to explore the creation of ethnic identities resulting from the imposition of colonial rule.

Such creations were called 'tribes', and many interests contributed to, and were served by, their invention. For colonial administrators, false historical assumptions about 'naturally tribal' Africans combined comfortably with practical administrative convenience. For Africans, the changes ushered in by colonial rule led both elites and the masses of peasant farmers and poor town dwellers to perceive advantages in belonging to 'tribal' political units, cultural fraternities, and welfare associations. The creation of these new 'tribal' entities and identities was accompanied by sharp and hard boundaries, and by divisions, rivalries, and attitudes of exclusiveness not present before, or at least not present in the same forms or to the same degree.

Of course, neither the new identities nor their consequences disappeared when colonial rule ended. Indeed, many of the particular characteristics commonly referred to as 'tribalism' in contemporary Africa – and often presumed in popular representations to be primordial and unchanging, peculiar to independent Africa, or both at the same time – are most of all an African *colonial* legacy.

The (Re)Construction of Ethnicity in Africa   29

This is important work, and has significantly advanced our understanding of both the constructivist approach to ethnicity in general (as relational, malleable, historical, and contingent) and the specific ways in which colonial rule affected the creation and transformation of ethnicity, or 'tribalism', in Africa. Why, though, has the historical work on ethnicity in Africa had this particular, mainly twentieth-century focus? At least four reasons come to mind, all related to the ways in which the academic discourse on ethnicity has developed, both generally and in Africa.

First is the initial impact and continuing influence of the overwhelmingly presentist nature of the disciplines in which the study of ethnicity emerged: anthropology, sociology, and political science. 'Anthropology', writes Eriksen, 'has a strong bias towards studying the present – and in their dealings with the past many anthropologists regard it as neither more nor less than present-day constructions of the past'.[86] Even more succinctly, political scientist Crawford Young refers to 'the tyranny of the present that permeates our [the political scientists'] discipline'.[87]

Second is the pervasive influence of the work of Anderson, Gellner, and Hobsbawm and Ranger in the early 1980s in shaping the constructivist approach to understanding ethnicity (even though ethnicity *per se* was not a particular concern of any of these works). In widely read books, these scholars all emphasised the role of 'modern' elements, particularly literacy, in the construction of the 'imagined communities' or 'invented traditions' of national or other collective identities and ideologies.[88] Whether expressed explicitly or by implication, this 'modernist' component became a major feature in subsequent representations of ethnicity.

A third impetus in the literature towards a focus on the recent past derives from a highly questionable (and large) step taken in many discussions of ethnicity beyond Barth's basic point that ethnic groups and boundaries only make sense in relational terms, as a result of social interaction rather than isolation. Such sources argue, or sometimes merely assert, that ethnicity can be considered primarily, or only, in the context of relationships within single polities, by which they usually mean 'modern' (colonial or post-colonial) states.[89]

A final reason (or set of reasons) that studies of ethnicity in Africa have focused on the recent past derives from three broad, underlying developments in African studies, including African history. The first was the increasing emphasis over the 1970s and 1980s on materialist and other structuralist perspectives. If this emphasis did not promote work on ethnicity, as we have seen, it was even less suited or inclined to explore Africa's pre-colonial past. The second development was the declining circumstances over the same period in much of Africa for conducting the sort of field work necessary for anything other than archival (mainly colonial) historical research, including increasingly harsh living conditions, greater health risks, and spiraling governmental impediments. The third is the increasing primacy of contemporary issues in the Africanist academy, as the continent since the 1970s has been beset by a succession of crises commanding attention.[90]

Together, all of these influences have contributed to a chronological emphasis in the study of African ethnicity, even by historians, that extends no farther back in time than the period of colonial rule. This focus, I would argue, is not only limited in chronology but conceptualisation, as it engenders a notion of ethnicity as a phenomenon that is purely 'modern', requiring for its very existence in Africa the presence of Europeans, colonialism, capitalism, and the modern state. This seems to me highly untenable as a general proposition.

The fundamental problem with this notion of ethnicity is that it grants too much power, too much importance, to colonial rule in Africa. As acknowledged above, colonialism (and its aftermath) have certainly shaped in major ways the nature and manifestations of modern ethnicity all across Africa. Still, as also noted, colonial rule in Africa did not occur on some continental *tabula rasa*, and its approximately sixty years neither erased nor totally overwhelmed all that had gone before. However powerful the colonisers, however distorted or manipulative their representations of ethnic identities, how often would (or could) these identities have been plucked from the air or created out of nothingness?

Writing of Kenya, Lonsdale succinctly states that '[e]thnic nationalisms have longer and more reflective histories than Kenyan nationalism. Kenyan political debate cannot afford to ignore them'.[91] Turning to the vast forest region of west-central Africa, Jan Vansina notes that some ethnic identities there seem 'to have existed only in the minds of French administrators'; '[o]n the other hand', he continues, 'not all ethnic references are of colonial vintage'.[92] Justin Willis reaches the same conclusion from his recent exploration of 'the micro-processes of formation of ethnic identity' among the Bondei of northeastern Tanzania.[93] Furthermore, in two recent West African studies, historian Sandra Greene and anthropologist Philip Burnham present complex, nuanced pictures of changing, socially constructed ethnic identities in southeastern Ghana and northern Cameroon, respectively. Both begin deep in the pre-colonial period (Greene as early as the late seventeenth century) and continue into the colonial and post-colonial eras.[94] All of this work helps affirm arguments I have made that the ideological and socio-historical forces involved in the construction and representation of ethnic identities in Africa are often, perhaps even usually, *not* confined solely to the colonial and post-colonial eras.[95]

This argument can be tested by recognising and collecting evidence dealing with the existence of forms of collective identity and consciousness predating colonial rule, and then investigating the always complex and changing dynamics involved in the construction of such identities. I have tried to do this with an East African people now called Acholi, living in northern Uganda (with related groups also called by that name in southern Sudan). As with the other sources just cited, it seems clear that while the specific actors and forces involved before and after colonial rule differ, many of the basic dynamics typically associated with constructivist views of ethnicity apply on both sides of the pre-colonial/colonial divide.

With respect to Acholi specifically, the basic argument can be summarised as follows.[96] Archaeological and linguistic evidence suggests that from early in the first millennium A.D., the area that becomes Acholi was settled mainly by Central Sudanic (or 'proto-Central Sudanic') speakers in the west and Eastern Nilotic ('proto-Eastern Nilotic') speakers in the east, though the linguistic frontier was hardly sharp or clear. Speakers of the Luo language that eventually became dominant in Acholi were limited before the late seventeenth century to a few peripheral areas. All of these early inhabitants were iron-working mixed farmers, organised into villages with localised patrilineages at their core, or, in some cases, into temporary groupings of two to four such village-lineages (often of mixed linguistic origins). Virtually nothing about the area or its peoples before the late seventeenth century suggested that a single society or collective identity would develop, or take the forms that it did.

Then, in the late seventeenth century a new socio-political order – and the basis of an eventual Acholi identity – began to be established, following the introduction of chiefly institutions and ideology into north-central Uganda by Luo-speaking Paluo from the neighbouring kingdom of Bunyoro-Kitara. Central to the new order were: (1) a set of notions about political leadership in which chiefs shared power and decision-making with the heads of the constituent lineages of the chiefdoms; (2) a system of redistributive tribute within each polity, with the chief at the centre; and (3) royal, often rainmaking, drums as symbols of sovereignty and authority. Over the eighteenth and early nineteenth centuries, some seventy chiefdoms were founded, spurring the development of a new social order and political culture, the spread of a new language (Luo), the evolution of a new collective identity, and the beginning of the establishment of new boundaries based on this emergent identity. Significantly, the iron ore necessary for tools and weapons was mainly located at, or just beyond, these emergent boundaries (to the west, northeast, southeast, and south), and trade for this iron created networks of movement and interaction that further reinforced the developing new identity.

This complex process was pushed along by three major droughts – probably during the 1720s, *circa* 1790, and the early 1830s. Each of these droughts radically altered material conditions and disrupted the social landscape, creating circumstances favouring the emergence or strengthening of chiefdoms, with their larger-scale political leadership and promise of greater stability and security. The droughts also furthered the formation of neighbouring identities against which members of an emergent Acholi could compete, compare, and define themselves.

Over the second half of the nineteenth century the area of emergent Acholi was incorporated into international trade networks through the activities of northern, Arabic-speaking ivory and slave traders. This trade brought new wealth into the area that was unevenly accumulated, with chiefs and interpreters being the major beneficiaries. The northerners also contributed to the further evolution of an Acholi identity, not only by introducing the 'Shuuli' name that eventually becomes Acholi, but by acting in ways that promoted Acholi as a meaningful ethnic and geographic entity.

When Britain established its rule during the early twentieth century, both ideological predisposition and practical utility prompted the colonisers to consider the Acholi a 'tribe' and to administer the area as a 'tribal' unit. From the beginning, the Acholi were marginal compared to Britain's concern with Buganda at the core of the colony. The role of Acholi in the colonial economy was confined mainly to the peasant production of cotton as a cash crop, the provision of recruits for the colonial army or police, and the provision of migrant labour for the more 'developed' Buganda. Both Protestant and Catholic missionaries were active in Acholi from early colonial rule, providing written Luo religious, educational, and historical texts, and producing a local educated elite, all of which fostered the further development of an Acholi identity within the colonial context of 'tribal' culture, consciousness, and politics.

I would hope that even this brief summary shows that the identity now called Acholi did not develop solely during the colonial period. Nor, of course, is it primordial or based on some set of cultural givens. As with all ethnic (or other collective) identities, Acholi identity is the ever-changing product of social and historical dynamics. If we want even to begin to understand this constructivist process, however, we certainly cannot begin our interpretation and reconstruction with the coming of British colonial rule.

This argument is not meant to convey the notion that all ethnic identities have the same, deep pre-colonial roots as Acholi, or even any significant pre-colonial roots at all. Ranger, for example, has made a strong case that many twentieth-century ethnic identities and divisions in Zimbabwe are *not* rooted in the pre-colonial past.[97] I am also certainly not proposing that we can understand colonial – or contemporary – ethnicity *only* in terms of pre-colonial identity formation. Ranger has recently commented that many post-colonialist accounts of Africa 'oddly privilege colonialism', and that there is a 'need to break down the barriers between postcolonial Africa and its past'.[98] Even as he quotes others who explicitly include 'pre-colonial' in their views of that past, Ranger then 'oddly privileges colonialism' himself by limiting his conception of the past no farther back than the colonial period.[99] Doing this, it seems to me, has predictable and even profound consequences: the virtually inevitable misreading of both pre-colonial and colonial identities. I would like to illustrate this with one recent example.

In the edited volume by Katsuyoshi Fukui and John Markakis, anthropologist Tim Allen presents a reasoned, logical, and seemingly persuasive (if not always clear) case for understanding current ethnic interactions among the Acholi and Madi along the Uganda-Sudan border. Allen writes that 'the Acholi and Madi are opposed as hostile "tribes", but not as individuals and lineages'.[100] Further, Allen suggests that 'Acholi and Madi perceptions of "tribal" conflict are imbued, on the one hand, with ideas about moral space set against the incursions of amoral "outside" forces in daily life and, on the other hand, with the impact of state formation and Christian-influenced historiography on conceptions of tradition'.[101]

What is missing in the essay as it attempts to interpret Acholi-Madi relations is any serious discussion of pre-colonial developments among either Acholi or Madi; thus, all explanations are colonial or post-colonial. The comfortable (but entirely unsupported, as well as inaccurate) assertion is made that 'both the Acholi and the Madi "tribes" were in fact colonial creations'.[102] An equally unsupported social-psychological interpretation is given for the relatively friendly relations during the colonial period between Madi and Acholi.

A much more direct and grounded analysis based on historical evidence would show that the people who gradually constructed an Acholi identity in the western part of Acholi over the eighteenth and nineteenth centuries were primarily of the same Central Sudanic origins as those farther west who became Madi. This analysis would also show that ongoing and largely amicable ties (of trade, inter-marriage, and other social interaction) continued into the colonial period.[103]

Based on a brief reference to the author's personal research into oral history, Allen's essay touches on this point, as well as on the existence of related lineages across ethnic boundaries. However, none of this is developed by utilising the historical reconstruction and analysis of other scholars. Finally, the development of colonial 'tribal' histories in Acholi and their relative lack in Madi is discussed in terms of its impact on current concepts of history and identity among both groups, while neither these histories nor their interpretations by later historians are applied to any of the questions being asked in the essay. All of this leads to mainly presentist arguments and interpretations that are incomplete, misleading, or simply wrong on several points. How often are similar assertions and arguments about the colonial role in the creation of identity flawed by lack of a serious exploration of pre-colonial foundations?

The only way to know is to bring the pre-colonial past to bear on understanding ethnicity in Africa. A failure to do this limits our ability to understand ethnic identity and consciousness in either historical or contemporary Africa. This is certainly the case with Acholi. The creation of an Acholi society and collective identity did *not* commence with colonial rule. The socio-historical developments that produced an 'Acholi' entity and identity began hundreds of years before that; indeed, the social order and political culture that came essentially to define an emergent Acholi had become widely and firmly entrenched even before 1800.

In introducing their recent collection of essays on ethnicity and conflict in northeastern Africa, Fukui and Markakis sum up succinctly one of the major deductions from these essays: 'that ethnic/tribal identities are essentially products of specific situations, socially defined and historically determined'.[104] They go on to note that bringing history to bear on ethnicity is 'a recent and promising development', that brings 'results [that] are often illuminating'.[105] They include pre-colonial history in this assessment, and I can think of no convincing reasons for excluding this portion of the past from the historical contextualisation necessary for understanding ethnicity. Indeed, only by considering the dynamics of both the pre-colonial and subsequent eras, I would argue, can we even begin to come to grips with one of the most complex and powerful social phenomena confronting – and often confounding – not only Africa but the late-twentieth-century world.

NOTES

I would like to thank Paris Yeros and Bruce Cauthen of the Association for the Study of Ethnicity and Nationalism and the London School of Economics for organising the conference that produced the essays in this volume, and for their invitation to me to participate. I would also like to thank the Department of History at the University of South Carolina for financial support to attend the conference, and colleague Mark Smith for his critical yet sympathetic reading of a draft version of this chapter.

1. Crawford Young, 'The Dialectics of Cultural Pluralism: Concept and Reality', in Crawford Young (ed.), *The Rising Tide of Cultural Pluralism: The Nation-State at Bay?* (Madison, WI: University of Wisconsin Press, 1993), pp. 7–8.
2. Crawford Young, 'Evolving Modes of Consciousness and Ideology: Nationalism and Ethnicity', in David Apter and Carl Rosberg (eds.), *Political Development and the New Realism in Sub-Saharan Africa* (Charlottesville, VA, and London: University Press of Virginia, 1994), p. 81. For two earlier arguments along these lines see Anthony D. Smith, *The Ethnic Revival* (Cambridge: Cambridge University Press, 1981), and Crawford Young, *The Politics of Cultural Pluralism* (Madison, WI: University of Wisconsin Press, 1976).
3. See, for example, Jan Pieterse, 'Variables of Ethnic Politics and Ethnicity Discourse', in Edwin N. Wilmsen and Patrick McAllister (eds.), *The Politics of Difference: Ethnic Premises in a World of Power* (Chicago, IL, and London: University of Chicago Press, 1996), pp. 25–44.
4. See Malcolm Chapman, Maryon McDonald, and Elizabeth Tonkin, 'Introduction', in Elizabeth Tonkin, Maryon McDonald, and Malcolm Chapman (eds.), *History and Ethnicity* (London and New York, NY: Routledge, 1989), p. 1, and Roger Just,

'Triumph of the Ethnos', in the same volume, pp. 71–88.
5. Philip Burnham, *The Politics of Cultural Difference in Northern Cameroon* (Washington, DC: Smithsonian Institution Press, 1996), pp. 3–4.
6. *Ibid.*, p. 4.
7. Even most scholars who see theoretical or conceptual problems in the existing literature on ethnicity also see the need (if often somewhat reluctantly) to continue to deal with the topic; that is, to try, in John Comaroff's words, 'to chart the dangers and possibilities inherent in the discourses and deeds of identity politics', and then move to the next and 'much more difficult [steps] of framing defensible alternatives' and taking 'those alternatives into the world of realpolitik'. John Comaroff, 'Ethnicity, Nationalism, and the Politics of Difference in an Age of Revolution', in Wilmsen and McAllister (eds.), *op. cit.*, in note 3, pp. 180–1. See also Marcus Banks, *Ethnicity: Anthropological Constructions* (London and New York, NY: Routledge, 1996), pp. 187–90.
8. See, especially, J. Clyde Mitchell, *The Kalela Dance* (Manchester: Manchester University Press, 1956); A.L. Epstein, *Politics in an Urban African Community* (Manchester: Manchester University Press, 1958); Max Gluckman, *Conflict and Custom in Africa* (Oxford: Blackwell, 1956); Max Gluckman, 'Tribalism in Modern British Central Africa', *Cahiers d'Etudes Africaines* (Vol. 1, No. 1, 1960), pp. 55–70; and Max Gluckman, 'Anthropological Problems Arising from the African Industrial Revolution', in Aidan Southall (ed.), *Social Change in Modern Africa* (London: Oxford University Press, 1961). Thomas Hylland Eriksen discusses these Copperbelt studies and notes that they drew on earlier research begun in the United States during the 1920s by a group of mainly urban sociologists, often called the 'Chicago School'. Thomas Hylland Eriksen, *Ethnicity and Nationalism: Anthropological Perspectives* (London and Boulder, CO: Pluto Press, 1993), pp. 20–33.
9. See Peter Skalnik, 'Tribe as Colonial Category', in Emile Boonzaier and John Sharp (eds.), *South African Keywords: The Uses and Abuses of Political Concepts* (Cape Town: David Philip, 1988), p. 68. This division is discussed by sociologists Benjamin B. Ringer and Elinor R. Lawless as 'The 'We-They' Character of Race and Ethnicity', in Benjamin B. Ringer and Elinor R. Lawless, *Race-Ethnicity and Society* (London and New York, NY: Routledge, 1989), pp. 1–27. Anthropological discussions include Chapman, McDonald, and Tonkin, *op. cit.*, in note 4, pp. 12–20, as well as Eriksen, *op. cit.*, in note 8, pp. 18–35, and Thomas Hylland Eriksen, *Us and Them in Modern Societies* (Oslo: Scandanavian University Press, 1992). See also the 'social identity approach' of social psychologists Michael A. Hogg and Dominic Abrams, *Social Identification: A Social Psychology of Intergroup Relations and Group Processes* (London and New York, NY: Routledge, 1988).
10. Skalnik, *op. cit.*, in note 9, p. 69.
11. *Ibid.*; Skalnik also notes how much early anthropology has contributed to the hold that these notions have in the popular mind.
12. See, for example, Morton Fried, 'On the Concepts of "Tribe" and "Tribal Society"', *Transactions of the New York Academy of Sciences* (Vol. 28, No. 4, 1966), pp. 527–40; June Helm (ed.), *Essays on the Problems of Tribe: Proceedings of the Annual Spring Meeting of the American Ethnological Society* (Seattle, WA: University of Washington Press, 1968); Aidan Southall, 'The Illusion of Tribe', *Journal of Asian and African Studies* (Vol. 5, No. 1/2, 1970), pp. 28–50, as well as the remainder of that issue, 'Special Number on the Passing of Tribal Man in Africa'.

13. Abner Cohen, *Custom and Politics in Urban Africa* (London: Routledge and Kegan Paul/Berkeley: University of California Press, 1969). Of 220 sources cited in Eriksen, *op. cit.*, in note 8, only 27 date from 1950 to 1968, most of which – apart from the Copperbelt studies – contribute only marginally to the developing literature on ethnicity. One exception is Clifford Geertz, 'The New Integration Revolution: Primordial Sentiments and Civil Politics in New States', in Clifford Geertz (ed.), *Old Societies and New States* (Glencoe, IL: Free Press, 1968). Two Africanist studies from this period not previously cited are Philip Mayer, *Tribesmen or Townsmen: Conservatism and the Process of Urbanization in a South African City* (Cape Town: Oxford University Press, 1961), and Leo Kuper and M.G. Smith (eds.), *Pluralism in Africa* (Berkeley, CA: University of California Press, 1969).
14. See James S. Coleman and C.R.D. Halisi, 'American Political Science and Tropical Africa: Universalism vs. Relativism', *African Studies Review* (Vol. 36, No. 3/4, 1983), pp. 25–62. Coleman himself (as recognised by Young, 'Evolving Modes of Consciousness and Ideology', *op. cit.*, in note 2, pp. 72–6) was a notable exception to this last generalisation. See James S. Coleman, 'The Problem of Political Integration in Emergent Africa', *Western Political Quarterly* (Vol. 8, No. 1, 1955), pp. 44–57, and especially James S. Coleman, *Nigeria: Background to Nationalism* (Berkeley, CA: University of California Press, 1958). Other exceptions included Immanuel Wallerstein, 'Ethnicity and National Integration', *Cahiers d'Etudes Africaines* (Vol. 1, No. 3, 1960), pp. 129–39; Paul Mercier, 'Remarques sur la signification du "triballisme" actuel en Afrique noire', *Cahiers Internationaux de Sociologie* (Vol. 31, 1960), pp. 61–80; Richard Sklar, 'The Contribution of Tribalism to Nationalism in Western Nigeria', *Journal of Human Relations* (Vol. 8, 1960), pp. 407–17; and Crawford Young, *Politics in the Congo* (Princeton, NJ: Princeton University Press, 1965), pp. 232–72.
15. Martin Klein, 'Review of *Cambridge History of Africa, Volume V: c. 1790 to c. 1870*', *Journal of African History* (Vol. 19, No. 2, 1978), p. 277.
16. *Ibid.*; see also John Tosh, *Clan Leaders and Colonial Chiefs in Lango* (Oxford: Clarendon Press, 1978), pp. 4–5. The dominance of such narrow, nationalist-influenced political history has been much criticised, from many different perspectives. Consider just three examples, A.J. Temu and Bonaventure Swai, *Historians and Africanist History: A Critique* (London: Zed Press, 1981); numerous contributions in Bogumil Jewsiewicki and David Newbury (eds.), *African Historiographies: What History for Which Africa?* (Beverly Hills, CA: Sage, 1987); and Ralph Austin, '"Africanist" Historiography and Its Critics: Can There Be an Autonomous African History?', in Toyin Falola (ed.), *African Historiography: Essays in Honour of Jacob Ade Ajayi* (Essex and Ikeja: Longman, 1993), pp. 203–17.
17. Fredrik Barth (ed.), *Ethnic Groups and Boundaries: The Social Organization of Culture Difference* (Oslo: Universitetetsforlaget/Boston, MA: Little, Brown, 1969).
18. In this regard, Eriksen acknowledges the importance of Barth's contribution. See Eriksen, *op. cit.*, in note 8, especially pp. 37–41; for his discussion of Barth's predecessors, see pp. 12–25 and 30–7. For a brief summary of criticisms of Barth's work, see Banks, *op. cit.*, in note 7, pp. 15–17. Also, contrast the role credited to Barth above with the provocative assessment by Richard Thompson that 'Barth's contribution to ethnic theory has not been substantial'. See Richard Thompson, *Theories of Ethnicity: A Critical Appraisal* (New York, NY: Greenwood Press, 1989), p. 8.

19. Fredrik Barth, 'Introduction', in Barth (ed.), *op. cit.*, in note 17, pp. 11 and 13, respectively.
20. *Ibid.*, pp. 10–16.
21. John Sharp, 'Ethnic Group and Nation: The Apartheid Vision in South Africa', in Boonzaier and Sharp (eds.), *op. cit.*, in note 9, pp. 79–80.
22. *Ibid.*, p. 80. Sharp draws especially on Benedict Anderson, *Imagined Communities: Reflections on the Origin and Spread of Nationalism* (London and New York, NY: Verso, 1983). Compare with John Comaroff who challenges the notion that this idea has produced any significant conceptual or analytical advance, in Comaroff, *op. cit.*, in note 7.
23. Ronald Cohen, 'Ethnicity: Problem and Focus in Anthropology', *Annual Review of Anthropology* (Vol. 7, 1978), p. 379.
24. See Cohen's reference to these studies, in *ibid.* Books with an African focus included Ronald Cohen and John Middleton (eds.), *From Tribe to Nation in Africa* (Scranton, PA: Chandler, 1970); Abner Cohen (ed.), *Urban Ethnicity* (London: Tavistock, 1974); Pierre van den Berghe (ed.), *Race and Ethnicity in Africa* (Nairobi: East African Publishing House, 1975); Brian du Toit (ed.), *Ethnicity in Modern Africa* (Boulder, CO: Sage, 1978); A.L. Epstein, *Ethos and Identity: Three Studies in Ethnicity* (London: Tavistock, 1978); Enid Schildkrout, *People of the Zongo: The Transformation of Ethnic Identities in Ghana* (Cambridge: Cambridge University Press, 1978); and William A. Shack and Elliot P. Skinner (eds.), *Strangers in African Societies* (Berkeley, CA: University of California Press, 1979).
25. These included Robert Melson and Howard Wolpe, *Modernization and the Politics of Communalism* (East Lansing, MI: Michigan State University Press, 1971); Ali Mazrui, *Cultural Engineering and Nation Building in East Africa* (Evanston, IL: Northwestern University Press, 1972); Victor Olorunsola (ed.), *The Politics of Cultural Sub-nationalism in Africa* (Garden City, NY: Doubleday, 1972); Nelson Kasfir, *The Shrinking Political Arena: Participation and Ethnicity in African Politics, with a Case Study of Uganda* (Berkeley, CA: University of California Press, 1975); A.O. Sanda (ed.), *Ethnic Relations in Nigeria: Problems and Prospects* (Ibadan: Caxton Press, 1976); and Holger B. Hansen, *Ethnicity and Military Rule in Uganda* (Uppsala: Scandanavian Institute of African Studies, 1977).
26. Cynthia Enloe, *Ethnic Conflict and Political Development* (Boston, MA: Little, Brown, 1973); Nathan Glazer and Daniel P. Moynihan (eds.), *Ethnicity: Theory and Experience*, Second Edition (Cambridge MA: Harvard University Press, 1975); and Young, *The Politics of Cultural Pluralism*, *op. cit.*, in note 2.
27. To cite just one or two examples in each of these areas, see, in sociology, R.A. Schermerhorn, *Comparative Ethnic Relations: A Framework for Theory and Research* (New York, NY: Random House, 1970), and Leo Kuper, *The Pity of It All: Polarization of Racial and Ethnic Relations* (London: Duckworth, 1977). In sociolinguistics, see Howard Giles (ed.), *Language, Ethnicity and Intergroup Relations* (London, New York, NY, and San Francisco, CA: Academic Press, 1975). A work in English in Soviet studies in the 1970s is Jeremy Azrael (ed.), *Soviet Nationality Policies and Practices* (New York, NY: Praeger, 1978). An important South Asian study was Paul Brass, *Language, Religion, and Politics in North India* (Cambridge and New York, NY: Cambridge University Press, 1974). A similarly important work focused on Europe was Michael Hechter, *Internal Colonialism: The Celtic Fringe in British National Development* (London: Routledge and Kegan Paul, 1975). Finally, a significant Americanist study to add to Glazer and Moynihan (eds.),

op. cit., in note 26, was Michael Novak, *The Rise of the Unmeltable Ethnics* (New York, NY: Macmillan, 1971).

28. A partial listing includes Smith, *op. cit.*, in note 2; Charles Keyes (ed.), *Ethnic Change* (Seattle, WA: University of Washington Press, 1981); Joseph Rothschild, *Ethnopolitics: A Conceptual Framework* (New York, NY: Columbia University Press, 1981); Donald L. Horowitz, *Ethnic Groups in Conflict* (Berkeley, CA: University of California Press, 1985); Paul Brass (ed.), *Ethnic Groups and the State* (London: Croom Helm, 1985); John Rex and David Mason (eds.), *Theories of Race and Ethnic Relations* (Cambridge: Cambridge University Press, 1986); Susan Olzak and Joane Nagel (eds.), *Competitive Ethnic Relations* (New York, NY: Academic Press, 1986); Anthony D. Smith, *The Ethnic Origin of Nations* (Oxford: Blackwell, 1986); Manning Nash, *The Cauldron of Ethnicity in the Modern World* (Chicago, IL: University of Chicago Press, 1989); and Tonkin, *et al.* (eds.), *op. cit.*, in note 4.

29. John Breuilly, *Nationalism and the State* (Manchester: Manchester University Press, 1982); Anderson, *op. cit.*, in note 22; Ernest Gellner, *Nations and Nationalism* (Ithaca, NY: Cornell University Press, 1983); Eric Hobsbawm and Terence Ranger (eds.), *The Invention of Tradition* (Cambridge: Cambridge University Press, 1983).

30. See Eriksen, *op. cit.*, in note 8. The articles or book chapters are Jay O'Brien, 'Toward a Reconstitution of Ethnicity: Capitalist Expansion and Cultural Dynamics in Sudan', *American Anthropologist* (Vol. 88, 1986), pp. 898–906; Richard Fardon, '"African Ethnogenesis": Limits to the Comparability of Ethnic Phenomena', in Ladislov Holy (ed.), *Comparative Anthropology* (Oxford: Blackwell, 1987), pp. 168–88; and J.D.Y. Peel, 'The Cultural Work of Yoruba Ethnogenesis', in Tonkin, *et al.* (eds.), *op. cit.*, in note 4, pp. 198–215. The occasional paper is Thomas Hylland Eriksen, *Communicating Cultural Difference and Identity: Ethnicity and Nationalism in Mauritius* (Oslo: University of Oslo Occasional Papers in Social Anthropology, 1988). See also two works by sociologists Pierre van den Berghe, 'Class, Race, and Ethnicity in Africa', *Ethnic and Racial Studies* (Vol. 6, No. 2, 1983), pp. 221–36, and M.G. Smith, 'Pluralism, Race and Ethnicity in Selected African Countries', in Rex and Mason (eds.), *op. cit.*, in note 28, pp. 187–225.

31. See Crawford Young, 'The Temple of Ethnicity', *World Politics* (Vol. 35, No. 4, 1983), pp. 652–62; Crawford Young, 'Nationalism, Ethnicity, and Class in Africa: A Retrospective', *Cahiers d'Etudes Africaines* (Vol. 26, No. 3, 1986), pp. 421–95; and Young, 'Evolving Modes of Consciousness and Ideology', *op. cit.*, in note 2. The books that he cites are Peter Osei-Kwame, *A New Conceptual Model for the Study of Political Integration in Africa* (Washington, DC: University Press of America, 1980); Donald Rothchild and Victor Olorunsola (eds.), *State Versus Ethnic Claims: African Policy Dilemmas* (Boulder, CO: Westview Press, 1983); and Jean-Loup Amselle and Elikia M'bokolo (eds.), *Au coeur de l'ethnie: ethnies, tribalisme et etat en Afrique* (Paris: Editions de la Decouverte, 1985). To these can be added Larry Diamond, *Class, Ethnicity and Democracy in Nigeria: The Failure of the First Republic* (Syracuse, NY: Syracuse University Press, 1988).

32. Coleman and Halisi, *op. cit.*, in note 14, p. 26.

33. Leroy Vail, 'Introduction: Ethnicity in Southern African History', in Leroy Vail (ed.), *The Creation of Tribalism in Southern Africa* (London: James Currey/Berkeley, CA: University of California Press, 1989), p. 2.

34. While decrying what he calls 'the banality of theory in conceptual discussions of ethnicity and nationalism', John Comaroff has situated this discussion – and the dynamics associated with such identities – more explicitly than anyone in the context

of our current revolutionary era; see Comaroff, *op. cit.*, in note 7. Contrast Marcus Banks' 'impression' that studies on ethnicity, at least in anthropology, 'are less common than they were in the heyday of the 1970s'; see Banks, *op. cit.*, in note 7, p. 1.

35. In addition to sources already cited, see, as a sample, Pierre van den Berghe (ed.), *State Violence and Ethnicity* (Nitwot, CO: University Press of Colorado, 1990); Paul Brass, *Ethnicity and Nationalism: Theory and Comparison* (New Delhi, Newbury Park, CA, and London: Sage, 1991); James G. Kellas, *The Politics of Nationalism and Ethnicity* (New York, NY: St. Martin's, 1991); Susan Olzak, *The Dynamics of Ethnic Competition and Conflict* (Stanford, CA: Stanford University Press, 1992); Malcolm Chapman (ed.), *Social and Biological Aspects of Ethnicity* (Oxford: Oxford University Press, 1993); Daniel P. Moynihan, *Pandaemonium: Ethnicity in International Politics* (Oxford: Oxford University Press, 1993); Walker Connor, *Ethnonationalism: The Quest for Understanding* (Princeton, NJ: Princeton University Press, 1994); Ted Gurr and Barbara Harff, *Ethnic Conflict in World Politics* (Boulder, CO: Westview, 1994); Larry Diamond and Marc F. Plattner (eds.), *Nationalism, Ethnic Conflict, and Democracy* (Baltimore, MD, and London: The Johns Hopkins University Press, 1994); Herbert W. Harris, Howard C. Blue, and Ezra E. H. Griffith (eds.), *Racial and Ethnic Identity: Psychological Development and Creative Expression* (New York, NY, and London: Routledge, 1995); Milton J. Esman and Shibley Telhami (eds.), *International Organizations and Ethnic Conflict* (Ithaca, NY: Cornell University Press, 1995); Linda Nicholson and Steven Seidman (eds.), *Postmodernism: Beyond Identity Politics* (Cambridge and New York, NY: Cambridge University Press, 1995); Rodolfo Stavenhagen, *Ethnic Conflicts and the Nation-State* (London: Macmillan/New York, NY: St. Martin's, 1996); and John Hutchinson and Anthony D. Smith (eds.), *Ethnicity: A Reader* (Oxford and New York, NY: Oxford University Press, 1996). Finally, see an important example of postmodernist subaltern studies from India, Partha Chatterjee, *The Nation and Its Fragments: Colonial and Post-colonial Histories* (Princeton, NJ: Princeton University Press, 1993), and a new postmodernist, "transculturation" study from Latin America, Silvia Spitta, *Between Two Waters: Narratives of Transculturation in Latin America* (Houston, TX: Rice University Press, 1995).

36. Bogumil Jewsiewicki, 'African Studies in the 1980s: Epistemology and New Approaches', in Falola (ed.), *op. cit.*, in note 16, p. 222.

37. In addition to the books dealt with in the second part of this chapter, two examples of recent general African history texts that incorporate ethnicity into their narratives are Basil Davidson, *Modern Africa: A Social and Political History*, Second Edition (London and New York, NY: Longman, 1989), pp. 70–5, and John Iliffe, *Africans: The History of a Continent* (Cambridge and New York, NY: Cambridge University Press, 1995), pp. 231–2; Bill Freund, *The Making of Contemporary Africa* (Bloomington, IN: Indiana University Press, 1984), pp. 152–4, is a slightly earlier example. Two recent broad thematic surveys that include explicit discussions of ethnicity are Robert H. Bates, V.Y. Mudimbe and Jean O'Barr (eds.), *Africa and the Disciplines: The Contributions of Research in Africa to the Social Sciences and Humanities* (Chicago, IL, and London: University of Chicago Press, 1993), and Frederick Cooper, Allen F. Isaacman, Florencia E. Mallon, William Roseberry, and Steve J. Stern, *Confronting Historical Paradigms: Peasants, Labor, and the Capitalist World Systems in Africa and Latin America* (Madison, WI, and London: University of Wisconsin Press, 1993).

38. Young, *op. cit.*, in note 2, p. 77.

39. See, for example, the Copperbelt studies cited in note 8; the Africanist sources from the 1960s in notes 12 and 13; and the Africanist sources from the 1970s in note 24 (excepting Pierre van den Berghe and A.L. Epstein).
40. See, for example, the sources in notes 24 and 25, plus the Rothschild and Olzak and Nagel sources in note 28. Young, 'Nationalism, Ethnicity, and Class in Africa', *op. cit.*, in note 31, pp. 447–8, adds that the instrumentalist approach also held an appeal for scholars working in another paradigm in political science theory – rational choice theory, citing as the main Africanist example Robert H. Bates, 'Modernization, Ethnic Competition, and the Rationality of Politics in Contemporary Africa', in Rothchild and Olorunsola (eds.), *op. cit.*, in note 31, pp. 152–71.
41. Two prominent examples of this are Okwudiba Nnoli, *Ethnic Politics in Nigeria* (Enugu: Fourth Dimension, 1978), and John Saul, *The State and Revolution in Eastern Africa* (New York, NY: Monthly Review Press, 1979). See also the discussion of ethnicity and class in Young, 'Nationalism, Ethnicity, and Class in Africa', *op. cit.*, in note 31; Paul Brass, 'Ethnic Groups and the State', in Brass (ed.), *op. cit.*, in note 28, pp. 1–56; Rex and Mason (eds.), *op. cit.*, in note 28; and Timothy M. Shaw, 'Ethnicity as the Resilient Paradigm for Africa: From the 1960s to the 1980s', *Development and Change* (Vol. 17, 1986), pp. 587–605.
42. Young, *op. cit.*, in note 1, p. 22.
43. Geertz, *op. cit.*, in note 13.
44. Epstein, *op. cit.*, in note 24, p. xi. See also sociologist Edward Shils, *Political Developments in the New States* (London: Mouton, 1962).
45. Harold Isaacs, *Idols of the Tribe: Group Identity and Political Change* (New York, NY: Harper and Row, 1975).
46. Moynihan, *op. cit.*, in note 35.
47. See, for example, Pierre van den Berghe, 'Race and Ethnicity: A Sociobiological Perspective', *Ethnic and Racial Studies* (Vol. 1, 1978), pp. 401–11, and R. Paul Shaw and Yuwa Wong, *Genetic Seeds of Warfare: Evolution, Nationalism, and Patriotism* (Boston, MA: Unwin Hyman, 1989). See also the much more nuanced Chapman (ed.), *op. cit.*, in note 35.
48. Young, *op. cit.*, in note 2, p. 79. In contrast to this basically positive depiction of how primordialism and instrumentalism can be combined, see John Comaroff, *op. cit.*, in note 7. Here, Comaroff decries a particular joining of instrumentalism and primordialism that he calls 'neo-primordialism', which concedes 'the historical and contingent nature of ethnicity and nationalism', while leaving intact 'the bedrock of essentialism' (pp. 164–5).
49. Young, *op. cit.*, in note 2, pp. 79–80. Although he would be typically considered a member of the constructivist camp, see Comaroff, *op. cit.*, in note 7, pp. 165–6, for a critical assessment of constructivist attempts to understand or theorise about ethnicity and nationalism.
50. Margaret Jean Hay, 'Local Trade and Ethnicity in Western Kenya', *African Economic History Review* (Vol. 2, No. 1, 1975), pp. 7–12.
51. John Lonsdale, 'When Did the Gusii (or Any Other Group) Become a "Tribe" – A Review Essay', *Kenya Historical Review* (Vol. 5, No. 1, 1977), pp. 123–33.
52. Carole Buchanan, 'Perceptions of Ethnic Interaction in the East African Interior: The Kitara Complex', *International Journal of African Historical Studies* (Vol. 11, No. 3, 1978), pp. 410–28.
53. Catharine Newbury, 'Ethnicity in Rwanda: The Case of Kinyaga', *Africa* (Vol. 48, No. 1, 1978), pp. 17–29.

54. John Iliffe, 'The Creation of Tribes', *A Modern History of Tanganyika* (Cambridge: Cambridge University Press, 1979), pp. 318–41, and Terence Ranger, 'European Attitudes and African Realities: The Rise and Fall of the Matola Chiefs of South-East Tanzania', *Journal of African History* (Vol. 20, No. 1, 1979), pp. 63–82.
55. Iliffe, *op. cit.*, in note 54, p. 324.
56. Vail, *op. cit.*, in note 33, p. 11.
57. Eriksen discusses this point within anthropology. See Eriksen, *op. cit.*, in note 8, pp. 93–7. Young notes also that such sentiments helped contribute to the emergence, across all disciplines, of the constructivist approach, with its inherently historical orientation. See Young, *op. cit.*, in note 2, pp. 79–80.
58. John Wright, 'Politics, Ideology and the Invention of "Nguni"', in Tom Lodge (ed.), *Resistance and Ideology in Settler Societies* (Johannesburg: Ravan Press, 1986), pp. 96–118.
59. Isabel Hofmeyer, 'Building a Nation from Words: Afrikaans Language, Literature and Ethnic Identity, 1902-1924', and William Beinart, 'Worker Consciousness, Ethnic Particularism and Nationalism: The Experiences of a South African Migrant, 1930–1960', both in Shula Marks and Stanley Trapido (eds.), *The Politics of Race, Class and Nationalism in Twentieth-Century South Africa* (London and New York, NY: Longman, 1987), pp. 95–123 and 286–309, respectively.
60. Two other early representatives of this shift, focusing on more contemporary issues relating to ethnicity in South Africa, were Gerhard Mare and Georgina Hamilton, *An Appetite for Power: Buthelezi's Inkhata and the Politics of 'Loyal Resistance'* (Johannesburg: Ravan Press, 1987), and John Sharp, *op. cit.*, in note 21.
61. Leroy Vail, 'Ethnicity, Language and National Unity: The Case of Malawi', in Philip Bonner (ed.), *Working Papers in Southern African Studies, Volume II* (Johannesburg: African Studies Institute, University of Witwatersrand, 1981), pp. 121–63.
62. Terence Ranger, 'Race and Tribe in Southern Africa: European Ideas and African Acceptance', in Robert Ross (ed.), *Racism and Colonialism* (The Hague: Martinus Nijhoff, 1982), pp. 121–42.
63. Landeg White, '"Tribes" and the Aftermath of the Chilembwe Rising', *African Affairs* (Vol. 83, No. 333, 1984), pp. 511–41.
64. Wim van Binsbergen, 'From Tribe to Ethnicity in Western Zambia: The Unit of Study as an Ideological Problem', in W.M.J. van Binsbergen and P.L. Geshiere (eds.), *Old Modes of Production and Capitalist Encroachment* (London and Boston, MA: Kegan Paul, 1985), pp. 181–234, and Robert Papstein, 'The Political Economy of Ethnicity: The Example of Northwestern Zambia', *Tijdschrift voor Geschiedenis* (Vol. 98, No. 3, 1985), pp. 393–401.
65. Patrick Harries, 'The Roots of Ethnicity: Discourse and the Politics of Language Construction in Southeast Africa', *African Affairs* (Vol. 87, No. 346, 1988), pp. 25–52.
66. Patrick Harries, 'Ethnicity, History and Ethnic Frontiers: The Inguavuma District in the 19th Century', *Journal of Natal and Zululand History* (Vol. 6, 1983), pp. 1–27, and Carolyn Hamilton and John Wright, 'The Making of the *AmaLala*: Ethnicity, Ideology and Relations of Subordination in a Precolonial Context', *South African Historical Journal* (Vol. 22, 1990), pp. 3–22.
67. *Ibid.*, p. 14.

68. Richard Waller, 'Interaction and Identity on the Periphery: The Trans-Mara Maasai', *International Journal of African Historical Studies* (Vol. 17, No. 2, 1984), pp. 243–84, and 'Economic and Social Relations in the Central Rift Valley: The Maasai Speakers and Their Neighbors in the Nineteenth Century', in B.A. Ogot (ed.), *Kenya in the Nineteenth Century* (Nairobi: Bookwise, 1985), pp. 83–151.

69. Catharine Newbury, *The Cohesion of Oppression: Clientship and Ethnicity in Rwanda, 1860–1960* (New York, NY: Columbia University Press, 1988).

70. Charles Ambler, *Kenyan Communities in the Age of Imperialism: The Central Region in the Late Nineteenth Century* (New Haven, CT: Yale University Press, 1988).

71. O'Brien, *op. cit.*, in note 29.

72. Terence Ranger, 'The Invention of Tradition in Colonial Africa', in Hobsbawm and Ranger (eds.), *op. cit.*, in note 29, pp. 211–62.

73. Fardon, *op. cit.*, in note 30.

74. The geographical focus of the sources is evident from their titles; see references below, in notes 75–83.

75. See Okwudiba Nnoli, *Ethnic Politics in Africa* (Ibadan: Vantage Publishers, 1990); Kenneth Ingham, *Politics in Modern Africa: The Uneven Tribal Dimension* (London and New York, NY: Routledge, 1990); Rene Lemarchand, *Burundi: Ethnocide as Discourse and Practice* (New York, NY: Woodrow Wilson Center Press/Cambridge: Cambridge University Press, 1994); William F.S. Miles, *Hausaland Divided* (Ithaca, NY: Cornell University Press, 1994); Harvey Glickman, *Ethnic Conflict and Democratization in Africa* (Atlanta, GA: African Studies Association Press, 1995); and E.E. Osaghe, *Ethnicity, Class and the Struggle for State Power in Liberia* (Dakar: Coderisa, 1996).

76. Gerhard Mare, *Brothers Born of Warrior Blood: Politics and Ethnicity in South Africa* (Johannesburg: Ravan Press, 1992); Roy R. Grinker, *Houses in the Rainforest: Ethnicity and Inequality Among Farmers and Foragers in Central Africa* (Berkeley, CA, and London: University of California Press, 1994); and Jean Davidson, *Gender, Lineage, and Ethnicity in Southern Africa* (Boulder, CO: Westview, 1997).

77. Katsuyoshi Fukui and John Markakis (eds.), *Ethnicity and Conflict in the Horn of Africa* (London: James Currey/Athens, OH: Ohio University Press, 1994), and Richard Werbner and Terence Ranger (eds.), *Postcolonial Identities in Africa* (London and Atlantic Highlands, NJ: Zed Books, 1996).

78. Rob Nixon, *Homelands, Harlem and Hollywood: South African Culture and the World Beyond* (London and New York, NY: Routledge, 1994).

79. These include Jan Vansina, *Paths in the Rainforests: Toward a History of Political Tradition in Equatorial Africa* (Madison, WI: University of Wisconsin Press, 1990); Justin Willis, *Mombasa, the Swahili, and the Making of the Mijikenda* (Oxford: Oxford University Press, 1992); James Quirin, *The Evolution of the Ethiopian Jews: A History of the Beta Israel (Falasha) to 1920* (Philadelphia: University of Pennsylvania Press, 1992); Ronald R. Atkinson, *The Roots of Ethnicity: The Origins of the Acholi of Uganda before 1800* (Philadelphia: University of Pennsylvania Press, 1994); Patrick Harries, *Work, Culture, and Identity: Migrant Laborers in Mozambique and South Africa, c. 1860–1910* (Portsmouth, NH: Heinemann/Cape Town: David Philip/London: James Currey, 1994); Paul S. Landau, *The Realm of the Word: Language, Gender, and Christianity in a Southern African Kingdom* (Portsmouth, NH: Heinemann/Cape Town: David Philip/London: James Currey, 1995); Vivian Bickford-Smith, *Ethnic Pride and Racial Prejudice in Victorian Cape Town: Group Identity and Social Practice, 1875–1902* (Cambridge and New York, NY: Cambridge

University Press, 1995); Sandra E. Greene, *Gender, Ethnicity, and Social Change on the Upper Slave Coast: A History of the Anlo-Ewe* (London: James Currey/Portsmouth, NH: Heinemann, 1996); and B. Marie Pirenbaum, *Family Identity and the State in the Bamako Kafu, c. 1800–c. 1900* (Boulder, CO: Westview, 1997).

80. Wim van Binsbergen, *Tears of Rain: Ethnicity and History in Central Western Zambia* (London and New York, NY: Kegan Paul, 1992), and Philip Burnham, *op. cit.*, in note 5.

81. David W. Cohen and E.S. Atieno Odhiambo, *Siyaya: The Historical Anthropology of an African Landscape* (London: James Currey/Athens, OH: Ohio University Press, 1989), and Bruce Berman and John Lonsdale, *Unhappy Valley: Conflict in Kenya and Africa* (London: James Currey/Nairobi: Heinemann Kenya/Athens, OH: Ohio University Press, 1992).

82. See Vail (ed.), *op. cit.*, in note 33; Philip Bonner, Isabel Hofmeyer, Deborah James, and Tom Lodge (eds.), *Holding Their Ground: Class, Locality and Culture in 19th and 20th Century South Africa* (Johannesburg: Ravan Press, 1989); and Thomas Spear and Richard Waller (eds.), *Being Maasai: Ethnicity and Identity in East Africa* (London: James Currey/Dar es Salaam: Mkuki na Nyota/Nairobi: East African Educational Publishing/Athens, OH: Ohio University Press, 1993). The first and third of these are edited by historians, but include contributions by anthropologists as well; the third is interdisciplinary in both editorship and content – as is Edwin Wilmsen, Saul Dubow, and John Sharp (eds.), 'Special Issue: Ethnicity and Identity in Southern Africa', *Journal of Southern African Studies* (Vol. 20, No. 3, 1994).

83. See the edited volumes by Fukui and Markakis (eds.), *op. cit.*, in note 77, and Louise de la Gorgendiere, Kenneth King, and Sarah Vaughan (eds.), *Ethnicity in Africa: Roots, Meanings and Implications* (Edinburgh: Centre for African Studies, Edinburgh University, 1996). The anthropological monographs are by Grinker and Davidson, both *op. cit.*, in note 76.

84. See historians Vansina, Atkinson, and Pirenbaum, all *op. cit.*, in note 79, and anthropologist van Binsbergen, *op. cit.*, in note 80.

85. The six volumes are by anthropologist Burnaham, *op. cit.*, in note 5; historians Willis, Quiren, and Greene, *op. cit.*, in note 79; historians Cohen and Odhiambo, *op. cit.*, in note 81; and historians Spear and Waller (eds.), *op. cit.*, in note 82. Of these, Burnham, Quiren, and Greene extend their discussion farther back than the mid- to late-nineteenth century. In addition, Berman and Lonsdale's richly textured study of colonial and post-colonial Kenya explicitly acknowledges and argues for the continuing importance of pre-colonial identities; see Berman and Lonsdale, *op. cit.*, in note 81. Also, each of the edited volumes by Vail and Fukui and Markakis, while concentrating mainly on ethnicity in the colonial or even contemporary contexts, includes a contribution extending back into the pre-colonial period; see Robert Papstein, 'From Ethnic Identity to Tribalism: the Upper Zambezi Region of Zambia, 1830–1981', in Vail (ed.), *op. cit.*, in note 33, pp. 372–94, and John Lamphear, 'The Evolution of Ateker "New Model" Armies: Jie and Turkana', in Fukui and Markakis (eds.), *op. cit.*, in note 77, pp. 63–92.

86. Eriksen, *op. cit.*, in note 8, p. 93.

87. Crawford Young, *The African Colonial State in Comparative Perspective* (New Haven, CT, and London: Yale University Press, 1994), p. 10.

88. Anderson, *op. cit.*, in note 22; Gellner, *op. cit.*, in note 29; and Hobsbawm and Ranger (eds.), *op. cit.*, in note 29. Anderson highlights a particular variant of literacy that he calls 'print-capitalism'.

89. This concept is present, for example, in Abner Cohen, 'Introduction: The Lesson of Ethnicity', in Cohen (ed.), *op. cit.*, in note 24; Chapman, McDonald, and Tonkin, *op. cit.*, in note 4; Ringer and Lawless, *op. cit.*, in note 9; and an important and insightful article by John Comaroff, 'Of Totemism and Ethnicity: Consciousness, Practice and the Signs of Inequality', *Ethnos* (Vol. 52, No. 3/4, 1987), pp. 301–22.

90. A recent, and readable, discussion of these developments is Jan Vansina's chapter, 'Professionals and Doctrines', in his *Living with Africa* (Madison, WI: University of Wisconsin Press, 1994), pp. 197–221.

91. Lonsdale, in Berman and Lonsdale, *op. cit.*, in note 81, p. 269.

92. Vansina, *op. cit.*, in note 79, pp. 19–20.

93. Justin Willis, 'The Making of a Tribe: Bondei Identities and Histories', *Journal of African History* (Vol. 33, No. 2, 1992), pp. 193–4.

94. Greene, *op. cit.*, in note 79; Burnham, *op. cit.*, in note 5.

95. Ronald R. Atkinson, 'The Evolution of Ethnicity among the Acholi of Uganda: The Precolonial Phase', *Ethnohistory* (Vol. 36, No. 1, 1989), pp. 19–43; and Atkinson, *op. cit.*, in note 79. The same point is also argued explicitly in Pier M. Larson, 'Desperately Seeking "the Merina" (Central Madagascar): Reading Ethnonyms and their Semantic Fields in African Identity Histories', *Journal of Southern African Studies* (Vol. 22, No. 4, 1996), pp. 541–60, and was suggested earlier in Peel, *op. cit.*, in note 30. Acknowledging that particular colonial and contemporary expressions of ethnic identities in Africa have been 'invented', Peel also argues that unless any such invention 'also makes genuine contact with people's actual experience, that is with a history that happened [including pre-colonial history], it is not likely to be effective' (p. 200).

96. This summary draws on Atkinson, *op. cit.*, in note 95; Atkinson, *op. cit*, in note 79; and Atkinson, 'Acholi', in John H. Middleton and Amal Rassam (eds.), *Encyclopedia of World Cultures, Volume IX: Africa and the Middle East* (New York, NY: G.K. Hall and Macmillan, 1995), pp. 3–7.

97. See, for example, Terence Ranger, *The Invention of Tribalism in Zimbabwe* (Gweru: Mambo Press, 1985), and Terence Ranger, 'Missionaries, Migrants and the Manyika: The Invention of Ethnicity in Zimbabwe', in Vail (ed.), *op. cit.*, in note 33, pp. 118–50.

98. Terence Ranger, 'Postscript: Colonial and Postcolonial Identities', in Werbner and Ranger (eds.), *op. cit.*, in note 77, pp. 271–81, especially pp. 273–4.

99. Pier M. Larson includes the Ranger sources cited above in note 97 in his criticism of research on ethnicity in Zimbabwe as 'particularly illustrative of the tendency to privilege European and African elites'. Larson, *op. cit.*, in note 95, p. 543, fn. 12.

100. Tim Allen, 'Ethnicity and Tribalism on the Sudan-Uganda Border', in Fukui and Markakis (eds.), *op. cit.*, in note 77, p. 112.

101. *Ibid.*

102. *Ibid.*, p. 123.

103. See Atkinson, *op. cit.*, in note 79, pp. 40–2 and 210–28.

104. Katsuyoshi Fukui and John Markakis, 'Introduction', in Fukui and Markakis (eds.), *op. cit.*, in note 79, p. 6.

105. *Ibid.*

3. A Non-ethnic State for Africa? A Life-world Approach to the Imagining of Communities

Thomas Hylland Eriksen

In this chapter, I address the process of social and political identification with particular reference to that vast continent conveniently summarised under the label 'sub-Saharan Africa'. The discussion is partly epistemological, partly analytic, and partly plainly policy-oriented. I will set out by outlining some standard social science models of nationhood and ethnicity, and will then proceed to a discussion of social and political identification and integration with reference to a few examples. I will then consider an important perspective, drawing on the phenomenological concept of *life-world* (*Lebenswelt*), which has been neglected in many scholarly analyses of collective identity formations.

How does a sense of group membership develop, and under which circumstances do groups behave as inverted refrigerators – emanating coldness outwards for every degree of heat painstakingly generated inwards? What is it about collective identification that makes it so susceptible to being exploited by warlords and Machiavellian power brokers? And – granted that ethnic group sentiment cannot be done away with by scholars and politicians fuelled by Enlightenment sentiment – how can all the energy invested into ethnic politics be harnessed for the progress of humanity?

Such are some of the typical questions asked by academics studying ethnicity and nationalism. Being one of those academics myself, I should add that something important is often missing from our scholarly diagnoses of contemporary ethnicity and nationalism. The main paradigm represented by academics is not only at odds with, but to a large extent incommensurable with, the experienced life-worlds of the people that we ostensibly study and, perhaps, for whom we make policy recommendations. It also, with a few notable exceptions, tends to caricature those life-worlds, often creating contrasts between a (benign, liberal) cosmopolitan attitude and a (totalitarian, irrational) localist or ethnicist attitude; a kind of contrast which is less marked in ongoing social life than in social science models, and which is both inaccurate and potentially politically harmful. Let us keep this in mind as we move on to the world of models, explanations, and empirical examples.

Towards the end of the article, I shall return to the discrepancy between local life-worlds and scholarly analyses.

Models of Ethnicity and Nationhood

It is widely held that the members of human groups have an 'innate' propensity to distinguish between insiders and outsiders, to delineate social boundaries, and to develop stereotypes about 'the other' in order to sustain and justify those boundaries.[1] If this is indeed the case, ethnicity can be conceived as being nearly as universal a characteristic of humanity as gender and age – unlike phenomena like nationhood and nationalism, which have been so conceptualised in the academic community as to concern the modern world only.[2] Marx and Engels held, probably correctly, that gender, age and the insider–outsider distinction, based on kinship in 'barbarian' societies were universal criteria of social differentiation.[3] If, on the other hand, ethnicity as we conceptualise it can be shown to be a product of a particular kind of society, it can, of course, not be regarded as an ahistorical and universal phenomenon. I have argued elsewhere that this discussion is a dead end.[4] In the present context, I would instead like to draw attention to the very process of collective identification, which is currently represented as a negotiable commodity in most of the world and which may, apparently, just as well end in nihilism, individualism, postmodernism, and hybridism as in vehement and stubborn identity politics with all the conventional trappings of firm boundary-markers and negative stereotyping of others – to mention some of the more extreme options.

By isolating 'ethnicity' as a focus for research, one easily loses everything else from sight. This is perhaps *the* cardinal sin committed by many students of ethnicity; and although one should not overestimate the importance of concepts generated by academic research, they can have very noticeable effects on the outside world through their potential as self-fulfilling prophecies. Concepts can serve as both intellectual tools of liberation and as straitjackets. Their only claim to legitimacy lies in their ability to help us conceptualise the outside world more accurately; when they cease to do that job, they are ready for replacement by others.

It has become a ritual exercise in social science theses and most theoretically ambitious papers on ethnicity and nationalism to interrogate the theories of nationalism developed by the late Ernest Gellner, Eric Hobsbawm, and Anthony D. Smith, concerning whether nationalism and ethnicity are 'old' or 'new' phenomena, and to which extent they are 'invented'.[5] While everyone seems to agree that nationalism is a child of that fusion between Enlightenment and Romanticism that we are accustomed to label Modernity, not everyone is convinced that it is this historically recent. For didn't already the Vikings distinguish between Dane, Swede, and Norwegian? And didn't the writers of the Bible attribute a certain saying about Jews and Greeks to Jesus Christ? And weren't the ancient Greeks pathologically xenophobic, as evidenced in the writings of Herodotos? To this, Modernists would reply that, although the collective self–other distinction harks back to the mists of human prehistory, the peculiarly reflexive character of the modern individual was missing, and that, besides, the nation-state places peculiar demands on its citizens, as well as abstract solidarity.

At this point, enter Benedict Anderson, famously quoted for the title of a book few seem to have read properly;[6] with all due respect, if they had, they would have realised that already on page six, Anderson notes that, in a certain sense, all communities beyond the family are imagined. In other words, to state that the nation is an 'imagined community' is pretty vacuous as a distinguishing mark. Rather than focusing on ethnic identity as the paradigmatic prerequisite for nationhood, as so many do, Anderson emphasises the impact of print technology and a capitalist system of distribution in his explanation of the development of imagined communities of an unprecedented scale, involving, through shared commitment, solidarity, and ritual communion, very large numbers of people who will never meet.

Although Anderson notes the similarity between ethnicity and nationalism as modes of belongingness, he does not explicitly relate nationalism to ethnicity; he does not talk of the 'ethnic origins of nations'.[7] An historian of South-East Asia, Anderson writes extensively about nationalist movements in the Philippines and Indonesia, countries which, if they are to be considered nations at all, are arguably non-ethnic ones.

Nations are conceptualised and defined in crucially different ways in different parts of the academic community. In the European press, incidentally, nationalism seems to have become virtually a synonym for xenophobia. In my own discipline, social anthropology, nationalism tends to be seen as identical with ethnic nationalism,[8] whereas political scientists often regard it as a chiefly civic kind of ideology, as what German intellectuals describe as *Verfassungspatriotismus* (Constitutional Patriotism). The two 'kinds' of nationalism, sometimes described as 'German' and 'French', or even 'East European' and 'West European', are not mutually exclusive in practice. Even the civic British nation, to the extent that it exists as an imagined community, has an easily identifiable dominant ethnic group, namely the English; just as the WASPs can be seen, with slightly greater difficulty, as the hegemonic ethnic group of the USA. This does not, however, mean that nations are by default built around the shared collective memories, territorial attachments, customs, and values of ethnic groups. I will shortly invoke an example which shows the opposite. Besides, any realistic discussion of nationhood in Africa must find its point of departure in a model of nationhood which does not equate national identity either with ethnic identity or with a subservient ethnic identity. In the African context, bickering about ethnic diversity as being somehow irreconcilable with nationhood, describing the African states as being 'unnatural', with 'artificial boundaries', would lead us nowhere analytically, if the ultimate aim is to understand the construction of identities *from the inside*. Such bickering would also reveal a rather weak understanding of empirically existing European nations, which, as it has been pointed out repeatedly since Walker Connor's seminal article on nationhood and ethnicity, are much less mono-ethnic than it has been customary to believe.[9]

The issue at this stage concerns the extent to which a sense of common identity can be developed in the poly-ethnic African countries, and which models of the nation can be reconciled with the facts on the ground.

In order to discuss this question properly, it is necessary to dwell briefly on the problem of cultural integration and its relationship to ethnicity and nationhood. Most theorists and commentators on nationalism describe it as an ideology which promotes cultural homogeneity and a subjective feeling of we-hood. The first clause is evidently true, but it needs qualifying. How much do the citizens of a nation need to have in common, culturally speaking, in order to be regarded as culturally homogeneous? The answer cannot be of an either-or kind, since shared culture is a matter of degree. Smith and others have stressed that a shared public culture is sufficient, but even if that much is conceded, there are some very real difficulties associated with the delineation of such a public culture.[10] Even societies regarded as homogeneous, such as mono-lingual countries, have greatly differentiated public spheres. The social philosopher Jon Elster once suggested that a society might be defined as a place where people stop at red traffic lights. This will certainly not be sufficient as a general definition of a nation, but it is difficult to tell exactly what is. This, obviously, is a core issue.

The second clause, regarding the subjective feeling of we-hood, is no less difficult to define in an unambiguous way, if not only because the compass and composition of the we-group shift situationally. In general, there is a widespread tendency, also present among academics, to conflate cultural similarity and subjectively defined nationhood. One may have a lot of the latter without much of the former, as when conservative Protestant fundamentalists in Western Norway and post-Marxist babyboomers in Eastern Norway take it for granted that they share the same culture, despite their very considerable differences at the level of objective culture. Conversely, the middle classes of Milan and Lyon may have a lot in common culturally, but not at the level of collective self-identity. The imagined community does not have an existence unless it is being *imagined actively* by its members. This does not mean that it is any more 'imaginary' than other communities, but that it can only exist at the inter-subjective level: it is defined *from within*. This is perhaps nowhere more evident than in the 'soft' African states, which only rarely come into being as relevant aspects of inter-personal life-worlds.

The common conflation of shared culture with shared ethnic identity makes the task of crafting accurate concepts even more difficult. Just as cultural similarity does not by itself lead to collective identification, ethnic similarity does not vouch for cultural similarity, even if there is often a strong correlation. As it has been pointed out many times, the most protracted and bitter ethnic conflicts are often staged between ethnic groups who, at the level of culture, are very similar, such as Hutus and Tutsis in Rwanda, or Orthodox, Catholics, and Muslims in Bosnia.

The role of history is a related question in discussions of nationalism and nationhood. To what extent do nations need a shared past as a foundation for their present collective identity? Although it is difficult to imagine a national ideology totally devoid of invocations of shared memories, their importance varies, and some theorists assert that the shared past is always a more or less arbitrary invention. In some nations, the future seems to play a more important role in popular national imagery than the past; twentieth-century Sweden and the United States are perhaps good examples of this. The governments of post-colonial African nation-states have also tended to stress ideas of progress and modernity rather than the mythical past in official national symbolism.[11]

Let me sum up this part of the discussion before moving on to the main example. There are several moot points in the discourse over nationalism with immediate relevance to the discussion about African nationhood.

(1) Whether or not ethnic groups are 'modern' is a contested issue. In the classic collection edited by Fredrik Barth, most of the contributions dealt with traditional societies.[12] For my purposes, however, I shall accept that ethnic corporations and ethnic imagined communities in Africa are recent developments, partly produced in the context of colonialism and associated with the rise of individualism, capitalism, and the state. Earlier corporations and collective identities, although they might have carried a label later seen as ethnic, were constructed according to a different logic.[13]

(2) The relationship between conceptualisations of ethnicity and nationalism is complicated. Some analysts see nations simply as ethnic groups writ large, with leaderships of state-building ambitions; others stress the civic, non-ethnic aspects of nations. Scarcely a single state is ethnically homogeneous, and many do not even have a dominant ethnic group. Here, I shall see the African nation as a supra-ethnic or poly-ethnic phenomenon, which may nevertheless be appropriated by ethnic groups in a number of ways, including the monopolisation of power and secession.

(3) The relationship between nationhood and culture has been insufficiently explored. Although Gellner brazenly, and probably correctly, stated that nationalism and successful nation-building inevitably

imply cultural homogenisation, the degree of cultural similarity varies both inside and beyond the boundaries of the state in question.[14]

(4) Cultural similarity, ethnic incorporation, and collective self-identity are granted unequal weight in rivalling conceptualisations of nationhood. In Hobsbawm's work, for example, collective self-identification takes on a paramount importance, while Smith stresses the sharing of customs and memories, frequently through an idiom of ethnicity.

(5) The role of historical continuity, whether real or imagined or both, is also a difficult aspect of nationhood, and one faced with deep gravity by the African states, many of them manifestly lacking a shared history.

A Quasi-African Success Story

Commenting on the genre of biography, Virginia Woolf lets the protagonist of her novel *Orlando* assume an enormous and seemingly unrealistic variety of social roles and identities, right down to the point of changing gender.[15] Yet, the narrator says towards the end of the book, she has written only a small fraction of the possible biographies that could be written about Orlando. In other words, people have many more facets than a single book might possibly reveal.

The people of Mauritius, I think it would be fair to say, collectively exploit a fair proportion of Orlando's vast role repertoire. Mauritius, a multi-ethnic island-state in the south-western Indian Ocean, has for historical reasons an ethnically very diverse population of about one million, four major religions, a large but uncertain number of languages, and no indigenous population.[16] Widely considered an economic miracle in the 1990s, Mauritius is also a stable multi-party democracy which has experienced several changes of government since independence in 1968.

Arriving on the island to carry out fieldwork early in 1986, I half expected to find a society where postmodern relativism was as deeply ingrained as the faith in technological progress had been in the Europe of the 1950s. Instead, I encountered a very wide range of perfectly solid and confident personal identities, often based on qualitatively different premises. The eclectic approach to identification which can be observed in a society such as Mauritius is evident already in the now obsolete colonial grid for dividing the population into ethnic categories. The last of several such classificatory exercises, abandoned officially in 1982, divided the Mauritian population into four mutually exclusive categories: Hindus, Muslims, Chinese, and 'General Population'. Two of them are religious categories, one refers to an ancestral country, and the final one is residual and contains most but not all of Mauritius' Catholics, with origins as diverse as France and Madagascar, and with no collective sense of ethnic community. However, if a common myth of origin is an important defining mark for an ethnic group, then the island has at least eight ethnic groups;[17] if one chooses to stress the endogamy rule, the number may rise to around twenty; whereas if ancestral language is to be invoked as a differentiating criterion, fifteen ethnic groups might be counted. This ought to make it clear, if there should be any doubt, that ethnicity is, and remains, a relational and situational kind of social phenomenon. However, the ethnic identities are not the only important identities in Mauritius, although they have justly or unjustly formed the focus of most research on identification in the island. Let me, by way of illustration, provide a list of the most important over-arching identities I have recorded during fieldwork in 1986 and in 1991–92.[18] By 'over-arching', I mean identities which may, in certain situations, overrule all other identities and appear as imperative in the sense that they induce action.

> (1) *Ethnic identity*. Although criteria for ethnic differentiation are not consistent with each other, there is always a close link between ethnic identity and kinship. Politics, jobs, and marriage are often, but far from always, regulated through an ethnic idiom.
> (2) *Class identity*. Trade unions frequently cut across ethnic lines, and two general strikes in independent Mauritius testify to their occasional efficacy. Also, the sense of belonging to a certain class rather than to an ethnic group is strong in parts of the urban middle class, which often intermarries and tends to regard itself as cosmopolitan. Shared professional identity, also not negligible under certain circumstances, can also be included here.
> (3) *Gender identity*. There are several feminist organisations, which have a certain impact on public debate and which explicitly try to bridge gaps between Indo-Mauritian and Creole women. Of course, gender identity is also highly relevant in a great number of everyday situations, probably most.
> (4) *Age*. Youth increasingly tend to share social idioms, networks and activities irrespective of ethnic background, in addition to, in most cases, going to multi-ethnic state schools.
> (5) *Religious identity*. Although the correlation between religion and ethnic identity is high, Chinese Catholics, Indo-Christians, and Muslim Creoles, among others, worship with members of ethnic groups other than their own.
> (6) *Local identity*. although the ethnic element is rarely entirely absent from local politics in Mauritius, villages are often united on single issues, and sometimes divided along non-ethnic lines.[19]
> (7) *Political identity*. Several political groups are explicitly based on non-ethnic premises, although national politics in Mauritius remains thoroughly ethnified.

(8) *Linguistic identity*. Although most Mauritians speak a French-lexicon Creole (*Kreol*) as their first language, other languages are also spoken in the island. Notably, French-speakers, regardless of ethnic affiliation, militate for the continued strong position of French in public life. Some of them would be, for example, Tamils by ethnic origin.
(9) *Kinship*. Much of what passes for ethnic organisation in Mauritius is simply kinship organisation, and a strong commitment to the family and kin group is found, both in ideology and in practice, in all ethnic groups in the island.
(10) *Supra-ethnic national identity*. Although this form of identification is most evidently present in parts of the growing urban middle class, among intellectuals, academics and the like, there have been historical situations where very large numbers of Mauritians have visibly associated themselves with the multi-ethnic nation rather than with their ethnic group. This is the case, for example, during and after the ritual following the death of Mauritius' first Prime Minister, Sir Seewoosagur Ramgoolam, and in connection with large international sports tournaments.[20] Significantly, during the controversy concerning whether Mauritius should change its Commonwealth status to that of a Republic (which happened on 12 March 1992), views did not diverge systematically along ethnic lines.

Mauritius now seems to be in the process of developing a common set of supra-ethnic, national myths and symbols which is invested with meaning and relevance by the bulk of its population, although ethnic identification still remains strong. Some of this mythical material harks back to the mists of colonialism, but some of it relates to the turmoil and social unrest in the years around Independence.[21] It is impossible to state whether this symbolic framework will, in the long run, prove too feeble and fragile to sustain a sense of unity among its ethnic and non-ethnic groups and networks. It is nonetheless clear that any viable Mauritian supra-ethnic nationalism will have to reconcile itself not only with ethnicity, but also with the emerging *non-ethnic* constituent parts of society. Ethnic, non-ethnic, and post-ethnic elements, in other words, coexist side by side in a precarious but, nonetheless, stable equilibrium.

Two complementary, and sometimes competing, models of the Mauritian nation coexist, and each has its symbols and rituals. One of them is commonly spoken of as *le pluriculturalisme mauricien*; this sees the nation as being made up by the very 'cultural mosaic' that it embodies, and locates nationhood at the interface between the constituent ethnic or cultural groups and their mutual respect. The other model lifts nationhood to a supra-ethnic level and depicts Mauritian nationhood in terms of the universal values and institutions that all Mauritians share: the political, legislative, and educational systems, the territory, and recently, the successful export economy. To the extent that these formal, or officially constructed, visions of nationalism are successful at the informal or popular level,[22] they appeal both to ethnic sentiment and to supra-ethnic nationhood; both to particularistic yearning for community and historical embeddedness and to the universalistic ideals of the bureaucratic state. Although it is by no means unproblematic to develop, and although it requires a great deal of compromise and improvisation as one goes along, a combination of these two nationalisms seems to solve many of the potential contradictions inherent in multi-ethnic states.

If the topic of this volume were xenophobia and exclusion in Europe, I would at this point have raised the question of what Europe can learn from Mauritius.[23] Here, it is more appropriate to ask what the forty-odd multi-ethnic states in Africa could learn from Mauritius. The answer is simple. The model can be learnt, quickly and freely. On the other hand, it is unlikely that it can be implemented wholesale through the application of mere political will, since several of the institutional and objective underpinnings of the Mauritian model are missing in most African countries. First, the boundaries of the Mauritian nation are not questioned, and no European *Besserwisser* ('smart-alec') or local identity politician can plausibly argue that its borders are 'artificial'. There can be no secession, no irredentism in such a small, isolated island, unlike the case of many post-colonial African states, with experienes ranging from Nigeria's Biafra war to the successful Eritrean secession and the idea of an Afrikaner *Volkstaat*. Second, the Mauritian population has a high level of education and a *de facto* high level of cultural integration, which makes a national public sphere possible. The media infrastructure – radio, TV, and, to some extent, newspapers – reaches most households. As a result, the political system is governed by a shared system of common denominators. Third, Mauritius is a country of such small scale that the gap between elite and masses, or between centre and periphery, is much smaller than in most African countries. Although many African countries, like Mauritius, practice power sharing between major ethnic groups, there is comparatively little social integration between elites and masses within each ethnic group.[24] Thus, power sharing at the ethnic group level is not tantamount to national integration, if the state bureaucratic elite is more or less cut off from ordinary people. Admittedly, nepotism remains a well established practice in parts of the Mauritian public sector, but, unlike the case of several African countries, it cannot be said that the state is run by kinship corporations.

I have mentioned unquestioned sovereignty, high levels of education and cultural integration, and small scale as factors which may partly account for the relative success of Mauritian nation-building. As regards the second point, it might be added that the dialect variations in Mauritian Creole tend to follow regional and not ethnic lines, and that, although cultural differences based on ethnicity invariably crop up during conversations and are sometimes observed as well, they rarely interfere with the functioning of the shared institutions of society. The message is, in a word, that if such shared institutions work reasonably impartially and according to universalistic principles, ethnic diversity is no obstacle to nation-building. Somalia could, in its tragic way, provide the mirror-image of this argument: the Somalis speak the same language, and share the same culture and ethnic identity in any reasonable meaning of the term, and yet their country has fallen into pieces because of a lack of functioning shared institutions.[25]

In this brief discussion of Mauritian nationhood, I have mentioned ritual a few times. Rituals are crucial confirmers and producers of collective identification in any society; they simultaneously create a sense of identity and justify a power structure. When rituals fail to engage people, as is the case with many state-sponsored Independence Day celebrations in post-colonial societies all over the world, the power structure they implicitly symbolise is not seen as legitimate or as relevant for identity, and people look elsewhere for their collective identification. In a recent book on ritual in contemporary Africa, none of the rituals analysed, with the possible exception of Nigerian witchcraft accusations as mediated by the popular press, seem to be credible candidates as nationally cohesive forces.[26] In creating *communitas*, to use Victor Turner's celebrated term,[27] among the members of single ethnic groups, rituals contribute to strengthening rather than weakening ethnic incorporation.

From the notion that ethnic identity is a threat to national cohesion in multi-ethnic societies, it would follow that ethnic rituals are dangerous centrifugal forces. The loyalty to the state would then be inversely proportional to the degree of loyalty to the ethnic group. This, indeed, is the view held by many politicians and theorists, not least in African countries. This is, nevertheless, a position which, by overestimating the political dimension of ethnicity and underestimating its dimension of identification, may paradoxically inspire a politicisation of ethnicity. A suppressed kind of cultural practice may easily re-emerge as a resentful political one. State intolerance towards ethnic rituals does not usually lead to popular support for state rituals, but rather to the creation of ethnic countercultures. This is one problem which has been avoided in the dual Mauritian construal of the nation, in which cultural expressions of ethnicity are positively encouraged and are not seen as a threat to nationhood; they are seen, instead, as complementary to it.

The paucity of rituals which are actually, and not merely officially, cohesive at the national level in many African countries, is a symptom, not a cause. The causes for the lack of national cohesion have to be found elsewhere – in the usually oligarchic and often kleptocratic political structures, in the widespread lack of *lingua francas* spoken by the bulk of the population, and in labour markets which fail to offer jobs to individuals who can no longer return to functioning clans and who therefore remain suspended in limbo between a lost traditional society and a mock modernity which reveals itself as little more than a showroom. The question is why it is that divisive and conflictual ethnicity emerges, or – as some would have it – re-emerges, in this kind of situation. In order to fully understand this, it is necessary to look more closely at the phenomenon of identification than I have done so far.

The Rationale of Social Identification

What is the self? What does the word 'I' mean, let alone the word 'we'? As Anthony P. Cohen has noted in an important recent book, mainstream social science has tended to avoid the question, taking individual agency for granted and regarding groups in society as 'social facts', even if they pay lip service to the fact that identification is *situational* and *relational*: given appropriate structural conditions, they need not be politicised.[28] Furthermore, social identity cannot be taken for granted by the analyst, but must always be investigated empirically; and which identity is construed as 'the most primordial' varies – whether, say, gender, ethnicity, kinship, or class is considered to be a person's most crucial criterion of belongingness in a particular society or a particular context. Therefore, an investigation of identification must begin with the individual and the meaningful relationships he or she enters into with others and with a world ordered through classificatory schemata.

People are loyal to ethnic, national, or other imagined communities not because they were born into them, but because such foci of loyalty promise to offer something deemed meaningful, valuable, or useful. This kind of perspective may be denounced as 'utilitarian' or 'individualist', or even 'reductionist'. I would like to argue that it is not. First, as I have argued with reference to Mauritius, ethnic identification is but one of several identities in which any individual engages. It is made relevant under particular circumstances over which the individual may not exert much control. Second, what is deemed valuable is culturally determined; it is defined from within. This means that there may be, and indeed often are, discrepancies between definitions of the good life, especially in societies where cultural diversity is considerable. Third, the 'instance' that finally perceives alternatives and chooses between them, is a human being, an individual, who, nevertheless, does not choose his or her own cognitive matrix, that is, his or her cultural context. Fourth, it may be that, say, kinship and natal villages may always command nostalgia and warm sentiment, but unless they are socially activated through some kind of resource flow perceived as relevant by the actor, they remain at the level of representations and do not emerge as social and political corporations. It is within this kind of framework that we may properly inquire into the circumstances in which classes and ethnic groups may emerge.

In other words, individuals choose their allegiances, but not under circumstances of their own choice. For them to invest symbolically, politically, or economically into a corporation or an imagined community, it must offer something in return. Which collectivities are at any point the most important both to individuals and to the functioning of society, is therefore an empirical question. This way of reasoning is not utilitarianist, since it emphasises the importance of the life-world context for action; it is, rather, tautologically true in the same sense as the Spencerian maxim of the survival of the fittest: people act, by definition, to achieve certain ends, but the ends are contextually defined.

On the question of why specifically ethnic corporations emerge, and why they tend to be poised against the state, Basil Davidson, reflecting on the traumas of post-colonial Africa, recently wrote that,

> [t]he jubilant crowds celebrating independence were not inspired by a 'national consciousness' any more than were the Romanian peasants and their coevals in the nation-states crystallized some decades earlier from Europe's old internal empires. They were inspired by the hope of more and better food and shelter.[29]

When these goods failed to materialise, they oriented themselves to new – or, in some cases, old – foci for social allegiance. For the great Pan-Africanists, the nation-state may have been too small. For very many Africans, it was far too big, unless they happened to live in a mini-state such as Lesotho or Mauritius, or if they had the kind of Western education and middle-class experiences which made the African nation-state seem relevant as an imagined community – or, again, if the state had something substantial to offer by way of education, employment, and security. For the vast majority of Africans, a community of this scale did not tally with their personal experiences, which were strictly local.

Generally, as every European critical of the Maastricht treaty or the EMU agreement would agree, when a large-scale community fails to deliver the goods, structures at the medium and low levels of scale emerge. Although these structures have always been present in African countries, they become increasingly invested with pragmatic potential as the higher level (the state bureaucracy) is weakened or simply severed from the majority of its citizens (who thereby become citizens in name only). We should keep in mind that a substantial part of what is conventionally described as African ethnicity is simply kinship; in other words, the failed nations are replaced by pre-existing structures, whose functioning has been transformed by historical changes, and whose political importance is inversely correlated with the strength and legitimacy of the state. That an individual in, say, Congo should place his bets on his clan rather than on the state, should offer no surprise, as ethnographic studies show.[30] In some parts of the world, notably North Africa and the Middle East, political Islam plays the same part: it stands for resentment to the corrupted and inefficient state and an alternative path to authentic belongingness, prosperity, and integrity.[31] In general, politicised countercultures are liable to take on an ethnic character in societies where kinship is the most important local principle of social organisation, since ethnicity is always, or nearly always, a form of metaphoric kinship.

Corporate kinship, in Africa and elsewhere, ideally works as a segmentary system. The segmentary model of identification, made famous in Evans-Pritchard's study of Nuer politics, but familiar to a vast number of people, including Jean-Marie Le Pen, depicts the modes of belonging of each individual as a set of concentric circles where loyalty, in absolute terms, becomes weaker as one moves outwards from the centre.[32] It is illustrated in the famous formula, 'it is I against my brother, my brother and I against our cousins; our cousins, my brother and I against our remote relatives'. In Evans-Pritchard's words, 'although any group tends to split into opposed parts these parts must tend to fuse in relation to other groups, since they form part of a segmentary system'.[33] Each level of allegiance is activated when circumstances make it relevant. The contraction of such a system of concentric circles indicates that structures at a high level of scale are weakening and breaking down. This seems to be happening in many African societies in the 1990s, where an increasing amount of capital – political, economic, and symbolic – seems to be flowing through the inner circles. The severing of links between elites and masses is one important indication, which is serious not just from the peasant's point of view, but also from a nation-building perspective. As noted by John Lonsdale in a recent discussion of Kikuyu ethnicity and Kenyan nationhood, 'the experience of state power seems necessary to the growth of nationhood'.[34]

An alternative view of social identification could represent a person's identities as a set of partly overlapping group allegiances. Such multiple identities cannot be placed in concentric circles in orderly ways; they can scarcely be represented graphically at all. They cut across each other: every person has a shared identity with different people at different times, according to the situation; one belongs to a profession, a political interest group, a neighbourhood, a kin group and so on. The most fundamental and universal human form of identification is arguably gender. In this kind of context, the status sets of individuals are not clustered about multiplex relationships to a limited number of people; they are diverse and flexible. The stiff and inflexible concept of culture typical of twentieth-century academia, depicting cultural systems as bounded and stable, has made it difficult to understand these complexities fully, since we have lacked tools enabling us to conceptualise group membership as something relative and relational.[35] As noted by Cohen, group boundedness has simply been taken for granted in virtually all anthropological studies of culture and in all social science studies of ethnicity – and, let me add, in modern identity politics worldwide.[36] A simple distinction between personal identity and group identity would nevertheless be sufficient to show that boundaries are relational and that groups, even if their existence is not necessarily negotiable, are situational at least regarding their relative importance.

The general policy implications of this analysis are obvious: cross-cutting ties and conflicting loyalties may contribute to reducing tension and conflict potential. A world of many small differences is safer, all other things being equal, than a world of a few major ones – such as the ones promoted by ethnic nationalisms. Here it may be noted that even a major theorist sympathetic to nationalism, namely Smith, stresses the need for states to encourage multiple and conflicting loyalties.[37]

It would seem, then, that if it is correct that the focus of social organisation in large parts of Africa is shifting from the grand, abstract imagined community to more manageable, tangible ones, political tension may be reduced. I do not think so, for the simple reason that the weakening of the state entails a weakening of that over-arching set of rules governing intergroup relations; that is, the universalistic structure, or common denominators, to which I referred in the Mauritian example. The division of labour between various institutions, functioning both at the macro and the micro level, which is characteristic of Mauritian society – and which, incidentally, is necessary to any society worth more than a few traffic lights – is skewed and incomplete in many African countries, where the highest level of scale is, to varying degrees, disengaged from the other levels.[38] In addition, the economic system operates at a level of very large scale, whereas low-level social integration is in no ways congruent with it and, thus, cannot monitor or control it efficiently.

If a sweeping statement can be allowed, let me offer the following: what is at stake for the majority of Africans is not primarily a vindication of their 'roots', popular culture and so on. In this, African ethnicity is quite different from West European ethnicity, insofar as kinship continues to play an important role, transcending public-private boundaries. This is to a much lesser extent the case in Europe, where ethnicity instead tends to be modelled on abstract, imagined communities in Anderson's sense. While meaning and *communitas* may certainly be scarce, more urgent concerns would in most cases be the satisfaction of basic needs, as well as compelling reasons for believing that one's personal ambitions will lead somewhere. When state institutions cease to deliver, kinship and, by extension, ethnicity is often the only alternative. It is chiefly in this context that we must understand the emergence of modern, sometimes militant African ethnicities as mass movements. The state would in this case be a Trojan horse concealing not identity politics but kinship organisation.

I began this essay by a comparison of different models of nationhood, with particular reference to the multi-ethnic, post-colonial states of Sub-Saharan Africa. Obviously, most African states did not easily fit the standard model of nations as culturally more or less homogeneous, historically constituted entities. Neither, of course, did most European, American, and Asian states. The crisis in the African state, I have subsequently argued, is no more a result of ethnic heterogeneity than the breakup of Yugoslavia was caused by ancient ethnic hatred.[39] Ethnic homogeneity can contribute to national cohesion, but as the contrasting examples of Mauritius and Somalia show, it is neither a necessary nor a sufficient condition. I have argued that insofar as presumedly shared state-level institutions – education, politics, labour market – do not function according to more or less universalistic principles and are perceived as such by the non-elite members of society, the state not only becomes illegitimate in a Weberian sense, but it also fails to form a sustained focus of loyalty and identification for the majority of its citizens. This may seem a banal insight, but it is meant as an urge for us, the academic community specialising in the study of other people's modes of identification, not to neglect the study of the subjective level of experience and of individual agency based on local life-worlds.

Coming to Terms with Essentialism

The social science project is, like the African nation-building one, essentially an Enlightenment one, but its subject-matter is largely constituted as a Romantic world in the wide sense; one drawing on unifying metaphors rather than on analytic dissecting tools for its cognitive power. In this divergence lies a great potential for misrepresentation and, as I think the African post-independence experience shows, political futility and disruption.

Theorists of culture have in recent years developed a critical attitude towards 'native' appropriations of the concept of culture for ideological purposes.[40] The classic anthropological concept of culture, originating in German romanticism (where Herder is the main reference[41]) and cultural relativism (from Franz Boas onwards[42]), depicts the world as an archipelago of more or less isolated cultures. Within this kind of model, culture becomes *reified*; it becomes like a fixed object, or a bounded vessel containing 'a people'. Against this model, theorists have posited a view which stresses the flow, ambiguity and unbounded character of systems of meaning.[43] One has tended to view kin groups and ethnic corporations as mere constructions, which they are in a certain sense, but not to their members, for whom they are resources which channel security, hopes, and dreams.

Native theories tend to be essentialistic, and argue for the objective, thinglike character of social and cultural identity. Criticism from an academic point of view does not change this. It may indeed seem that we, as theorists, represent perspectives which may be analytically valid but which are politically futile, as post-independence African experiences, whereby politicians and theorists eagerly applied European models to their societies, may show. It may, of course, be the case that the theory is *avant-garde*, but there can be no doubt that there are profound and systematic differences between the experiences, life-worlds, and structures of relevance (*Relevanzstrukturen*[44])upon which theorists and categories of 'natives', respectively, draw in their constructions of identity. Extrapolating from our own experiences of the world, we run the risk of generalising from our own, highly specialised experiences. As a result, large parts of the population about which we theorise would feel alienated from our theoretical models and would question their validity, since their own experiences and models of the world are radically different – not only from ours, but also from our representations of theirs!

The professional academic mode of engaging with the world could be described as detached, logical, disinterested and discursive. The academic discursive field is supra-spatial, or disengaged from place. By contrast, local modes of engaging with the world are experience-based, sensual, engaged, practical, and often kinship based. These world views are intrinsically connected with concrete places. They are often stigmatised (by cosmopolitans) as fascist, racist, reactionary and so on, after having been caricatured as much more solid and absolute than they may actually be.

Perhaps, it would be more accurate to state that both modes of engaging with the world are practical, but derive from qualitatively different kinds of practices, different embedded experiences, and thus different interests in a wide sense. The city-dweller walks on tarmac and lives in a flat; the rural dweller walks on soil and lives in the family's farm.[45] The urban social network is based on the public sphere of anonymous individuals, while the rural one is based on kinship and neighbourhood. It is perfectly understandable that different groups, with radically different experiences, do not develop the same ways of relating to kinship, resources, belonging, and identity. It is therefore the source of some worry that recent criticisms of ethnic and nationalist ideologies have not incorporated an understanding of such variations in our frequently one-sided dismissals of 'indigenous essentialisms', because the bias proper to the life-worlds of intellectuals hampers a sensitive understanding of such processes. *Blut und Boden* (blood and soil) may be a perfectly appropriate metaphor for the collective interests of rurals in contemporary African life-worlds, just as human rights may be more important to urban dwellers. Furthermore, the sheer force of argument is scarcely sufficient to make people change their views on identity, belonging, and loyalty. The rationale behind subjective identification with a collective entity is simply, as I have discussed at length, that it has something to offer which is deemed valuable, meaningful, or useful within a context of experience. Mauritians are not by birth more civilised, more tolerant, more industrious, or more democratic than, say, Togolese or Angolans, but for structural reasons, they are able to relate to identity options which make such virtues seem sensible and beneficial.

Conclusion

Tailbiting occurs in two very different ways where ethnicity is considered. While ethnopoliticians and their supporters bite the tails of others, scholars increasingly tend to bite their own. Scholars encounter risks of self-referential inconsistency, circular argument, and infinite regress, and ought to find no easy consolation in the alternatives of stringent positivism and reductionist objectivism. It remains a fact that ethnic groups are created from within – subjectively and intersubjectively – and also that a mere examination of the objective conditions for their genesis does not provide a full explanation for their existence. Many of us pay lip service to rather fuzzy ideas of 'interplay' between objective and subjective, or historical and structural, factors; but it is another matter altogether to demonstrate the actual complexity of ethnic phenomena.

What is crucial at this point is that we academics become able, not necessarily to sympathise with, but at least to understand what it is that makes people tick: in order to carry out an analysis of an entire society, we must first be able to understand the subjective experiences upon which people act.

A largely implicit theme in this essay, announced at the beginning, has been the contrast between social science models of ethnicity and nationalism, on the one hand, and ongoing group identification in actual societies, on the other. Social scientists, from political scientists to anthropologists, have excelled in developing sophisticated formal models of societal formations and cultural systems of classification. At the same time, they have paid much less attention to modelling and understanding the ongoing flow of social life as defined from within – and if they have done the latter, as many anthropologists would insist that they have, they usually fail to demonstrate the relationship between the levels.[46] Addressing the relationship between macro processes and local life-worlds, a classic problem in social analysis, is essential for any proper understanding of ethnicity.

In many of our societies, including, in this case, both European and African ones, it seems that the academic, political, and economic élites are moving in one direction and the rest of the population in another, and simplistic academic models of the world do not exactly mitigate this problem. An important task for analysts must therefore consist in relaying an understanding of life-worlds, not just the way they are described by locals, but to come as close as possible to the ways in which they are *experienced*. Only then can we claim to have understood African ethnicity, and only then should our policy recommendations carry any weight.

NOTES

I would like to thank the participants of the ASEN conference on 'Ethnicity and Nationalism in Africa' and, in particular, Paris Yeros, for comments and criticism.

1. See, for example, Lawrence Hirschfeld, *Race in the Making: Cognition, Culture, and the Child's Construction of Human Kinds* (Cambridge, MA: MIT Press, 1996).
2. See Benedict Anderson, *Imagined Communities: Reflections on the Origin and Spread of Nationalism*, Second Edition (London: Verso, 1991), and Ernest Gellner, *Nations and Nationalism* (Oxford: Blackwell, 1983).
3. This view is evident in Karl Marx and Friedrich Engels, *Manifest der Kommunistischen Partei* (Berlin: Dietz Verlag, 1968 [1848]), but also in later works by both authors.
4. See Thomas Hylland Eriksen, 'What Is Happening to the Concept of Ethnicity?', *Razprave in Gradivo* (No. 29–30, 1995), pp. 165–77.
5. See Gellner, *op. cit.*, in note 2; Eric Hobsbawm, *Nations and Nationalism since 1780*, Second Edition (Cambridge: Cambridge University Press, 1992); and Anthony D. Smith, *The Ethnic Origins of Nations* (Oxford: Blackwell, 1986).
6. Anderson, *op. cit.*, in note 2.
7. Smith, *op. cit.*, in note 5.
8. See, for example, Marcus Banks, *Ethnicity: Anthropological Constructions* (London: Routledge, 1996).
9. See Walker Connor, 'A Nation Is a Nation, Is a State, Is an Ethnic Group, Is a...', *Ethnic and Racial Studies* (Vol. 1, No. 4, 1974), pp. 378–400.
10. See Anthony D. Smith, *Nations and Nationalism in a Global Era* (Cambridge: Polity, 1995), Anthony Giddens, *Beyond Left and Right* (Cambridge: Polity 1994), and Hobsbawm, *op. cit.*, in note 5.
11. See, for example, Basil Davidson, *The Black Man's Burden: Africa and the Curse of the Nation-State* (London: James Currey, 1992).
12. Fredrik Barth (ed.), *Ethnic Groups and Boundaries: The Social Organization of Cultural Difference* (Oslo: Scandinavian University Press, 1969).
13. See, for example, Riachard Fardon, 'African Ethnogenesis: Limits to the Comparability of Ethnic Phenomena', in Ladislav Holy (ed.), *Comparative Anthropology* (Oxford: Blackwell, 1987), pp. 168–88.
14. See, for example, Gellner, *op. cit.*, in note 2, pp. 35ff.
15. Virginia Woolf, *Orlando* (London: Hogarth Press, 1928).
16. See Thomas Hylland Eriksen, *Communicating Cultural Difference and Identity: Ethnicity and Nationalism in Mauritius* (Oslo: Occasional Papers in Social Anthropology, No. 16, 1988); Thomas Hylland Eriksen, *Us and Them in Modern Societies: Ethnicity and Nationalism in Mauritius, Trinidad and Beyond* (Oslo: Scandinavian University Press, 1992); and Larry Bowman, *Mauritius: Democracy and Development in the Indian Ocean* (Boulder, CO: Westview Press, 1990).

17. French, African, (North Indian) Hindu, Tamil, Muslim, Hakka-speaking, Cantonese-speaking, and *gen de couleur* (mixed Euro-African).
18. See Eriksen, *Communicating Cultural Difference and Identity, op. cit.*, in note 16, and Thomas Hylland Eriksen, 'Nationalism, Mauritian Style: Cultural Unity and Ethnic Diversity', *Comparative Studies in Society and History* (Vol. 36, No. 3, 1994), pp. 549–74.
19. See Eriksen, *Communicating Cultural Difference and Identity, op. cit.*, in note 16.
20. See Eriksen, 'Nationalism, Mauritian Style', *op cit.*, in note 18.
21. See Thomas Hylland Eriksen, *Ethnicity and Nationalism: Anthropological Perspectives* (London: Pluto, 1993).
22. See Thomas Hylland Eriksen, 'Formal and Informal Nationalism', *Ethnic and Racial Studies* (Vol. 16, No. 1, 1993), pp. 1–25.
23. For such a discussion, see Thomas Hylland Eriksen, 'Modernity and Ethnic Identity: Fragmentation and Unification in Europe Seen Through Mauritius', *L'Express Culture & Research* (No. 5, 1995), pp. 12–15.
24. See, for example, Göran Hydén, *No Shortcuts to Progress* (London: Heinemann, 1983), and Kajsa Ekholm Friedman, *Catastrophe and Creation: The Formation of an African Culture* (London: Harwood, 1991).
25. See Ioan M. Lewis, *Blood and Bone: The Call of Kinship in Somali Society* (Lawrenceville, NJ: Red Sea Press, 1994).
26. Jean and John Comaroff (eds.), *Modernity and its Malcontents: Ritual and Power in Postcolonial Africa* (Chicago, IL: University of Chicago Press, 1993).
27. Victor Turner, *The Ritual Process: Structure and Anti-structure* (Chicago, IL: Aldine, 1969).
28. Anthony P. Cohen, *Self Consciousness* (London: Routledge, 1994).
29. Davidson, *op. cit.*, in note 11, p. 185.
30. See Kajsa Ekholm Friedman, *Den magiska världsbilden: Om statens frigörelse från folket i Folkrepubliken Kongo* [The Magical World-view: On the Liberation of the State from the People in the People's Republic of Congo] (Stockholm: Carlssons, 1993).
31. See, for example, John Esposito, *The Islamic Treat: Myth or Reality?* (New York, NY: Oxford University Press, 1995).
32. E.E. Evans-Pritchard, *The Nuer* (Oxford: Clarendon Press, 1940).
33. *Ibid.*, p. 148.
34. John Lonsdale, 'Moral Ethnicity, Ethnic Nationalism and Political Tribalism: The Case of the Kikuyu' (Unpublished ms., University of Cambridge, 1996), p. 9.
35. The conceptualisation of culture, or cultures, as discrete, stable, and homogeneous runs through much of twentieth-century anthropology, from Franz Boas to Cliford Geertz and Claude Lévi-Strauss. See Franz Boas (ed.), *General Anthropology* (Boulder, CO: D.C. Heath, 1938), Clifford Geertz, *The Interpretation of Cultures* (New York, NY: Basic Books, 1973), and Claude Lévi-Strauss, *Race et Histoire* (Paris: Plon, 1952).
36. Cohen, *op. cit.*, in note 28.
37. Anthony D. Smith, *National Identity* (Harmondsworth: Penguin, 1991), and also Anthony D. Smith, *Nations and Nationalism in a Global Era* (Cambridge: Polity, 1995).
38. See Göran Hydén, *op. cit.*, in note 24.

39. For a convincing argument regarding Yugoslavia, see Tone Bringa, *Being Muslim the Bosnian Way: Identity and Community in a Central Bosnian Village* (Princeton, NJ: Princeton University Press, 1995).
40. See, for example, Jonathan Friedman, *Cultural Identity and Global Process* (London: Sage, 1994).
41. Johann Gottfried von Herder, *Auch eine Philosophie der Geschichte zur Bildung der Menschheit* (Frankfurt-am-Main: Suhrkamp, 1968 [1774]).
42. Boas, *op. cit.*, in note 35.
43. See, for example, Ulf Hannerz, *Cultural Complexity* (New York, NY: Columbia University Press, 1992).
44. See Alfred Schütz and Thomas Luckmann, *Strukturen der Lebenswelt, Band I* (Frankfurt-am-Main: Suhrkamp, 1979).
45. In the words of my colleague, Eduardo Archetti, it is impossible to develop *roots* in an environment where one walks on tarmac and not on soil. Eduardo Archetti, personal communication.
46. This shortcoming can be traced back at least to Barth's 'Introduction', in Barth (ed.), *op. cit.*, in note 12. Interestingly, in a more recent statement, Barth makes a similar point about levels and their interrelationships; see Fredrik Barth, 'Enduring and Emerging Issues in the Analysis of Ethnicity', in Hans Vermeulen and Cora Govers (eds.), *The Anthropology of Ethnicity* (Amsterdam: Het Spinhuis, 1994), pp. 11–32.

4. Nationalism and Ethnicity in the Horn of Africa

John Markakis

Both nationalism and ethnicity have earned the attention of social scientists because of their political prominence. The discussion here focuses specifically on the role of these two closely related, and often confused, phenomena in struggles for power. The state is at the centre of such struggles, whose bone of contention is, more often than not, access to state-controlled resources. Not infrequently, conflict is the result, particularly where resources are scarce and diminishing. Conflict involving nationalism and ethnicity rarely brings out the best in human nature; the reverse is the norm. Seeking to explain such behaviour, some scholars peer into the murky depths of the human psyche with its unfathomable emotions and uncontrollable passions, and pin the blame on the mindless subjectivity which presumably rules the behaviour of people in the throes of nationalism and ethnicity.[1] Others see the elemental logic of biology at work.[2] The conflictual aspect tends to cast an ethical shadow on our perception of nationalism and ethnicity, often obliging social scientists to add normative assessments to the study of these phenomena. Being entirely subjective, such additions seldom facilitate comprehension.[3]

Irrefutably, emotions influence human behaviour. Attempts to take them into account in a given instance confront two problems. First, by the nature of the subject, any assessment of their weight in the calculus of motivation is itself impressionistic, not to say subjective. Second, such attempts tend to isolate the phenomena they are studying, to reify and isolate them from the situations that give birth to them. As Thomas Hylland Eriksen comments in this volume, 'by isolating "ethnicity" as a focus for research, one easily loses everything else form sight'.[4] In other words, effect is detached from cause. In order to avoid tunnel vision of this sort, the discussion that follows proceeds on the assumption that the political manifestation of nationalism and ethnicity is socially defined and historically determined. This means that one can comprehend and explain why they become hegemonic political forces by investigating the context in which this occurs. This will be demonstrated with reference to the Horn of Africa, a region awash in national and ethnic conflicts.[5]

Nationalism

In his influential work on *Nationalism and the State*, John Breuilly writes that 'nationalism is, above all else, about politics and...politics is about power. Power, in the modern world, is principally about the control of the state. The central task, therefore, is to relate nationalism to the objectives of obtaining and using state power'.[6] This is a useful, albeit incomplete, definition of a phenomenon that has yet to be precisely defined. It is incomplete because it tells us not what nationalism is, but what it is about. It is useful as a working definition, because it addresses a relationship that is empirically established and, furthermore, it links it to power, an attribute of the state which is an indisputable fact as well. By contrast, the usual approach is to theorise about the relationship of nationalism to the nation, without the benefit of having an adequate definition of either.

The advantage of this approach is obvious to those whose work concerns sub-Saharan Africa. We have states in Africa and we have nationalism, and there is an established historical relationship between the two. There is nothing particularly obscure or mystifying in this relationship. This is not the chicken or egg puzzle posed by Anthony D. Smith when he asks, '[d]oes nationalism create nations, or do nations form the matrix and seedbed of nationalism?'[7] We know the modern state appeared in Africa first in its colonial guise. We know also that it was the incubator of nationalism, and that the nationalist aim was to obtain and use the power of the state created by colonialism. Having achieved this, African nationalists made 'nation building' a priority thus apparently confirming Ernest Gellner's view that nationalism 'invents nations where they do not exist'.[8] Whether nations exist in Africa or not is a contentious issue that cannot be settled here. Suffice it to say, the nation was not an actor when nationalism entered the political stage in Africa, and the nationalists themselves assumed it did not exist.

Given the presumed lack of 'nations' in the sub-continent, the appearance of nationalism there puzzled observers initially. Some saw it as plain imitation of Western ideological fashion, a view implying an extremely narrow social context as well as artificiality.[9] Most observers regarded nationalism in Africa as a reaction to the iniquities of the colonial situation. Thomas Hodgkin, for example, thought the term could be applied generally to any opposition to European rule.[10] The 'anti-colonial' view of African nationalism, which became the established version, implies a catholic and undifferentiated peoples' struggle for freedom. This is misleading because it exaggerates the scope of the nationalist movement, and draws attention away from its social composition which, in turn, provides the main clue to its character and to the nature of the post-colonial state.

Nationalism in Africa was not, as often depicted, a massive popular crusade driven by the desire to undo what colonialism had wrought. In fact, its constituency was socially circumscribed, with distinct regional, ethnic, class, and gender features. As Franz Fanon critically observed, nationalism was an urban phenomenon with limited impact on the rural masses.[11] It mobilised social groups spawned during the colonial era by the modernising sector of the economy and the activities of the state. It was not inappropriate for the first nationalist organisation in the Sudan to call itself the 'Congress of Graduates'. Its counterpart in Somalia was called the 'Somali Youth League' to highlight its modern appeal. These groups were intrinsically linked by vested interests to the colonial economy. They were similarly attached to the state, because defense of their interests required access to the state; that is, power to influence decisions made at that level. It was precisely the denial of access inherent in the colonial situations that was the mainspring of nationalism.

Not all Africans were swept into the nationalist current. There were regions, ethnic groups, and social classes which were little involved or not at all. Usually, these were regions where the modern economy had not penetrated and, for that reason, the colonial state maintained only a token presence. Needless to say, the same regions were by-passed by economic and social developments during the colonial period, and on the eve of independence were relatively deprived of material and social resources. This is true of Southern Sudan, Northern Somalia, Northern Kenya, and most of the lowlands in the Horn where pastoralists and agro-pastoralists live; all these regions have been subject to perennial conflict during the post-colonial era.

Political developments by-passed these regions as well, and they found themselves outside the nationalist movement also. Sudanese nationalism flourished in the central riverain region in the North where cotton had become king. It had no echo in the South where no sign of development appeared under colonialism or later. The highlands of Kenya where commercial farming flourished were the cradle of a nationalist movement whose appeal never reached the vast lowlands in the north where pastoralism prevails. Likewise, Somali nationalism matured in the South, where commercial farming and urbanisation made advances under Italian rule. The Somali Youth League had no following in the North, a purely pastoralist region untouched by any sort of development under British rule.

Belated awareness of their comparative disadvantage led some regions and ethnic groups to oppose the nationalist current by seeking to delay independence, others organised political movements to compete with the nationalists, still others sought protection in federal arrangements, and a few rebelled at the dawn of independence. Confronted with the prospect of replacing British colonial rule with Northern Sudanese Arab domination, Southern Sudanese first sought to delay the independence of the colony, then asked for a federal system of government only to be rebuffed, and finally rebelled. Violent conflict had already broken out in 1955, before independence was proclaimed in 1956, setting off a civil war that still rages three decades later.

Northern Somalia formed its own clan-based nationalist organisation to compete with the Somali Youth League whose base was in the South. The expressed desire of the North for a decentralised form of government was overruled by the more populous and economically developed South in a referendum held after unification of the two colonies in 1960. Northern resentment was expressed immediately afterwards in a military mutiny that took place in 1961. The union of the two Somali regions proved an exceedingly unhappy one, and was dissolved with bloodletting in 1991. The demand for a federal system of government was supported by the Sab communities of cultivators in the South, who correctly anticipated the domination of the independent Somali state by the pastoralist clans. One consequence of that domination in the years that followed has been the gradual loss of Sab lands to those who wielded state power.

The Somali in Northern Kenya demanded union with their kinsmen in the Somali Republic. Rebuffed, they launched a violent struggle for secession on the eve of Kenya's independence in 1964. Their region has been under emergency rule ever since. Kenya entered independence with a short-lived federal constitution demanded by the smaller ethnic communities grouped in the Kenyan African Democratic Union, which feared domination by the Kikuyu-Luo coalition in the Kenyan Africa National Union. Fear of Somali domination persuaded the Afar to reject independence for Djibouti in the 1967 referendum, and the enclave did not become independent until a decade later when that danger seemed to have receded. In fact, the Somali came to dominate the mini-state in the 1980s, and eventually drove the Afars to rebellion in the beginning of the 1990s.

The objectives of African nationalism were limited and concrete. Far from seeking to dismantle the state, nationalists aimed to safeguard it. It is correct, therefore, to say, as P.M. Holt said of the Sudanese nationalist movement, that it was 'essentially not the supplanter but the successor' to the colonial regime.[12] This explains the preservation of the economic edifice created by colonialism, as well as the endurance of the state structures that it founded. Adherence to the colonial blueprint meant that material and social disparities between regions, ethnic groups, and social classes, which had appeared during the colonial period, subsequently widened and became a source of political conflict that undermined all nationalist regimes in the Horn of Africa, caused the collapse of the state in Somalia, dismembered Ethiopia, and now threatens the existence of Sudan and Djibouti.

The post-colonial state is the epicentre of the conflict. To no small degree, this is due to the prominence of its role in the production and distribution of resources, a prominence that made it the focus of social conflict. The stagnation of the private sector of the economy made access to state power essential for the material and social welfare of people. True for the continent and all types of regimes, this reached exaggerated proportions in the Horn of Africa under the radical military regimes that ruled Sudan, Somalia, and Ethiopia in the 1970s and 1980s, when all resources came under state ownership and control. Obviously, not all groups had equal access to state power, and some had none at all. More often than not, power rested with those who inherited it from colonialism and their political descendants. It is no secret what use they have made of it. To quote Julius Ihonvbere, '[t]he state is used for accumulation as against legitimation purposes. Its structures, institutions and instruments are easily employed by the dominant forces to repress, exploit, suppress and marginalise the masses.'[13]

It is not entirely correct to say the state has not been used for legitimation purposes. In fact, dominant groups sought legitimacy through the 'nation-state' building exercise in the first two decades of independence. On the ideological level, nationalism sought to transcend and supplant the communal pluralism inherited by the state in Africa, as if to prove Ernest Barker right when he said that '[i]t is not nations which make states, it is states that create nations'.[14] Myth is of the essence in nationalism everywhere, and the nation building exercise in Africa was steeped in it. Of all the states in the Horn, Ethiopia's rulers invested more in weaving a colourful nationalist mythology, complete with the familiar fable of a three thousand year old state, which gained worldwide currency. In fact, Ethiopia, as we know it today, is not older than most African states, having been formed during the imperialist scramble in the late nineteenth century. The difference is that Ethiopia is not the creation of Europeans but of Africans who responded to the challenge of imperialism and successfully joined the scramble. These were the Abyssinians, whose history does reach back to antiquity, and whose Christian kingdom ruled the northern plateau for many centuries. The Abyssinian family comprises two branches, Amhara and Tigray, who share a common ancestry, culture, and history, but speak different languages. It was the Amhara, by far the larger of the two, who led the expansion that doubled the territory and population of the Abyssinian kingdom, and it was they who dominated what thereafter was officially called the Ethiopian Empire.

The expansion covered territories inhabited by a melange of ethnic groups with a rich variety of cultures and a multitude of languages. Many of them were adherents of Islam. Land scarcity in the badly eroded northern plateau was a factor in the expansion, which was followed by the appropriation of most of the better lands in the conquered territories. These lands and the indigenous peasantry that lived on them were distributed to the Abyssinian ruling class, clergy, and soldiery. Land expropriation condemned the non-Abyssinian peasantry to quasi-serfdom, and effected an explosive conjunction of class and ethnic contradiction whose potential for conflict is not yet exhausted. The state promoted its own version of Ethiopian nationalism, whose cultural ingredients, not surprisingly, were purely Amhara. Indeed, for the imperial regime, Ethiopia was Abyssinia writ large. Likewise, Sudanese nationalism extolled the Arab culture and language of the Northern Sudanese who ruled the Sudan after the departure of the British. In Ethiopia and the Sudan, national integration was tantamount to assimilation into the culture of the dominant groups, a point to which we will return later.

The resort to nationalism to gain legitimacy for ruling groups proved a disastrous failure. This was due, to no small degree, to the authoritarian excesses committed in the name of national unity. In practice, nationalism sanctioned the drive to centralisation, authoritarianism and the ultimate resort to violence through which dominant groups sought to perpetuate their hold on state power. In was on the grounds of national unity that all pleas by subordinate groups for decentralisation and local autonomy were rejected, and the outcome in several instances was violent conflict.

Eritrea is a good example. The former Italian colony was administered by Britain during 1941–1952. While the Great Powers bargained over its fate, Ethiopia made a strong bid for annexation, which divided the inhabitants of Eritrea along religious lines. The Christians, who belong to the Tigray community and made up roughly half of the population, opted for the most part for union with Ethiopia. The Muslims, who belong to several ethnic groups and made up the other half, understandably wanted nothing to do with Ethiopia and opted for independence. What happened in Eritrea was not greatly different from what was happening elsewhere in Africa at the same time, where nationalist movements divided along regional, ethnic, or communal lines. The division in Eritrea occurred along sectarian lines, and each side sought outside support in its bid for local predominance. The Muslims sought support from Italy, the former master, and the Christians from Ethiopia, the future master.

Following complex international manoeuvres and local confrontations, the United Nations imposed a federal arrangement in 1952, making Eritrea a self-governing region joined to Ethiopia. The arrangement provided full parity in all fields for all communities in Eritrea, and was initially accepted by all political factions. However, Eritrean self-government was a gross anomaly in the feudal domain of Haile Selassie, and the Ethiopian government wasted no time in undermining the arrangement. It subverted the Eritrean government, violated its constitution, diverted its resources, imposed the Amhara language and banned the use of Tigray, banned Arabic and restricted the operations of Quranic schools, and used violence against those who opposed the drive to reduce Eritrea to the status of a simple Ethiopian province. The federation was finally abolished in 1962.

The first Eritrean nationalism organisation had already appeared two years earlier. The Eritrean Liberation Front began as a Muslim affair, for it was this community that suffered first and most by the imposition of direct rule by Ethiopia. In time, the nationalist movement was embraced by the Christians who, as it became clear, had not bargained to turn Eritrea into an Ethiopian province ruled by imperial retainers, and to have their own language banned in the process. The Eritrean case is sometimes cited in support of the view that economic factors are not significantly linked to the rise of nationalism, because the former Italian colony was relatively more developed than Ethiopia when the two were joined in the federation. This ignores the fact that the nationalist rebellion was launched in the impoverished lowlands of western Eritrea and that pastoralists were its first recruits, and that the Eritrean economy deflated after 1952, forcing hundreds of thousands of Eritreans to emigrate in order to find employment.

Reliance on the state apparatus for repression enhanced the political role of the soldiers, until they were emboldened to seize direct control of the state. This happened in the Sudan and Somalia in 1969, and in Ethiopia in 1974. Classified as 'radical', in order to distinguish them from the conventional military interventions devoted to the preservation of the socioeconomic status quo, the military regimes in all three countries sought popular legitimacy through wide ranging reform measures, which included sweeping economic nationalisation; in the case of Ethiopia, land was included. State nationalism having already proved a shaky ideological prop, these regimes sought to reinforce it with an infusion of revolutionary socialism, and all three proclaimed their conversion to 'scientific Marxism'. At the same time, centralisation and authoritarianism in government reached their apogee. It was of no avail. All three were involved in manifold conflicts with their subjects, which reached genocidal proportions in some instances.

The familiar invocation of 'national salvation' by ruling juntas in Africa symbolises a continued reliance on nationalism by those who wield state power. To bolster its fading appeal, nationalism is sometimes mixed with other ideological brews, like socialism and religion. The latest military intervention in the Sudan enlisted Islam in its fundamentalist version for this purpose. Whatever it may be elsewhere, nationalism in Africa is the ideology of the state. More precisely, it is the ideology of those who wield state power. Properly speaking, in the African setting this phenomenon should be called 'state nationalism', to distinguish it from the notion that prevails abroad that nationalism naturally emanates from what is called the 'nation'. In the work cited above, Breuilly makes a conceptual distinction between 'state led nationalism' and 'anti-state nationalism', which is spurious. We can have nationalism without the nation, but not without the state. If nationalism rejects one state, it is only for the sake of another, real or imagined.

Ethnicity

While ethnicity appears in many guises, it is its political manifestation that has gained it prominence lately, and it is this that interests us here. In this context, ethnicity has the same relation to the state as nationalism. That is, its objectives are to obtain and use state power in order to gain access to resources commanded by the state. It was noted earlier that the pattern of resource distribution in the post-colonial state is iniquitous, that this pattern is maintained through the use of state power, and favours those who have access to it. Ethnicity has proved an effective means of political mobilisation for those who seek access to state power in order to change the existing pattern of resource distribution.

The similarity between ethnicity and nationalism does not end there. Ethnicity appears to have the same relationship to the 'ethnic group' that nationalism has to the 'nation'. Conceptually, the ethnic group is no more securely anchored than is the nation. Attempts at definition range from the primordial and the bio-social to the situational and instrumental.[15] Some see the ethnic group as the preeminent natural and unalterable unit of social organisation whose boundaries are rigidly fixed. Others see it as a transient and flexible form of social interaction with shifting boundaries, to which people have recourse when it best serves their interests. In the latter view, ethnicity, like nationalism, is the ideology or strategy used to mobilise a group in the pursuit of collective goals. As far as they go, attempts at definition of both the nation and the ethnic group use not only the same kind of criteria – cultural and historical – but the very same criteria – language, religion, customs, and collective memory. Indeed, fervent nationalists see no difference between nation and ethnic group.

Such striking similarities inevitably lead from comparison to convergence, and thence to confusion. Those who, like Smith, believe that 'the central question in our understanding of nationalism is the role of the past in the creation of the present', see in the ethnic group the seed, or core, of the nation, and speculate about the ethnic origin of nations.[16] In this 'historicist' perspective, the ethnic groups is the precursor of the nation, while ethnicity merges analytically with nationalism to produce 'ethno-nationalism'.[17] This line of reasoning implies ethnic conflict is inevitable in plural societies since, according to Smith, 'in modern times, even the smallest ethnic communities have adopted an aggressive, if not always expansionist, posture'.[18] Clifford Geertz went further to suggest that every ethnic group is a potential candidate for nationhood.[19] Obviously neither is correct, because symbiosis is the rule, not the exception, among ethnic groups in Africa. Furthermore, in most instances where ethnicity has become a significant political force, it has not espoused the ideological goal of ethnic sovereignty.

The Tigray Peoples Liberation Front (TPLF), now the dominant political force in Ethiopia has chosen to reconstruct, rather than destroy, the imperial state. Despite intense and sometimes violent rivalry, both the Afar and the Somali in Djibouti are committed to the preservation of the mini-state. In fact, separatism in the Horn was manifested mainly among the Somali who were inspired by irredentism and the desire to unite with their kinsmen in the now defunct Somali Republic. The *de facto* secession of Northern Somalia in 1991 cannot be attributed to ethnicity but to clannishness. Among the many ethnic movements that have appeared in the Horn, scarcely any have ethnic sovereignty as their goal. A notable exception is the Oromo Liberation Front (OLF) in Ethiopia, which claims to represent the largest ethnic group in the Horn. However, the OLF has not raised significant support for this goal among the Oromo people.

In the debate on the nature of ethnicity, a consensus has emerged concerning two of its key features. One concerns the formation of ethnic identities, and the other, the functions ethnicity performs in the contemporary setting. It is generally agreed that ethnic identities are social constructs defined by the historical conditions in which they emerge; they are 'the ever-changing product of social and historical dynamics', as Ronald R. Atkinson puts it.[20] What we see today are not the atavistic remnants of an earlier age bound to disappear with modernisation, but fairly recent creations shaped by social and political change.

The historical point of reference for contemporary ethnicity in Africa is the colonial period. This is not simply determined by the largely fortuitous reasons that Atkinson reviews critically. It is mainly because this period is a watershed in the modern history of Africa, when Africans were obliged to react and adapt to radically changed circumstances. The forging of new ethnic identities and the dissolution of old ones, as well as the change in the functions that ethnicity is required to perform, were part of this reaction, as Africans adapted to the exigencies of the colonial situation. This is not to say that ethnic identities of pre-colonial vintage did not survive, nor that new identities were woven entirely of new cloth. It is to say simply that ethnic identities are subject to change, and so are the functions ethnicity is required to perform. For Africans who found themselves in the emerging urban sector during the colonial period, for instance, ethnicity acquired new contours as well as functions. The 'invention of tribes' during that period was not simply the result of administrative expediency on the part of alien rulers, but also the African response to radical changes in the socioeconomic and political environment.

Though colonialism may be the historical point of reference, nearly half a century of independence has also left its mark on ethnicity, as Africans were obliged once again to adapt to changing conditions. One aspect of this response was the politicisation of ethnicity; that is, the use of ethnicity for purposes of group mobilisation in social conflict involving the state. Certainly, the political role of ethnicity is not a novelty. It has long been one of the factors determining political choice in Africa and elsewhere in the world. In recent years, however, ethnicity appears to have become the only factor that determines political choice in African societies afflicted with poverty, social tension, and political unrest.

What accounts for the political hardening of ethnicity? Is it due to the intervention of 'ethnic entrepreneurs', or to the 'false consciousness of the masses'.[21] If the logic of the argument set out here holds, the widespread resort to ethnicity as the basis of political mobilisation is a reaction and adaptation to the manifold, protracted, and deepening crises of contemporary Africa. The first chapter in the modern history of Africa has ended. The era of nationalism, with its promise of nation-building, development, and democracy is over, its promise sadly unfulfilled. With the fading of nationalism and the demise of regimes whose claim to legitimacy was based on it, the pattern of distribution of state power forged during decolonisation is bound to change. Intense competition and sometimes violent struggle is how change is brought about. This is what the recent, much publicised and misleadingly labeled 'democratisation' movement in Africa is all about.

Group mobilisation in contests for state power is often done effectively along ethnic lines. Resort to ethnicity in the ongoing struggle seems inevitable. As indicated earlier, in many instances the nationalist regimes themselves constituted ethnic monopolies of state power and resources. This was and still is the case in the Sudan, where the Arabs of the North have ruled since independence. It was the case in Ethiopia, where the Amhara who build the empire ruled it single-handedly until a few yeas ago. It was the case in Kenya where a Kikuyu-Luo coalition held the reins of power for many years, and in Djibouti where the Somali emerged predominant. In the case of Somalia, it was a coalition of clans that controlled the state and looted the country.

In such cases, ethnicity was a determining factor in the constitution of what Ali Mazrui calls 'the ethnocratic state', long before it was adopted as a political weapon by the opposition.[22] Ruling groups proscribed and anathematised ethnicity as the antithesis to nationalism. Such condemnation and legal proscription was partly inspired by the political threat it was perceived to represent. 'Politics then involves the attempts by state elites to proclaim the illegitimacy and subversive nature of ethnic affiliations, and to undermine opposition groups by branding them as ethnically based.'[23] Ethnic and regional political organisations regularly emerged in the Sudan during its brief periods of democratic rule, aspiring to represent the marginalised communities of the Beja, the Fur, and the people of the Nuba Mountains. They were routinely banned by the military whenever they seized power in the name of 'national unity'. The Siad Barre regime (1969–91) in Somalia proclaimed the death of clannishness and carried out a mock burial of this menace to Somali unity. Adept as any in manipulating ethnicity, Kenya's rulers are fond of addressing the '*wanachi*' ('people'), as if the latter were quite free of ethnic sentiment. In Ethiopia under the imperial regime mention of ethnic diversity was frowned upon, and dwelling on the history and culture on non-Abyssinian ethnic groups was considered subversive.

Exclusion from power and relative resource deprivation serves to heighten the cultural identity and solidarity of subordinate groups, the leavening process in the political maturing of ethnicity. In the ethnocratic states of the Horn, this process acquired additional momentum due to the cultural suppression carried out in the name of national integration. It was not surprising that the 'national' culture promoted by ruling groups was their own ethnic culture writ large. In Ethiopia, Coptic Christianity and the Amharigna language were the twin hallmarks of state nationalism, while in the Sudan it was Islam and the Arabic language. It was easier for a camel to go through the eye of a needle, than for an Ethiopian who was not a Christian and did not speak Amharigna to enter the charmed circle of power and privilege in his country, and the same was true in the Sudan for someone who was not Muslim and did not speak Arabic. In Ethiopia all other languages were banned in print, broadcast, and public meetings, and Islam was ignored. In the Sudan, a determined Islamisation and Arabisation drive was launched with independence, and continues to this day.

When the hold of dominant groups on state power begins to slip, and the struggle to redistribute power begins, the political ripening of ethnicity, that is, political mobilisation along ethnic lines, is inevitable. The collapse of the imperial regime in Ethiopia in 1974 saw the formation of several ethnic political organisations, some of which declared war on its military successor. The Tigray Peoples Liberation Front (TPLF) was one of them. Along with the Eritrean nationalists, it waged the war that finally toppled the military regime. The collapse of the latter witnessed a veritable explosion of ethnic mobilisation, although this time it was actively encouraged by the new regime under TPLF control. Ethnicity became the hallmark of political opposition in Kenya, as the nationalist regime in that country began to falter. In Djibouti, an Afar movement, the Front for the Restoration of Unity and Democracy (FRUD), took up arms to challenge the Somali monopoly of state power, when Hassan Gouled Aptidon, the autocratic Somali state president, appeared weakened by advanced age and illness. In Somalia, the decline of the Siad Barre regime threw all Somali clans into a frenzy of politico-military mobilisation.

The role of ethnic entrepreneurs who are keen to make political capital out of ethnicity is not insignificant. Ethnic movements, like nationalist ones, are organised, led, and ideologically inspired by intellectuals and petty bourgeois elements. A survey carried out recently by this author in Ethiopia showed that the leading figures in all ethnic organisations were schoolteachers, civil servants, and traders. Their efforts would not bear fruit unless the ethnic appeal elicits a strong response from the people to whom it is addressed. The proven effectiveness of ethnicity as a principle of political mobilisation is due to the instant recognition and ready response it elicits from masses of people. Is this an irrational response?

It was said earlier that in parts of sub-Saharan Africa ethnicity seems to have become the only factor determining political choice. Furthermore, it was said that the reason for this turn of events is to be sought in the situation that gives rise to it, not in ethnicity itself; that is, it is to be sought in the profound and deepening crisis confronting many African societies today. In this situation, ethnicity is required to perform functions that other institutions have failed to perform. What alternatives are available to the ordinary African, when the state is unable to protect its own subjects; worse yet, when the state itself is a menace to them? Given the largely traditional pattern of societies in the sub-continent, to what other association or institution can the African turn for emotional security, social solidarity, political protection, and support in the daily struggle to obtain the necessities of life?

Unfortunately, the political salience of ethnicity has produced a generalised and highly misleading exegesis of social conflict in Africa, under the label of 'ethnic conflict'. It is unfortunate because it provides a facile explanation and diverts attention from the real causes of conflict. Since ethnic identities are culturally defined, the implication is that cultural differences are involved in the generation of conflict. While it is true that such differences are an essential factor because they draw the dividing lines between rival groups, they are not sufficient cause. While conflict often takes an ethnic form – with rival groups deriving their identity and political solidarity from cultural affinity – its substance, more often than not, is a struggle for power and resources, and seldom a clash of cultures. Ethnicity may provide the ideology of conflict, but, like all ideologies, it is not the cause but the symptom of social disorder. It is in the nature of this disorder that we need to look for the causes of 'ethnic conflict'.

We have noted substantial similarities between nationalism and ethnicity. Are they one and the same thing? Is ethnicity a variant of nationalism? Sub-nationalism, neo-nationalism, and dissident nationalism are terms used in this connection. If we remain true to the conventional definition of nationalism, which is premised on the attainment of a homogeneous, sovereign nation-state, then the answer to both questions has to be negative. The Western nation-state model has been shown to be inappropriate to the requirements of Africa's pre-industrial societies, whose fabric is woven with ethnic strands of many colours. Nor is the ethnic-state a logical alternative for a region with a legion of ethnic groups of all sizes and manner of spatial distribution, whose identities, upon closer inspection, have a tendency to dissolve into smaller components like clans and lineages. Comparatively few ethnic groups in black Africa are candidates for nationhood, and few of them have such aspirations. In fact, instances where a separate state has been sought concern not ethnic groups, but regions representing coalitions of groups – Eritrea, Southern Sudan, Biafra, Katanga – and in one instance clans – Somaliland.

If few ethnic groups aspire to their own state, many seek political recognition, cultural emancipation, and a fair share of material and social resources from the states which they share with others. These are the commonplace goals of ethnic group mobilisation, the goals of ethnicity. Their pursuit need not disturb the political process or threaten the integrity of the state, unless groups are excluded from this process. This brings us back to the post-colonial state, under whose rule ethnicity rose to political prominence. The unitary and highly centralised structure of this state, and its harshly authoritarian rule were designed to restrict political competition and avoid challenges to the status quo. The decline of the post-colonial order ushered in a period of intense competition which will eventually produce a new pattern of power distribution within states, as well as cause the break-up of some existing states and the appearance of new ones. In what seems to be the opening of the second chapter in the modern political history of the continent, Africans are playing a leading role. It is to be hoped they will forge systems of government to suit their society, rather than try to change society to suit imported models.

A Case in Point

After many years of struggle to overthrow the old order, and following the secession of Eritrea, Ethiopia is now going through the difficult process of working out the structural design of a new political order. The process of reconstruction will be a long and difficult one, and the initial phase presided over by the Tigray Peoples Liberation Front (TPLF) is only the beginning. The fact that this phase is dominated by one ethnic group means that forging a stable pattern of power distribution is a task yet to be completed. Consequently, it is too early to evaluate the Ethiopian experiment, or to predict its success. However, it is useful to take note of some factors upon which success or failure might be predicated.[24]

The emerging outline of the new state is a highly decentralised federal system, whose constituent units are ethnic groups. The choice of ethnicity as the foundation of the state is unorthodox, to say the least. However, it is a realistic one, a response to domestic requirements. Since the option of force was exhausted by previous regimes, there seemed to be no other way to hold the Ethiopian state together in 1991, when the coalition led by the TPLF took power. The TPLF's commitment to the preservation of the Ethiopian state is explained by the logic of the situation. Asked why the option of independence for Tigray was rejected, the leader of the TPLF, referring to the material impoverishment of the province, said simply that '[w]e looked at Tigray and saw there is nothing there'.[25] Objective conditions dictated a similar choice for other ethnic movements in that country.

The reconstructed state is 'multi-national', admitting a variety of cultural traditions, and making it possible for its citizens to claim different national (ethnic/cultural) identities. Thus, Ethiopian citizenship has no specific national connotation. The uncoupling of nationality and citizenship signals a rejection of what Basil Davidson called 'the curse of the nation-state' that has afflicted post-colonial Africa.[26]

If ethnicity was all about culture, the Ethiopian formula could be a recipe for success. However, ethnicity is mainly about state power, and success or failure hinges upon whether or not the new arrangement will make power accessible to the larger groups on an equitable basis. As written, the Ethiopian constitution grants political recognition to ethnic groups regardless of size, and affords wide scope for group autonomy and self-government, including the right of ethnic groups to use their own official language. The question is whether the political process will adhere to the constitutional prescription, or it will become the facade for a new monopoly of power.

Furthermore, power is the bone of contention because it commands access to resources, and resources have to be produced before they can be distributed. Its productive capacity crippled by the long conflict, its land afflicted with drought and erosion, and its population growing at a rate of three per cent annually, Ethiopia is now the poorest country in the continent. Economic recovery will take a long time, and the struggle for material and social resources will be intense during this period. This is the spectre that haunts political life throughout Africa, and it casts a heavy shadow over Ethiopia.

Ethnicity has proved its political effectiveness in opposition to the post-colonial order. However, its efficacy as the basis of government has yet to be tested. It should be noted that the choice of ethnicity in designing a new political order is based on a twofold assumption. One is that ethnic groups can be clearly distinguished and neatly separated on the basis of conventional cultural criteria. In Ethiopia, for instance, language was used to delineate ethnic units. As the introduction to this section makes clear, there is reasonable doubt about this assumption which is regarded by some as the invention of anthropologists. Following Fredrik Barth's insight, ethnic boundaries are now seen as the product of social interaction and, indeed, of political competition.[27] If that be the case, the reasons leading to the political empowerment of ethnicity in a particular instance, as in Ethiopia, may also reinforce ethnic boundaries and strengthen group solidarity. Such a process of 'ethnification' made considerable progress in Ethiopia in the past decade.

Whether it will have enduring political significance will depend on the validity of the second assumption, which is that ethnic groups are adequately integrated internally on the basis of common interests and have the required political coherence to serve as the building blocs of a stable political system. There can be no generalisation about this, since, as noted above, the functions that ethnicity is required to perform vary with circumstances.

NOTES

1. See, for example, Daniel Patrick Moynihan, *Pandemonium* (Oxford: Oxford University Press, 1993), and Crawford Young (ed.), *The Rising Tide of Cultural Pluralism: The Nation-State at Bay?* (Madison, WI: University of Wisconsin, 1993).
2. Pierre Van den Berghe, *The Ethnic Phenomenon* (New York, NY: Praeger, 1981), and Malcolm Chapman (ed.), *Social and Biological Aspects of Ethnicity* (Oxford: Oxford University Press, 1993).
3. Elie Kedourie's indictment of nationalism as an unmitigated evil, and Tom Nairn's portrayal of it as a two-faced Janus capable of good or evil, are typical examples of normative assessment; they tell us not what nationalism is, only what it is capable of doing. Elie Kedourie, *Nationalism* (London: Hutchinson, 1960), and Tom Nairn, 'The Modern Janus', *New Left Review* (No. 94, 1975).
4. Thomas Hylland Eriksen, 'A Non-ethnic State for Africa? A Life-world Approach to the Imagining of Communities', in this volume, p. 46.
5. For the background to the conflicts in this region, see John Markakis, *National and Class Conflict in the Horn of Africa* (Cambridge: Cambridge University Press, 1987).
6. John Breuilly, *Nationalism and the State* (Manchester: Manchester University Press, 1993) p. 1.
7. Anthony D. Smith, 'Gastronomy or Geology? The Role of Nationalism in the Reconstruction of Nations', *Nations and Nationalism* (Vol. 1, No. 1, 1995), p. 3.
8. Ernest Gellner, *Thought and Change* (London: Weidenfeld and Nicholson, 1964), p. 169.
9. Elie Kedourie (ed.), *Nationalism in Asia and Africa* (London: Weidenfeld and Nicholson, 1971).
10. Thomas Hodgkin, *Nationalism in Colonial Africa* (London: Muller, 1956).
11. Franz Fanon, *The Wretched of the Earth* (Paris: Maspero, 1961).
12. P.M. Holt, *A Modern History of the Sudan* (London: Weidenfeld and Nicholson, 1961), p. 171.
13. Julius Ihonvbere, 'The "Irrelevant" State, Ethnicity and the Quest for Nationhood in Africa', *Ethnic and Racial Studies* (Vol. 17, No. 1, 1994), p. 43.
14. E. Barker, *National Character and the Factors in its Formation* (London: Methuen, 1939).
15. See the surveys by Thomas Hylland Eriksen, *Ethnicity and Nationalism: Anthropological Perspectives* (London: Pluto, 1993), and Marcus Banks, *Ethnicity: Anthropological Constructions* (London: Routledge, 1996).
16. Smith, *op. cit.*, in note 7, p. 18, and Anthony D. Smith, *The Ethnic Origin of Nations* (Oxford: Blackwell, 1986).
17. Walker Connor, *Ethnonationalism: The Quest for Understanding* (Princeton, NJ: Princeton University Press, 1994).

18. Anthony D. Smith, *The Ethnic Revival in the Modern World* (Cambridge: Cambridge University Press, 1981), p. 15.
19. Clifford Geertz, 'The Integrative Revolution', in Clifford Geertz (ed.), *Old Societies and New States: The Quest for Modernity in Africa and Asia* (New York, NY: Free Press, 1963).
20. Ronald R. Atkinson, 'The (Re)Construction of Ethnicity in Africa: Extending the Chronology, Conceptualisation, and Discourse', in this volume, p. 32.
21. For two such interpretations, see J. Rothchild, *Ethnopolitics* (New York, NY: Columbia University Press, 1981), and Archie Mafeje, 'The Ideology of Tribalism', *Journal of Modern African Studies* (Vol. 9, No. 2, 1971), pp. 253–61, respectively.
22. Ali Mazrui, *Soldiers and Kinsmen in Uganda: The Making of a Military Ethnocracy* (Beverly Hills, CA: Sage, 1975).
23. David Brown, 'Ethnic Revival: Perspectives on State and Society', *Third World Quarterly* (Vol. 11, No. 4, 1989), pp. 1–17.
24. For a discussion of recent developments in Ethiopia, see John Young, 'Ethnicity and Power in Ethiopia', *Review of African Political Economy* (Vol. 23, No. 70, 1996), pp. 531–42.
25. Meles Zenawi, then President, now Prime Minister of Ethiopia;, in interview with the author, 1994.
26. Basil Davidson, *The Black Man's Burden: Africa and the Curse of the Nation-State* (London: James Currey, 1992).
27. Fredrik Barth, 'Introduction', in Frederik Barth (ed.), *Ethnic Groups and Boundaries: The Social Organization of Cultural Difference* (Oslo: Scandinavian University Press, 1969).

5. Rethinking Ethnicity: Identification, Hybridity and Democracy

Aletta J. Norval

> [T]hat is the condition of being 'coloured' in South Africa...'halfway between...being not defined'....[T]he coloured South African subject represents a hybridity, a difference 'within', a subject that inhabits the rims of an 'in-between' reality....[1]

Homi Bhabha's description of the ontological condition represented by coloured identity in South Africa raises important issues for the analysis of ethnicity. Starting from what is clearly a 'constructivist' position, namely, that social differences are 'not simply given to experience through an already authenticated cultural tradition', but are 'the signs of the emergence of community envisaged as a project', Bhabha draws a series of far-reaching conclusions.[2] His analysis not only locates the importance of cultural hybridity as a perennial feature of the identity of marginalised groups and minority perspectives, but goes further to draw strong normative conclusions from this location of hybridity. Most importantly, he argues that, to understand cultural difference as the product of minority identities which are 'split', estranged from themselves, must also lead one to recognise the extent to which this very fact of estrangement places those who occupy such sites in a privileged position to question dominant traditions and to widen spaces of democratic critique. This position is also articulated more widely in contemporary literature which draws on post-colonial theory. Nikos Papastergiades, for instance, drawing on Bakhtin, notes that a hybrid text 'always undoes the priorities and disrupts the singular order by which the dominant code categorises the other', such that the language of hybridity becomes a means for resistance to the monological language of authority.[3] In this article, I will endeavour to explore the consequences of these issues for theorising ethnicity. While recognising the importance of the idea of hybridity for contemporary theorisations of ethnicity, I will argue that the idea, as articulated in Bhabha's work, fails to distinguish between ontological and political claims. As a result, he limits the possibilities of thinking through the potential for democratic articulations of this idea. That is, by assuming that there is a coincidence between ontological claims of hybrid, post-colonial identities and politics of resistance, Bhabha forecloses two distinct possibilities of relevance to the articulation of democratic politics. These are, first, that the ontological claim may hold not only for post-colonial identities but for all identities, and, second, that a democratic politics does not follow from such claims, but needs to be articulated and constructed as a political project. By way of introduction, I will trace out a genealogy of the theoretical developments which acted as conditions of possibility for the emergence of this theoretical perspective.[4] In so doing, I will also give attention to the specific modes of analysing ethnicity to which the different perspectives gave rise. The second part focuses in more detail on the consequences of, and problems with, post-colonial arguments as they relate to ethnic identity. Through an engagement with Bhabha and his critics, I intend to articulate bodies of theoretical work which have tended to develop in isolation from one another. In conclusion, I will challenge some of the central political and normative assertions of Bhabha's argument, and will draw on recent work in radical pluralist democratic theory so as to develop an alternative account of the relation between ethnic identities and the possibility of a deepening of democracy. Throughout, I will draw on examples from the South African context to elucidate my arguments, and to foreground the question of context and particularity in relation to the treatment of ethnic forms of identification.

Ethnicities Old and New: From Identity to Identification

[K]nowledge is not made for understanding; it is made for cutting.[5]

Theoretical accounts of the phenomenon of ethnicity have a long trajectory, too long to be outlined in full here. A few remarks on this trajectory are, however, necessary so as to situate current theorisation in a proper context. It is important to note the fact that the history of the theorisation of ethnicity is not a progressive and cumulative one. Rather, it is intimately bound up with political concerns and normative judgements. Moreover, any attempt to reconstruct this trajectory ought to take the form of a genealogy. That is, it has, of necessity, to start from where we are, from our current concerns and our present commitments, making visible the conditions under which particular theorisations emerge and become disseminated. In this respect, it is worth noting that much recent work on the politics of ethnic and cultural identity starts from a concern with the question of *recognition*. Charles Taylor puts it in the following manner:

> [a] number of strands in contemporary politics turn on the need, sometimes the demand, for *recognition*....And the demand comes to the fore in a number of ways in today's politics, on behalf of minority or 'subaltern' groups, in some forms of feminism and in what is today called the politics of 'multiculturalism'. The demand for

recognition...is given urgency by the supposed links between recognition and identity....The thesis is that our identity is partly shaped by recognition or its absence, often by the *mis*recognition of others....[6]

Any discussion of ethnicity today must take cognisance of this starting-point, and must engage seriously with theoretico-political questions concerning identity, the specificity of ethnic forms of identification, and the relation between such identifications and the struggle for an extension of democratic participation in contemporary politics. The focus on recognition is, as Taylor makes clear, a feature of our current situation. This holds not only for Europe and the Americas, where these issues are intimately bound up with multicultural politics, but also, increasingly, in other contexts, including post-apartheid South Africa, where demands for the recognition of ethnic identities raise particularly difficult questions. Given this general context, it is appropriate to trace out a genealogy of the theorisation of ethnicity in terms of the fortunes of the concept of *identity*.

Traditional debates on ethnic identity can be situated on a continuum of views ranging from primordialism to instrumentalism. That is, from views that ethnic identity stems from the givens of social existence – blood, speech, custom – which have an ineffable coerciveness in and of themselves,[7] to a view that ethnic identity is nothing but a mask deployed strategically to advance group interests which are often economic in character.[8] In the latter case, analytical emphasis tends to fall on unmasking the processes through which elites mobilise groups so as to further their own self-interest. Analyses of the history of apartheid abound with examples of both these positions. Liberal historiography has, for instance, tended to take the former view. Afrikaner identity was taken as such a primordially given identity which, paradoxically, would wither away with economic modernisation.[9] Neo-Marxist analyses, on the other hand, have tended to treat both ethnic and racial forms of identification as mere masks for the furthering of economic interests.[10] What they called for was an uncovering of the real, objective interests behind subjective ethnic identifications. Both types of analysis signally failed to address the dimension of ethnic identification as worthy of analysis in and of itself. Consequently, the question of *identity* was consistently reduced to a level of analysis which was deemed to be somehow more fundamental, deeper, and politically more significant than identity itself.

Both the primordialist and instrumentalist accounts of ethnicity remained trapped in the strictures of the distinction, widely deployed in the social and human sciences, between the objectively given and the subjectively constructed. This distinction has continued to inform early constructivist accounts of ethnicity and, as a consequence, these accounts have tended to suffer from similar problems to those they set out to overcome; while attention was now given to the processes through which ethnic mobilisation came into being, they continued to be treated as epiphenomena which had to be unmasked. This position is exemplified in Edwin N. Wilmsen's comments on ethnic identity:

> [e]thnic identification can never be explanatory; it is necessarily a constituted phenomenon. That is to say that ethnicity and identity refer to diametrically opposite processes of locating individuals within an arena of social formation – the one to objective conditions of inequality within an arena of social power, the other to subjective classification on a stage of social practice....[E]thnicity takes on a cogent existential and experiential reality which sociocultural features are reified into a justificatory premise for inequality.[11]

More recent theorisation has, however, advanced considerably in rethinking the relation between the objective and the subjective and, in so doing, has put into question the coincidence between 'objective' and economic conditions, on the one hand, and the subjective and identity, on the other.

This recasting of the distinction has been made possible by a theorisation and an investigation of the imaginary constitution of society which breaks with the topographical conception of the social underlying the traditional subjective/objective distinction.[12] On this reading, far from being simply 'given', objectivity is nothing but that which is socially constituted, and which has become *sedimented* over time. The feature of 'objectivity', thus, may be attributed to any sedimented social practice or identity. Positing objectivity in this manner has the further consequence of opening the space for the thought of *desedimentation*: any sedimented practice may be put into question by political contestation, and once its historically constituted character is revealed, it loses its naturalised status as 'objectively given'.[13] The consequences of this shift for the analysis of the phenomenon of ethnicity are far-reaching. Once the givenness and objectivity of identity is put into question, and a purely subjectivist account of ethnic identity is problematised, the way is open to develop a theoretical account of ethnic *identification*. As Sara Ahmed argues, when we can no longer assume that the subject simply 'has' an identity, in the form of a properly demarcated place of belonging, what is required is an analysis of the processes and structures of identification whereby identities *come to be seen* as such places of belonging.[14]

There are, however, many forms that such a constructivist position may take, and it is important to outline them so as to come to a closer understanding of the possibilities and limitations of this approach.[15] A common type of constructivism takes the form of linguistic monism, whereby 'linguistic construction is taken to be generative and deterministic'.[16] In this case, constructivism is reduced to a verbal action which creates that which is being constructed in a godlike fashion. The difficulties arising from this position are many. First, if the act of construction is understood as a purely verbal act, it is unclear how such an act would be linked to the materiality of the real, since ethnic markers place certain limitations on what could 'constructed' verbally. Second, it immediately raises the question as to *who* is doing the constructing. If verbal construction determines being, then it seems that there must be a subject doing the construction, a subject which, moreover, must be understood as standing outside the process of construction. Alternatively, the process of construction could, in a structuralist fashion, be attributed to an impersonal force, such as 'Culture or Discourse or Power, where these terms occupy the grammatical site of the subject after the "human" has been dislodged from its place'.[17] Both these alternatives, however, reintroduce the very problems associated with more traditional approaches to ethnicity. More specifically, in both cases, construction is still understood as a unilateral process initiated by a prior subject, thus reinforcing a top-down view of the production of ethnic identity which leaves little, if any, space for human agency and resistance.

In order to outline an alternative account of constructivism, it is necessary to specify clearly what main features such a position would have to contain. In the first instance, it has to break with the view of ethnic identity as either imposed or merely subjective. It must, therefore, provide us with an account of the subject and of identification which takes cognisance of wider power relations, while not reducing contingent identities to an imposition on an inert subject. In the second place, it must avoid linguistic determinism, and must, therefore, contain a plausible account of materiality and its role in the production of images for identification. It is possible to articulate such an account by drawing on the work of contemporary political theorists, including Benedict Anderson's concept of 'imagined community', Ernesto Laclau and Chantal Mouffe's work on the construction of imaginary horizons of meaning and processes of identification, William Connolly's work on contingency and pluralisation, and Judith Butler's work on materialisation.

In *Bodies that Matter*, Judith Butler argues that, in order to counter linguistic determinism, one needs to reintroduce a conception of matter as materialised, as a process that becomes stabilised over time. The pertinence of the notion of materialisation is best understood through the example of the problem of 'the body' and the manner in which regimes of regulatory production contour the materiality of bodies. This issue arises, as must be clear by now, from objections to constructivist accounts which argue that they ignore that which is materially 'given'. So, for instance, it may be objected that these accounts of ethnic identity ignore the material visibility of colour and of cultural practices, and tend to absorb them into accounts of the linguistic meaning conferred upon such phenomena. The result is that one either ends up with an 'epiphenomenal' account, by which ethnicity is that which overlays what is already materially given, or one subordinates materiality to linguistic determinism such that the visibility of these phenomena is treated as entirely non-material. To counter these views, Butler argues that the theoretical options 'are not exhausted by presuming materiality, on the one hand, and negating materiality, on the other'.[18] Rather, matter – that which is given prior to construction – must be understood as always *posited* or *signified* as *prior*. The body signified as prior to signification, is then always already an effect of signification. In this manner, she puts into question the 'as suchness', the brute givenness of matter, the body, and colour. Signifying acts delimit and contour matter. This, however, is not to say that the body, colour, matter, does not matter. On the contrary, as Butler argues,

> [t]o call a presupposition into question is not the same as doing away with it; rather, it is to free it from its metaphysical lodgings in order to understand what political interests were secured in and by that metaphysical placing, and thereby to permit the term to occupy and to serve different political aims.[19]

To argue that racial or ethnic identity in this sense, is constructed, and that attention needs to be given to the materialisation of categories such as the body, colour, and other ethnic markers as a result of political practices is, thus, not also to assert that they are unimportant or irrelevant. Similarly, to emphasise the *contingency* of socially inscribed identities does not mean that they are fungible, that they may be picked and chosen as if from a supermarket shelf.[20] To the contrary, it directs attention to the historical, social, and political processes through which images for identification are constructed and sustained, contested and negotiated. One consequence of this shift towards *identification* is that the focus of analysis of ethnic identities is laterally displaced. It is no longer adequate simply to ask, 'in whose interest are ethnic identities constituted?' Rather, we need to inquire into the processes through which ethnicity becomes a significant site of identification, which may or may not entail a construction of the 'interests' of a particular group.

The construction of Afrikaner identity during the 1940s and 1950s is a case in point. As I argued earlier, much work on apartheid ideology has historically started from the presupposition that the construction of Afrikaner ethnic identity was aimed primarily at gaining economic resources and control over such resources.[21] This approach, as pointed out, tended to reduce ethnic forms of identification to mere masks for other, pre-given interests. Following the arguments outlined above on a constructivist approach proper, one needs to investigate why and how claims to such identification were produced, why they emerged at this or that particular point in time, and how, if at all, they were interlinked to the production of certain (economic) interests. Wilmsen's claim that ethnic identification can never be explanatory since it is necessarily a constituted phenomenon is thus subverted. All interests are constructed. What is pertinent to the political analysis of ethnicity is to investigate *how* identities *and* interests are constructed in contexts of uneven power relations.

This takes us back to the remark by Taylor with which I introduced this section. Taylor argued that the distinguishing mark of political struggles around identity today is the fact that these struggles are articulated around demands for recognition.[22] Implicit in this claim is a distinction between struggles for recognition and struggles around issues concerning redistribution. This claim, and the very distinction between recognition and redistribution, have obvious relevance for the understanding of the politics of ethnic identification. As argued earlier, analyses of the politics of redistribution and economic interests have classically served to denigrate questions of identity understood as claims for recognition. Should this separation be retained, then approaching contemporary politics of ethnic identification from the perspective of an emphasis on recognition alone would serve only to reinforce criticisms that constructivist perspectives cannot deal with material interests. If, however, as Taylor does indeed argue, the politics of recognition is intimately bound up with 'denunciations of discrimination and refusals of second class citizenship', then that very distinction is put into question.[23] In short, once one accepts that material interests themselves need to be socially constituted, as well as entailing a significant dimension of identification, the problem is reformulated in a manner consistent with a constructivist position which takes as its starting-point the imaginary constitution of society. The traditional distinction between instrumentalist and primordialist approaches to the question of ethnicity is problematised insofar as both come to be seen as part and parcel of the process through which forms of ethnic identification come into being and are subjected to contestation. It is perhaps *this* which is the most significant element of the politics of ethnic identification today. Claims and demands made in the name of ethnic groups cannot be understood without giving attention to the dimension of identification; and identification, while it may be closely associated with felt discrimination and the unequal distribution of resources in society, cannot be reduced to the latter.

The position of coloured South Africans in post-apartheid society is a case in point. The critique of policies of 'affirmative action', from within the coloured community, no doubt, is intimately associated with the structural position they occupy, and with the concerns that they will 'lose out', once again, since they are not 'black enough' and may, therefore, be excluded from the corrective action. To reduce the debate raging within these circles to a mere concern with material interests would, however, be to negate the extent to which the very question, possibility, and nature of coloured identity is at stake.[24] This is evident in disputes concerning the very appellation 'coloured'. The tragic history of the enforced separation of 'coloureds' from 'whites' during the 1950s, and the subsequent efforts by apartheid ideologues to argue for the existence of a 'Coloured nation', called forth an identification with 'blackness'. That is, in response to the attempt to impose a very specific conception of 'Coloured identity', a large part of the people designated as 'Coloured' by the Population Registration Act resisted that imposition by identifying as black South Africans and, therefore, as part of the oppressed and excluded. This identification was not, however, entirely unproblematic. The appellation 'so-called Coloured', which was widely used in liberation discourse, not only served an inclusionary function. It simultaneously foreclosed the possibility of addressing the specificity of the political, economic, and cultural position of coloured South Africans. As a result we have witnessed, since the late 1980s, an increasingly vocal debate on the nature and specificity of coloured identity.[25] Part of this process consists in retracing the very processes through which coloured identity has been demarcated and constructed historically;[26] it consists in a reclaiming of a subaltern history which places its concerns squarely in the domain of the concerns of post-colonial theory.

Ethnicity and Hybridity

> To wear with pride the name they were given in scorn.[27]

Post-colonial theories of identity are explicitly situated within the context of contemporary concerns with diaspora, displacement, and the politics of cultural difference. So, for instance, one finds an emphasis on displacement as the starting-point for re-thinking questions of identity in the work of Stuart Hall, Gyatri Spivak, and Homi Bhabha. Hall utilises this perspective to extricate the concept of ethnicity from its anti-racist paradigm, 'where it connotes the immutable difference of minority experience'.[28] For Hall, it becomes a term which 'addresses the historical positions, cultural conditions and political conjunctures through which all identity is constructed'.[29] Ethnicity becomes a concept connoting the 'recognition that we all speak from a particular place, out of a particular history, out of a particular experience....We are all, in a sense, *ethnically* located and our ethnic identities are crucial to our subjective sense of who we are'.[30] For Hall, then, what is important is to show the extent to which ethnicity is something which is not the exclusive characteristic of the other, but which marks every identity as such.

Bhabha, by contrast, continues to focus on the consequences of displacement for the *minority* subject. His development of the concept of hybridity serves to act as a signifier of the irreducibility of cultural difference.[31] Hybridity is not to be understood as an admixture of pre-given identities or essences. Rather, it signifies the attempt to capture the non-purity of identity, the non-coincidence of the self with itself, and the unhomeliness of existence which arises as an effect of colonial power. The production of hybridisation, moreover, 'turns the discursive conditions of dominance into the grounds of intervention'.[32] Thus, the limits of ethnocentricity which characterises Western cultures have, for Bhabha, become the enunciative boundaries of a multiplicity of dissonant and dissident voices. It is from here that the concepts of homogenous cultures and national communities, the very logic of identity conceived as pure, intact and self-sufficient, are being challenged and subverted. Bhabha thus moves almost seamlessly from a conception of hybrid identities – exemplified in the experience of displacement – to a politics of resistance, based on transgressive discourses which aim to unsettle liberal multiculturalist and appropriative political strategies.

While Bhabha's work on hybridity, ambivalence, and indeterminacy is theoretically sophisticated, he has been increasingly taken to task for political naiveté.[33] These criticisms all seem to converge on what Rod Edmond has called a 'disturbing political blindness', a Whiggism in which 'the ethnocentric certainties of the past are being marvelously dissolved by the indeterminacies of the present'.[34] More specifically, Bhabha's easy celebration of the condition of displacement, unhomeliness, and hybridity evokes continued criticism from those who argue that these locations, for many, are experienced as threatening, and as a condition of existential angst, rather than as a vital condition enabling critique. Bhabha treads far too easily over the fact that identities are markers of uneven power relations, and that so-called hybrid identities may inspire an acute sense of 'being inadequate to any available cultural identity'.[35] The phenomenon of 'passing for white' which marked one response by the South African coloured community to the initial demarcation and purification associated with the institution of apartheid serves as a historical reminder of the difficulties of living with ambiguous identities in a world in which purity and exclusivity is the dominant norm. These anxieties do not arise only in contexts such as that of apartheid South Africa, in which extreme forms of identitarian logics are at work. Sara Ahmed, commenting on living in Britain today, argues that a mixed race, hybrid identity may constitute a trajectory of migration and loss.[36] Jayne O. Ifekwunigwe similarly points to the phenomenon of 'diaspora angst'.[37] These criticisms should not be dismissed too easily, for they raise the question as to the ontological and existential consequences of occupying sites of hybrid identity in a world in which, far from opening itself to the other, we are witnessing a tendency to (re)essentialise identities. It is not accidental that new forms of fundamentalism emerge in a context of greater and greater globalisation;[38] the disruption of old certainties and traditional identities, by no means, lead inexorably to an acceptance of greater diversity, not to speak of reaching a position where cultural difference, in Bhabha's sense, may find a space of articulation.

One possible way out of this aporia may be to introduce a distinction between 'organic' and 'intentional' forms of hybridity where organic, unconscious hybridity would be a feature of all cultures, while intentional hybridities are disruptive of the dominant sense of order and continuity, relativising singular ideologies, cultures, and languages.[39] This distinction, articulated by Ahmed, goes some way towards overcoming the problem associated with Bhabha's uncritical celebration of hybridity and unhomeliness. The idea of a paradoxical 'organic hybridity' reinforces the focus on hybridity as a generalised logic, a feature of *all* cultural, ethnic, and other identities, and steers clear of the all-too-easy trap of equating hybridity with 'mixed-race' or *metis(se)* identities. All depends, however, on the manner in which 'intentional hybridities' are to be understood. If it marks a return to the intentional subject as the origin of identity, the very nature of hybridity as such would be put into question. If, however, such intentional hybridities are understood as discursively constructed within a domain of power relations and a struggle for hegemony, it has the potential of adding a dimension of political analysis which is absent from Bhabha's account.

However, before exploring this in more depth, it is necessary to return to the roots of the idea of hybridity so as to make visible its ignoble theoretical and political roots in the colonial and modernist mentality which privileged purity over non-pure forms of identity. As Papastergiadis shows, hybridity has shadowed every organic theory of identity, and was deeply inscribed in nineteenth-century discourses of scientific racism where it served as a metaphor for the negative consequences of racial encounters.[40] This was the case also in South Africa, where fear on the part of apartheid ideologues with respect to 'mixed identities' informed the very drive to purity, and it continues to inform far-right thinking on the question of cultural identity. Two examples, one from the 1940s and one from the early 1990s, will suffice. Geoffrey Cronje, a scientific racist, argued with regard to the 'Coloured community' that they were in a position 'between heaven and earth, neither fish nor fowl, between the tree and the bark'.[41] This condition, according to Cronje, arose out of a lack of a separate, pure identity, and was the root of conflict in South Africa. The solution to this problem was clear: races had to be separated so as to ensure their purity and continued peaceful co-existence. This thematic is continued, though without the overt racial references, in the discourses of the contemporary far-right. The Freedom Front places their demand for 'Afrikaner' self-determination in the context of 'cultural strife': 'the peculiar and pronounced sense of cultural identity that has developed within the Afrikaner community was the result of cultural interaction and alienation that had to do with this massive cultural clash that characterised

[the] 20th century'.⁴² And, they argue, the painful events in the former Yugoslavia, Rwanda, and Burundi, are reminders not to divert one's eyes from the 'realities of civilisation conflict'.⁴³ The 'mixing' of identities and the failure to protect them from contamination can only lead to conflict between 'cultures'.

Given this drive to purity, and the continued denigration of 'mixed identities' which accompanies it, the question necessarily arises as to whether it is possible, as post-colonial theorists would have it, 'to wear with pride the names they were given in scorn'? Moreover, the further question arises as to whether we can now be confident that hybridity has been moved out from the loaded discourse of 'race', and situated within a more neutral zone of ethnic identity.⁴⁴ That is, whether we can successfully reinscribe old names as markers for positive and vital identities? Here the argument advanced by Jacques Derrida with reference to such 'old names', bearing the traces of the metaphysics of identity and logocentrism, may be of some use.⁴⁵ Derrida argues that the principle of reinscription – redeploying old names in a new context – has the important advantage of reminding us of the problems associated with them in the first instance. Thus, rather than simply inventing new names, the redeployment of old ones can have distinct political advantages. This question cannot, however, be approached merely from the vantage-point of purely theoretical arguments. Answers to these questions must be considered in the political context of the very discourses which aim to construct such hybrid identities. In other words, there is no simple 'in principle' argument which can solve what is, in essence, a problem of reconstruction and renegotiation which requires the formulation of political projects adequate to the task.

Ethnicity, Post-national Identities and Democracy

If ethnicity in one sense represents a repudiation of false universalism which paraded as the universal subject but was in reality stratified and exclusionary, what then emerges on the horizon beyond ethnicity? What would be the points of reference for a new universalism that starts out from cultural pluralism?⁴⁶

What is needed...is a processual theory of hybridity, one that goes beyond the recognition that monological discourses are in permanent tension with a 'sea of heteroglossia'. Such a theory must differentiate...between a politics that proceeds from the legitimacy of difference, in spite and despite the need for unity, and a politics that rests on a coercive unity, ideologically grounded in a single monolithic truth.⁴⁷

In a post-national age, an age characterised by a shift of allegiance from the nation to units smaller or larger than the nation,[48] it is particularly pertinent to reopen the questions as to the politics of ethnicity, its relation to other forms of politics associated with this age, and the possibility of critical engagements with it. Constructivist accounts have often been charged with remaining locked within the specific discursive formations which they set out to analyse. If this were the case, it would be impossible to engage in a critical fashion with discourses of ethnic identification, for one would not be able to gain any distance from the claims put forward. This accusation, however, remains trapped within the old distinction between the subjective and the objective as outlined above. Once that untenable distinction is problematised, the very possibility and desire to develop a critique 'from nowhere' is also renounced. This does not, however, mean that criticism is no longer possible.[49] If it is possible, it is because the very process of constituting, negotiating, criticising, and recasting ethnic identities never occurs in a seamless fashion. Of necessity, ethnic discourse, like other discourses, contains traces of its own construction, and it is the task of the genealogist to investigate the ignoble processes through which those discourses come into being and attempt to conceal their own historically constituted characters.[50]

It is precisely here that the question posed above arises, namely, the need to distinguish between a politics that arises from the legitimacy of difference and a politics resting on coercive unity. If there is anything that can be learnt from the history of apartheid, it is that such a politics of legitimate difference can only avoid the problem of coercive unity insofar as it is inserted into a *democratic* context, a context in which identity is open to challenge, negotiation, and renewal. While accepting that an understanding of the hybridity and ambiguity of identity in no way leads inexorably to a democratic politics, a democratic context – more than any other – facilitates accentuating 'exposure to contingency and increases the likelihood that the affirmation of difference in identity will find expression in public life'.[51] It is precisely in this sense that the idea of 'intentional hybridity' becomes pertinent to contemporary politics, for, insofar as the constitutive hybridity or plurality of identity is foregrounded *qua* political issue, the homogenising tendencies of liberal democracies may be explicitly thematised and problematised. The deepening of democratic spaces are then crucial to this project if one is to avoid the assimilationist tendencies of modern liberalism and encourage the radical pluralism advocated by post-colonial and radical democratic theorists alike.[52] In this respect, it is important not simply to remain caught in conventional liberal pluralist imaginaries, but to focus on the possibility of extending pluralism, thereby turning its appreciation of established diversity into an active process of *pluralisation,* an active cultivation of difference.[53] This conception of pluralisation could be related to the distinction, pointed out earlier, which Bhabha introduces between 'cultural difference' and 'liberal cultural diversity'.[54] Pluralisation, in this sense, would refer to subjecting static conceptions of 'cultural diversity', based on categories such as gender, race, class, and ethnicity as givens, to the disruptive effects of a conception of difference as irreducible, and to actively cultivating the visibility of the deeply split nature of identity politically. Connolly's conception of pluralisation provides a context in which it is possible to bring together (1) the idea of hybridity as an ontological condition constitutive of all identity, with (2) the notion of an intentional hybridity which foregrounds the need to give a political articulation to hybridity, in (3) a context of a project aiming to radicalise democracy. In this way, it becomes possible to retain important insights from contemporary theories of hybridity, but to eschew their more politically naïve tendencies.

The active cultivation of difference is necessary, first and foremost, because there is always the danger that ethnic forms of identification may become exclusionary and self-enclosed. This possibility arises from the very context in which ethnic forms of identification often emerge: in response to (equally) exclusionary and homogenising nationalistic projects.[55] There is, however, not only the danger that ethnic identifications become exclusionary *vis-à-vis* other groups, but that they *already* contain exclusions within them. Much of the work on the relation between gender and ethnicity, and sexuality and gender, for instance, attests to this.[56] The ethos of pluralisation, which depends upon a deepening of existing pluralisms, would thus not only have to foster and cherish, rather than simply encounter, difference within 'minority cultures'. As argued earlier, it would also have to challenge the presumption that dominant groups do not have ethnic identities; that is, the presumption that they have homogenous and seamlessly unified self-referential traditions. One of the most important arguments to come out of post-colonial theory is the one concerning the fact that we *all* have ethnicities. Danielle Juteau underlines this by pointing out that as long as ethnicity is regarded as a characteristic of minority groups, dominant groups remain in a position to treat

> ethnicity as a specific attribute of some (read subordinate) collectivities while *they* incarnate universal culture and humanity as a whole....By saying that we are all ethnic, we can remind dominant groups that they too are culturally specific and that their 'universal' projects actually correspond to their own sense of history and culture and identity and to their own material interests.[57]

But is it not precisely this challenge to the universality of traditional sedimented identities which have led to the growth of fundamentalisms? As Connolly points out, if fundamentalism is understood to be 'any movement that insists upon the certainty and exclusionary character of its own identity', it emerges, above all, as a reaction to the historic trend toward multiculturalism.[58] How, then, is one to advance an argument for the recognition of the hybridity and contingency of identity in general, and avoid this problematic outcome?

There is no simple solution to this problem. The possibility of the construction of spaces of pluralisation, and the concomitant renegotiation of the tensions between universality and particularity, depends upon the fostering and deepening of a democratic culture which allows for and encourages a critical interrogation of identity.[59] This project remains one which is deeply political in character, and the specific form that it may take depends largely on the very context in which the issue first arises. The possible political 'solutions' to the issue of pluralisation would thus look very different in, for instance, the North American and South African contexts. Whereas, in the former, the politics of multiculturalism emerged in response to the perceived inability of liberal assimilationism to respect differential identities, in the latter, the politics of difference has to contend with the legacy of apartheid. Whilst in both cases the democratic context acts as a minimal, albeit generalised, condition of possibility for the fostering of pluralisation, the specificity of the requirements for its institution will always already be context specific.[60] The particularity of the context will thus shape and give body to the universality underlying the demand for the deepening of democratic forms of interaction and participation. An example may be useful to illustrate this. Connolly argues, with reference to the USA that, if it is to move from a 'majority nation presiding over numerous minorities in a democratic state' to a 'democratic state of multiple minorities contending and collaborating with a general ethos of forbearance', there will have to be a shift in the self-recognition of the dominant constituency, such that the historically contingent character of the language, faiths, and canonical text which have inspired it, will become visible. Such a culture of pluralisation would encourage an enlarged set of cultural identities to appreciate the elements of '*social construction* in what they are, the profound *dependence* they have on those differences that endow them with specificity, and the deep *contestability* of the cultural assumptions that vindicate what they are (*e.g.*, as Christians, Jews, Kantians, Muslims, atheists, masculine, feminine,...*etc.*, *etc.*)'.[61]

The same argument can, and should be, advanced with regard to the question of the specificity of ethnicity and ethnic forms of identification in 'Africa'. By way of conclusion, then, it is pertinent to ask after the function of the signifier 'Africa' in these debates. Once again it may be useful to remind ourselves of the role of that signifier in the colonial imagination in general, and in the apartheid imaginary specifically.[62] In the latter, 'Africa' acted as a signifier of ontological uprootedness, and of human uncertainty, which stood in sharp contrast to Pan-Africanist discourses which, at the time, attempted to construct a unity based upon a principle of 'colour consciousness'. Contemporary debates on hybridity are, once more, re-enacting these older debates, while inscribing them in a novel context. I can do no better than conclude with the words of Kwame Anthony Appiah who suggests, in this respect, that

> [i]f an African identity is to empower us...what is required is not so much that we throw out falsehood but that we acknowledge first of all that race and history and metaphysics do not enforce an identity: that we can choose, *within broad limits* set by ecological, political, and economic realities what it will mean to be African in the coming years....[I]n thinking about how we are to reshape it [African identity], we would do well to remember that the African identity is, for its bearers, *only one among many.* [...] [*B*]*eing African is...one amongst other salient modes of being, all of which have to be constantly fought for and rethought.*[63]

This recognition of the many possible forms of identification, none of which has an *a priori* centrality, which increasingly do not correspond to either specific national states or geographically specific entities, and which do not necessarily address themselves to the traditional arenas of struggle, is what is most characteristic of what I would call post-national identities. And it is within this arena that contemporary struggles around ethnic identity have to be understood, and have to be articulated politically, if we are to realise a greater pluralisation of democracy.

NOTES

I would like to thank David Howarth and Paris Yeros for their helpful comments on earlier drafts of this chapter.

1. Homi Bhabha, *The Location of Culture* (London: Routledge, 1994), p. 13.
2. *Ibid.*, p. 3.
3. Nikos Papastergiadis, 'Tracing Hybridity in Theory', in Pnina Werbner and Tariq Modood (eds.), *Debating Cultural Hybridity: Multi-Cultural Identities and the Politics of Anti-Racism* (London: Zed Books, 1997), p. 267.
4. For a discussion of Michel Foucault's conception of 'genealogy', see Hubert L. Dreyfus and Paul Rabinow, *Michel Foucault: Beyond Structuralism and Hermeneutics* (Brighton: The Harvester Press, 1982), Chapter 5.
5. Michel Foucault, *Language, Counter-memory, Practice* (Ithaca, NY: Cornell University Press, 1977), p. 154.
6. Charles Taylor, 'The Politics of Recognition', in Amy Gutman, (ed.), *Multiculturalism and 'The Politics of Recognition'* (Princeton, NJ: Princeton University Press, 1992), p. 25, emphasis in original.
7. Clifford Geertz, *The Interpretation of Cultures: Selected Essays* (New York, NY: Basic Books, 1973), p. 259.

8. While my examples of instrumentalist conceptions of ethnic identity in this section draws mostly on neo-Marxist work, similar tendencies are present also in other approaches to the question. See, for instance, the instrumentalist account of a rational choice theory approach to ethnicity in Michael Hechter, 'Rational Choice Theory and the Study of Race and Ethnic Relations', in John Rex and David Mason (eds.), *Theories of Race and Ethnic Relations* (Cambridge: Cambridge University Press, 1986), pp. 264–79. This instrumentalism also informs Stephen Steinberg's study of race, ethnicity, and class in America. See Stephen Steinberg, *The Ethnic Myth: Race, Ethnicity and Class in America* (Boston, MA: Beacon Press, 1989).

9. See, for instance, Michael C. O'Dowd, 'The Stages of Economic Growth and the Future of South Africa', in Lawrence Schlemmer and Eddy Webster (eds.), *Change, Reform and Economic Growth in South Africa* (Johannesburg: Ravan Press, 1977), pp. 28–50.

10. The most sophisticated work in this genre is that of Dan O'Meara, *Volkskapitalisme: Class, Capital and Ideology in the Development of Afrikaner Nationalism, 1934–1948* (Johannesburg: Ravan Press, 1983). I have discussed this work, as well as the whole 'race-class debate' in depth elsewhere. See, *inter alia*, Aletta J. Norval, *Deconstructing Apartheid Discourse* (London: Verso, 1996), pp. 1–100.

11. Edwin N. Wilmsen, 'Introduction', in Edwin N. Wilmsen and Patrick McAllister (eds.), *The Politics of Difference: Ethnic Premises in a World of Power* (Chicago, IL: University of Chicago Press, 1996), p. 6.

12. See, especially, Benedict Anderson, *Imagined Communities: Reflections on the Origins and Spread of Nationalism* (London: Verso, 1983); Cornelius Castoriadis, *The Imaginary Institution of Society* (Oxford: Oxford University Press, 1987); Ernesto Laclau and Chantal Mouffe, *Hegemony and Socialist Strategy* (London: Verso, 1985). All of these works emphasise the constitutive character of the symbolic processes at the heart of the institution of images of social unity.

13. This means that any sedimented practice or identity is *partially* fixed. That is, its fixity is a result of articulatory practices which, in the final instance, can only be provisional. This very fact means that such sedimented practices and identities allow space for rearticulation and contestation, and thus space for subjectivity. It is also important to note that the idea of sedimented identities, for instance, does not entail that such identities can be characterised in terms of 'necessary and sufficient' elements. To the contrary, the idea of sedimentation seeks to avoid such essentialist forms of characterisation by focusing on the political processes through which partial stabilisations come into being.

14. Sara Ahmed, '"It's a Sun-tan, Isn't It?" Autobiography as an Identificatory Practice', in Heidi Safia Mirza (ed.), *Black British Feminism: A Reader* (London: Routledge, 1997), p. 157, emphasis in original.

15. This is necessary so as to be able to counter confused and facile caricatures drawn of social constructionism. For an example of a recent muddled account of social constructionism and its implications for the analysis of ethnicity, see Aidan Campbell, 'Ethical Ethnicity: a Critique', *The Journal of Modern African Studies* (Vol. 35, No,. 1, 1997), pp. 64–73. Campbell, for instance, portrays social constructionist accounts of ethnicity as nothing but an imposition of Western concerns on the African continent, aimed at discrediting African nationalism. On this reading, social constructionism simply valorises the local (ethnicity) at the expense of the national. Implicit in this reading is, first, a highly questionable dichotomy between the local and

the global; second, an assumption that nationalism is not subject to processes of social construction at all; and, third, a political argument which equates the idea of the malleability of identity with political manipulation from outside. Campbell, moreover, seeks to tar social constructionists with the brush of a new modern imperialism and quasi-biological determinism. It may not be amiss to speculate that his antagonism to social constructionist arguments arises more from his particular political prejudices than from any discernable understanding of such arguments.

16. Judith Butler, *Bodies that Matter: On the Discursive Limits of Sex* (New York, NY: Routledge, 1993), p. 6.
17. *Ibid.*, p. 9.
18. *Ibid.*, p. 30.
19. *Ibid.*
20. Will Kymlicka, for instance, argues that this is precisely the view of liberal assimilationist doctrines which regard ethnic identity as being comparable to choices of job. See Will Kymlicka, *Multicultural Citizenship: A Liberal Theory of Minority Rights* (Oxford: Claredon Press, 1995).
21. In *Deconstructing Apartheid Discourse*, I discuss this process in depth. Here, it is important to point out that one of the central features of apartheid discourse was a 'modification' of the horizon of racial exclusion through the introduction of a concern with ethnicity and cultural identity. See Norval, *op. cit.*, in note 10, Chapters 1–3.
22. For a critical discussion of the form of liberalism that Taylor advocates, see William E. Connolly, 'Pluralism, Multiculturalism and the Nation-state: Rethinking the Connections', *Journal of Political Ideologies* (Vol. 1, No. 1, 1996), pp. 61–64.
23. Taylor, *op. cit.*, in note 5, p. 39.
24. The political character of practices of naming is very clear in this instance. It makes a significant difference whether, for instance, one writes 'Coloured' or 'coloured'. The former, in this context, is used where the appellation is regarded as one attributed by the dominant discourses of Afrikaner nationalism, while the latter is used to refer to cases where an identity is claimed by members of the community. The former was widely resented and was oppressive insofar as it attempted to create a separate community, opening the way for discriminatory practices. The latter, to the contrary, signifies an attempt to reclaim a name, and a space for community identification in the context of a democratic, non-racial society.
25. See, for instance, the debates on coloured identity in *Sechaba*, the official organ of the ANC, during the mid-1980s, which is discussed in Immanuel Wallerstein, 'The Construction of Peoplehood: Racism, Nationalism, Ethnicity', *Sociological Forum* (Vol. 2, No. 2, 1987), pp. 373–9. The issues arising in these debates became even more salient during the 1990s after the general election which brought the ANC to power. In 1995, coloured members of the ANC Youth League in the Western Cape left the League and set up new Community Youth organisation focusing on the needs of the youth in coloured communities in the Western Cape. They argue that this split was necessary since their interests were not represented within the old organisation. In particular, they point to the failure of the ANC to live up to the philosophy of non-racialism within its organisational structures. The emphasis within these structures on 'African' (read black African) leadership, regardless of actual demographic tendencies in membership numbers and to the exclusion of leaders from the coloured communities, was one of the immediate factors leading to the split. Other issues, however, also contributed to it, such as, most notably, the tendency amongst black Africans to set up hierarchies of oppression, presenting Africans as 'the most

oppressed section of society', and differences in community cultures and views on the role and character of political activism. For a fuller discussion of these issues, see Annelise Burgess, 'Breakdans van die Kaapse Left', *Die Suid-Afrikaan* (No. 53, 1995), pp. 14–15; and Annelise Burgess and Sandile Dikeni interviewing Eugene Paramoer, 'Kleurling Jeug Toyi-Toyi uit die ANC', *Die Suid-Afrikaan* (No. 53, 1995), pp. 16–17.

26. Contemporary debates on coloured identity have occurred largely in daily newspapers and in other popular media. For a study of the issues as they were treated historically by different political groupings in this community, see the collection of documents in Pierre Hugo, *Quislings or Realists? A Documentary Study of 'Coloured' Politics in South Africa* (Johannesburg: Ravan Press, 1978). Finally, for a recent attempt to trace out the specificity of social and cultural histories, see, for instance, Vivian Bickford-Smith, *Ethnic Pride and Racial Prejudice in Victorian Cape Town: Group Identity and Social Practice, 1875–1902* (Cambridge: Cambridge University Press, 1995).

27. Salman Rushdie, quoted in Papastergiadis, *op. cit.*, in note 3, p. 258.

28. Stuart Hall, 'New Ethnicities', in Kobena Mercer (ed.), *Black Film, British Cinema* (London: Institute of Contemporary Arts, 1988), p. 5.

29. *Ibid.*

30. *Ibid.*

31. Bhabha distinguishes cultural difference, which has its origins in post-structuralist and psychoanalytic thinking, from liberal cultural diversity. The latter operates within a conceptual frame which assumes that all cultural diversity may be understood on the basis of a particular universal concept – human being, class, race – and that diversity can be contained and domesticated, whereas the former signifies irreducible, non-domesticable difference.

32. Bhabha, *op. cit.*, in note 1, p. 112.

33. Robert Young, for example, takes Bhabha to task for effectively belittling colonial resistance by suggesting that it has to be 'read between the lines'. See Robert Young, *White Mythologies: Writing History and the West* (London: Routledge, 1990), pp. 141–56. See also Aletta J. Norval, 'Homi Bhabha, Hybridization and the Political', in Jenny Edkins, Nalini Persram and Veronique Pin-Fat (eds.), *Sovereignty and Subjectivity* (Boulder, CO: Lynne Rienner, forthcoming 1998).

34. Rod Edmond, 'Much Ado About Difference', *Radical Philosophy* (No. 72, July/August 1995), p. 39.

35. Ahmed, *op. cit.*, in note 14, pp. 153–67.

36. *Ibid.*, p. 157.

37. Jayne O. Ifekwunigwe, 'Diaspora's Daughters, Africa's Orphans? On Lineage, Authenticity and "Mixed Race Identity"', in Mirza (ed.), *op. cit.*, in note 14, p. 127.

38. Papastergiadis makes a similar point when he argues that, to understand both the disturbing anxiety generated by cultural hybrids and the productive and enabling force of hybridity, there needs to be a close scrutiny of the creation of differences, precisely where there is renewed circulation of equivalences, or an exaggerated outburst of hostility towards the 'intimate enemy'. See Papastergiadis, *op. cit.*, in note 3, p. 267.

39. The distinction between organic and intentional forms of hybridity disrupts the pure/non-pure dichotomy which informs identitarian thinking. The fact that it allows us to distinguish between ontological and political claims has two distinct advantages. It makes it possible to show that, first, no single politics follows necessarily from ontological claims and, second, that hybridity is not just a feature of minorities, but a characteristic of all identities.

40. Papastergiadis, *op. cit*, in note 3, pp. 257–79.
41. Geoffrey Cronje, *Regverdige Rasse-Apartheid* (Stellenbosch: CSV Boekhandel, 1947), p. 87.
42. Constand Viljoen, 'Parameters for Self-determination in the South African Context', Freedom Front, 28 November 1995.
43. Constand Viljoen, 'Die Beginsels van Selfbeskikking en 'n Volkstaat in 'n Demokratiese Samelewing'. Paper delivered to the Press Club of South Africa, Johannesburg, 24 August 1995.
44. Papastergiadis, *op. cit.*, in note 3, p. 257.
45. Jacques Derrida, *Positions* (London: The Athlone Press, 1981), p. 71.
46. Jan Nederveen Pieterse, 'Varieties of Ethnic Politics', in Wilmsen and McAllister (eds.), *op. cit.*, in note 11, p. 26.
47. Pnina Werbner, 'Introduction: The Dialectics of Cultural Hybridity', in Werbner and Modood (eds.), *op. cit.*, in note 3, p. 21. The quote continues: '[s]econd, it must explain how and why cultural hybrids are still able to disturb and "shock"...in a postmodern world that celebrates difference through a consumer market that offers a seemingly endless choice of "unique" identities, subcultures and styles'.
48. Nederveen Pieterse, *op. cit.*, in note 46, p. 26. This shift of allegiance does not rule out the possibility of new nationalist struggles also emerging; however, it does challenge the presupposition that those are either the most important or most dominant forms of struggle in politics today.
49. I have recently treated this issue in depth via a discussion of the work of Michael Walzer. See Aletta J. Norval, 'Deconstruction and Criticism', in Iain Mackensie and Shane O'Neill (eds.), *Reconstituting Social Criticism* (Basingstoke: Macmillan, forthcoming 1998).
50. While agreeing with the claim that ethnic and racial discourses always entail a misrecognition of their genesis, and that intellectuals are aware of this, Kwame Anthony Appiah argues that a distinction between this critical awareness and the political need of a respect for the myth of origins, must be retained. Raising the question as to whether these truths – that identity is a product of history, and contains ignoble myths of origin – ought to be uttered, he responds as follows: 'I am enough of a scholar to feel drawn to truth telling...enough of a political animal to recognise that there are places where the truth does more harm than good'. Kwame Anthony Appiah, 'African Identities', in Linda Nicholson and Steven Seidman (eds.), *Social Postmodernism: Beyond Identity Politics* (Cambridge: Cambridge University Press, 1995), p. 105. This hesitancy between 'telling the truth' and endorsing 'ennobling lies', however, relies on a questionable discourse which privileges the traditional intellectual and his access to truth.
51. William E. Connolly, *Identity/Difference: Democratic Negotiations of Political Paradox* (Ithaca, NY: Cornell University Press, 1991), p. 193.
52. Elsewhere, I have discussed in depth the relation between 'third wave' pluralism – as found, for instance, in the works of Laclau and Mouffe and Connolly – and the theories of pluralism which informed the original 'plural society' thesis. See Aletta J. Norval, 'Minoritarian Politics and the Pluralisation of Democracy', *Acta Philosophica* (Vol. 14, No. 2, 1993), pp. 121–40.
53. William E. Connolly, *The Ethos of Pluralization* (Minneapolis, MN: University of Minnesota Press, 1995), pp. xiv–xv. It is important that Connolly, as well as other radical democrats taking this position, does not argue that one should break with liberal democracy *tout court*. Rather, it is a matter of deepening, extending, and

radicalising the democratic tradition. For instance, in his earlier work, *Identity/Difference*, Connolly argues that the conception of the political (which continues to inform his work on pluralisation) as a means through which identity and difference can be expressed and contested, criticises and draws on both liberal individualism and civic liberalism. For instance, from the civic tradition it draws 'appreciation of the hermeneutic character of ethical and political discourse, wherein debate and argumentation proceed from preconceptions and convictions already present in the life of the self', while from the theory of liberal individuality it draws the understanding 'that the claims of individuality often clash with the claims of conventionality'. Connolly, *op. cit.*, in note 51, p. 92. Laclau and Mouffe make a similar point in *Hegemony and Socialist Strategy*, when they argue that they aim, not to renounce liberal-democratic ideology, but on the contrary, 'to deepen and expand it in the direction of a radical and plural democracy'. Laclau and Mouffe, *op. cit.*, in note 12, p. 176.

54. See note 31.

55. As Connolly puts it, 'the demand for a hard core…can itself produce irreconcilable conflicts, particularly when it encounters contending forms of dogmatism posing exclusionary demands on the same ground'. Connolly, *op. cit.*, in note 20, p. 58.

56. See, for instance, the many interventions in this domain by Nira Yuval-Davis, including 'Ethnicity, Gender Relations and Multiculturalism', in Werbner and Modood (eds.), *op. cit.*, in note 3, pp. 193–208.

57. Danielle Juteau, 'Theorising Ethnicity and Ethnic Communalisms at the Margins: From Quebec to the World System', *Nations and Nationalism* (Vol. 2, Part 1, 1996), p. 55.

58. Connolly, *op. cit.*, in note 22, pp. 53–4.

59. For a discussion of the rethinking of the relation between particularity/universality, see Ernesto Laclau, 'Universalism, Particularism and the Question of Identity', in John Rajchman (ed.), *The Identity in Question* (New York, NY: Routledge, 1995), pp. 93–110.

60. Connolly, *op. cit*, in note 22, pp. 60–1.

61. *Ibid.*, p. 67.

62. I have explored this question in depth in Aletta J. Norval, 'Decolonization, Demonization and Difference: The Difficult Constitution of a Nation', *Philosophy and Social Criticism* (Vol. 21, No. 3, 1995), pp. 31–51.

63. Appiah, *op. cit.*, in note 50, p. 108, emphasis added. The very idea of individual 'choice' suggested here by Appiah is problematic. While we may be able to 'choose' identities, such possibilities always already occur withing contexts which are discursively structured and sedimented. This is not to suggest, however, that change and 'choice' is not possible. Rather, it is to argue that it is only under conditions where there is a degree of desedimentation, that this becomes a possibility. In addition, as I have argued earlier, a democratic context offers the best possibility for realising such 'choices'.

6. Towards a Normative Theory of Ethnicity: Reflections on the Politics of Constructivism

Paris Yeros

The most important contribution of 'constructivism' to the study of ethnicity has been the relocation of the ethnic phenomenon firmly in the realm of social and political processes which are constituted by acting human subjects.[1] Indeed, this reconceptualisation has gained such wide currency that to reassert it nowadays is a cliche. In this chapter, I will argue that, despite their collective advances, constructivists have yet to begin systematically to address their most fundamental differences. These differences – masked by the broad label of 'constructivism' – are to be found in the normative contents of their theories and their political implications. For beneath the shared constructivist predisposition, one finds a variety of normative positions that remain underthematised and underexplored. These normative positions unavoidably impact the ways in which we explain and evaluate ethnic identity, pronouncing it variously as either modern or traditional, imported or autochthonous, imposed or reconstructed, inclusive or exclusive – in short, as either a more or less legitimate form of identity and politics. Whatever the pronouncement, theories which seek to explain the ethnic process are moral theories insofar as they themselves lend to, or detract from, the legitimacy of ethnicity.

The purpose of this chapter is to propose the need specifically for a 'normative' approach to ethnicity. I will outline what this means in the first part. As a form of theory, a normative approach is one that, in the first instance, is not concerned with what ethnicity *is*, or with explaining an 'emergence' of ethnicity as an historical phenomenon. Rather, it is concerned with distinguishing deliberately what sorts of political claims in the ethnic process are morally defensible, that is, of a counter-exclusionary nature. By implication, a normative approach does not view ethnicity as having a singular socio-political function and moral standing. A deliberately normative way of thinking, I will argue, is a precondition for the formulation of an ethically-conscious methodology, one that makes explicit the political purpose of explanation and is designed to serve the interests of the politics that it endorses. I do not, however, intend here to put forth an ethics of any specific sort, although the analysis is clearly a post-positivist one and invariable points away from naturalist ethics.[2]

In order to show the need for a normative way of thinking, I will proceed, in the second and main part of the chapter, to discuss some of the ways in which ethnicity has been explained by constructivists. Here, I will critique four influential constructivisms, including transactionalism, instrumentalism, inventionism, and moral ethnicity approaches. I will argue that such theories that seek to explain what ethnicity *is* have a tendency to impute to it a singular socio-political function and, hence, a constant moral standing. Moreover, such explanatory theories attempt to establish the validity not only of their explanatory claims, but also of their moral ones, by reference to empirical evidence. I will argue that, without being equipped with an explicit normative position, an 'empirical' approach to theory, even if constructivist, is liable to essentialise ethnicity as an historical phenomenon and to foreclose on ethical debate with respect to political claims made in the name of ethnicity.

In the third and final part of this chapter, I will argue that normative theory is capable of combining ethical concerns with empirical inquiry. My claim is that such a combination would be possible by taking a clear position first on what politics one wishes to defend and then by adjusting one's methodology in the interest of such politics. Here, I will suggest an 'advocative' approach to ethnography.

Preconditions for a Normative Approach to Ethnicity

A distinction can be drawn between two forms of theory: empirical theory and normative theory. The two forms differ in their objectives and methods, as well as their capacity to answer certain questions. In the study of ethnicity, constructivists are often found in an uncomfortable grey area between the two. For, to be a constructivist, one is not automatically committed to either the normative or the empirical form of theory. The form of theory that one adopts is ultimately evident in the theoretical objectives of the theorist and the methods that he or she employs.

Empirical theory fashions itself on the basis of the assumptions and methods of the natural sciences, in order to 'capture', explain, predict, and control a social reality. It seeks to discover general laws in the workings of society, whose validity it establishes or refutes by empirical observation. As such, empirical theory is concerned with establishing *what is*. Normative theory, by contrast, encompasses those approaches that are concerned with the moral dimensions of social life. Normative theory does not assume that reality is self-existent and that it is there to be 'captured'. As such, it does not ask *what is*, but *what ought to be*. Most crucially, normative theory does not subscribe to the distinction itself between the *is* and the *ought*. It does not view the two as separate and complementary domains of inquiry, but as convergent and inextricable: one cannot ask and explain what is, without employing concepts that themselves are moral.[3]

Empirical theory proceeds on the basis of a positivist methodology and an empiricist epistemology. It assumes a distinction between fact and value, the separability of the knower from the known, and, hence, the autonomous existence, value, and meaning of facts. Facts exist independently of the concepts used to select them and describe them, and facts do not gain their relevance, value, and meaning in the act of their selection and description. On the basis of these assumptions, facts can be collected, correlations between variables can be discovered, and testable theoretical propositions can be formulated in nomological terms. These propositions, as general laws of social behaviour, are true insofar as they continue to correspond to the facts.

Political practice is coneived by empirical theory as a technical matter. Thus, politics consists of the employment of 'scientific' knowledge as a means to an end. The end itself is not deemed problematic; rather, it is assumed to be commonly held in society. This non-problematisation of valued ends is fully in accordance with the positivist assumption that 'values' are not a worthy domain of inquiry. In the words of Isaiah Berlin,

> [i]n a society dominated by a single goal there could in principle only be arguments about the best means to attain this end – and arguments about ends are technical, that is, scientific and empirical in character: they can be settled by exprience and observation or whatever other methods are used to discover causes and correlations; they can, at least in principle, be reduced to positive sciences. In such a society no serious questions about political ends or values could arise, only empirical ones about the most effective paths to the goal....[T]he only society in which political philosophy in its traditional sense, that is, an inquiry concerned not solely with elucidation of concepts, but with the critical examination of presuppositions and assumptions, and the questioning of the order of priorities and ultimate ends, is possible, is a society in which there is no total acceptance of any single end.[4]

The distinction between fact and value, the reliance on a correspondence theory of truth, the production of generally applicable nomological knowledge, the denial of the political character of theory, and the depoliticisation of valued ends are common among many of those who are known as constructivists. An empirical constructivist proceeds in his or her inquiry by singling out particular agents as being primarily responsible for the reproduction of ethnic identity. With regards to the specific approaches that will concern us in the next section, these selected agents may be colonial administrators, missionaries, intellectuals, peasants, or the state. Furthermore, these selected agents are deemed to be active in the realm of the 'political'. And their precise political behaviour is presumed to adhere to the laws of an *a priori* conceptual model, be it, for example, of a transactionalist, functionalist, rational-choice, or Marxist derivation. However, this conceptual model often does not view *itself* as being in the realm of the political. It need not view itself as having a political purpose, capacity, or influence. It is in such a proclaimed *a*political form that a constructivist theory bears the hallmarks of empirical theory. The choice of agents and institutions is justified by reference to 'hard' facts which have autonomous value and meaning, while the conceptual model itself which gives meaning to these facts gains a transcendental quality. Thus the theorist will claim that the act of theorising and the concepts employed are unrelated to the object of study. That is, the object of study exists independently of the concepts used to describe it; that the concepts themselves are not influenced by the theorist's interest in the object of study; and that the theorist is capable of discerning an 'actual' social process, and proceed to explain it, without morally evaluating it and without impacting it, or intending to do so.

Given these explanatory objectives and positivist methods, the empirical constructivist asks and discovers what ethnicity *actually is*. He or she is likely to conclude that ethnicity serves one general function – be it the maintenance of group boundaries, the engendering of social solidarity, the pursuit of material goods, or the legitimisation of a hierarchical social structure – though ethnic identity itself may be malleable and may manifest itself in particular situations.[5] This knowledge of ethnicity that empirical theory produces claims to be of general utility. That is, having been produced by a universal method of validation, it can be used by anyone interested, and be put in the service of an assumed uncontested political end. With the available knowledge of ethnicity, the achievement of a given political end becomes a technical matter.

This project of ascertaining an 'essence' in ethnicity as an historical phenomenon is where empirical theory differs most crucially from normative theory. Normative theory is concerned precisely with the *normativity* of theoretical constructs, that is, the values that they generate, and the validity of the political ends which they assume. Thus, normative theory considers theoretical practice itself as political practice. And as political practice, it is concerned not with explaining an assumedly self-existent reality which adheres to general laws of society. Instead, it is concerned with *understanding* the moral concepts through which social action becomes meaningful to the agents themselves; with *evaluating*, unavoidably, the moral basis of the social and political reality thus performed; and, finally, with the wider questions regarding the practical role of theory in *social transformation*.

The normativity of empirical theories of ethnicity becomes clearer as we unpack their inner workings. The mere explanation of what ethnicity *is* assumes that ethnicity is one thing, that it involves particular agents in its reproduction, and that it has a specific function. Such an explanatory approach assigns to ethnicity, first, a specific moral standing, and, second, a moral standing with specific political implications. As I will demonstrate in detail in the next section, in selecting particular agents, a theory privileges them ontologically as the subjects that are capable of political action; it privileges their claims to the moral substance of the particular ethnic identity; and it reifies the relationship between these agents and the rest of the community as the primary axis – at the exclusion of others – along which moral values and ethnic identity are generated. As such, the explanatory approach does not 'capture' *the* reality of ethnicity. It reifies the claims of the privileged agents as *the* claims that constitute the moral substance of the group as a whole. The law-like extrapolation of these claims to the group as a whole is performed in accordance with dictums of the *a priori* conceptual model. This, in turn, either challenges or endorses the legitimacy of these claims, as well as the ethnic process as a generality, depending on the manner in which it judges the function of ethnicity – again, for example, as either maintaining group boundaries, engendering social solidariy, maximising material goods, or legitimating a hierarchical social structure. Thus, in contrast to its amoral and apolitical claims, 'a given framework of explanation', as Charles Taylor has demonstrated at length, 'tends to support an associated value position, [and] secretes its own norms for the assessment of politics and society'.[6]

Rather than identifying and explaining laws of social behaviour, empirical theory constitutes them on the basis of its own values. Taylor continues elsewhere to characterise theories as 'self-defining':

> [t]heory…has an important use to define common understandings, and hence to sustain and reform political practices, as well as serving on an individual level to help orient themselves…[T]his self-definition is essentially a definition of norms, goods or values; and there are in each case practices of which it is the essential enabling condition.[7]

To acknowledge this, however, is also to beg the larger question. How *should* one conceptualise society? Being sensitive to the theories and moral categories that enable the practices of social agents – that is, understanding the meanings attributed to the social practices by the agents themselves – is an important predisposition among normative theorists, especially, of course, those trained precisely in the interpretive tradition.[8] Understanding the 'self-understandings' of others aims to avoid grafting one's own self-understanding upon that of others via the employment conceptual models which assume, and thereby constitute, general laws of society.[9] Understanding, furthermore, aims in principle to create a two-way cultural dialogue, a broadening of the intersubjective realm of meanings through which the terms of discourse gain common relevance.

Understanding as a methodology, however, is not unproblematic either. It remains, unavoidably, a value-laden exercise, variably inclined along the spectrum between scientism and relativism. Taylor's version is no exception in this regard. In his essay on 'Understanding and Ethnocentricity', for example, Taylor does not avoid the positing of distinct and autonomous cultures, such as a 'Western' one and a 'primitive' one, the latter of which then becomes the object of understanding.[10] He goes on to appeal to 'a language of perspicuous constrast' in research by which he intends to perspiciously describe 'our' and 'their' form of life, in order to present the alternative possibilities to all of us.[11] The point here is that, even if we were to adhere to such an approach, we would be treading on a number of evaluative assumptions: that there are 'distinct' (as opposed to syncretic 'hybrid') cultures which are, perhaps, bounded political communities, homogeneous, and uncontested; and that there are such self-evident things as 'West' and 'primitiveness', however defined, and that these are not discursive constructs of power relations, which, in turn, do not pervade the exercise of understanding itself.[12]

To avoid such assumptions, it is useful to give a central place to another of Taylor's conceptualisations of society. This offers the possibility of conceptualising society as a political community that is capable of both consensus and contest, and it also breaks down reifications of cultural boundedness, homogeneity, and difference. It has important implications for the study of ethnicity, and it is worth quoting him at length. Taylor argues that,

> [t]he intesubjective meanings which are the background to social action are often treated by political scientists under the heading of 'consensus'. By this is meant convergence of beliefs on certain basic matters, or of attitude. But the two are not the same. Whether there is consensus or not, the condition of there being one or the other is a certain set of common terms of reference....[I]ntersubjective meanings are a condition of a certain kind of very profound cleavage....[B]oth convergence of belief or attitude or its absence presupposes a common language in which these beliefs can be formulated, and in which these formulations can be opposed....[C]ommon meanings are quite other than consensus, for they can subsist with a high degree of cleavage; this is what happens when a common meaning comes to be lived and understood differently by different groups in a society. It remains a common meaning, because there is the reference point which is the common purpose, aspiration, celebration. Such is, for example, the American Way, or freedom as understood in the USA. But this common meaning is differently articulated by different groups. This is the basis of the bitterest fights in society, and this is also what we are seeing in the US today. Perhaps one might say that a common

meaning is very often the cause of the most bitter lack of consensus. It thus must not be confused with convergence of opinion, value, attitude.[13]

If we were to accept such a view– and, in due course, I will argue that we should – understanding as a methodology does not tell us where is the appropriate place to start one's inquiry, how to constitute conceptually those whom one wishes to understand, whose political claim in this social process to endorse or challenge, and, in this context, what the purpose of our theory should be. Thus, while understanding serves the important purpose of sensitising the theorist to the 'self-understandings' of others, I would argue that it is not normative enough.[14]

Given that understanding does not address the above questions, it is liable to confront the same evaluative problems that explanatory theory does in the study of ethnicity. In approaching ethnicity as an object of study, one must begin somewhere, and this somewhere has moral implications. An emprical theory, as mentioned earlier, begins by selecting particular agents as being responsible for the reproduction of ethnicity, those that are deemed politically capable. Inherent in this theoretical act are several moral judgements that need to be brought out. The act of investing certain agents and institutions with the ability to influence the consciousness and identity of others risks assuming that their power becomes uncontested and, indeed, *legitimate* from the perspective of the members of the relevant political community. If the theorist does not find this assumed legitimacy problematic, the theorist necessarily endorses it, by investing with moral significance the relevant political order, the power of the privileged agents and institutions – be they colonial administrators, missionaries, intellectuals, peasants, or the state – and the assumed primary axis along which moral values and ethnic identity are generated. These assumptions, I believe, bedevil empirical and interpretive approaches alike.

One may also find the assumed legitimacy of a particular identity problematic, and may wish to challenge it, or 'unmask' it. This project is more directly interested with social transformation, and creates a moral energy of a different sort. Besides identifying who is capable of political action, along which axis political action takes place, and where political action should be directed, the theory, in this second case, must specify who is *responsible* for political action. This means that the among the concerns of theory should be questions regarding to whom the theory should be addressed; who should be the subject of political action; and what should be the role of the theorist in the political process – that is, whether the theorist has a 'critical' as opposed to what I would call an 'advocative' role in relation to the addressees of his or her theory.[15]

The exercise of 'unmasking' the ethnic process assumes precisely a critical role for theory. I argue that this has three problems. First, critical theory risks becoming politically impractical, unless the theorist specifies how he or she is also a capable political actor, in the capacity of a social theorist. This means that the theorist has to demonstrate what access he or she has to the addressees. Second, critical theory lacks the capacity to be sensitive to the moral categories which are meaningful to the addressees themselves, assuming as it does that they have a false sense of reality. Third, critical theory assumes that there exists a consensus and that the sources of moral contestation are external to the relevant political community.

I would like to make the case, instead, for an advocative approach to theory. Basic to this is the conceptualisation of society as drawn from Taylor above. It conceives of society as a political community which is capable of both consensus and contestation, and whose sourses of contestation, therefore, are internal. The purspose of such a normative theory is, first, to be sensitive to the 'self-understandings' and political needs of others; second, to be explicitly evaluative; and, third, in the interest of social transformation, to bring into the analytical foreground the politics that it wishes to endorse. As such, it does not identify addressees that are to be 'awakened', but theorises the agents whose politics it chooses to defend as capable of contesting the meaning of their political community.

To recapitulate, I have drawn a sketch of what empirical theory claims to be able to do. As I argued, it claims to be able to detach itself from the social process, to not generate moral values, and to not have political purpose and influence. As such, it claims to be able to establish what ethnicity is, by indicating what agents and institutions bring it about. This knowledge is then made available as general knowledge, on the basis of which one is to design technical means towards a given, presumed uncontested political end. As an alternative to empirical theory, I have presented the preconditions for a normative approach. This understands theory itself as political practice, by refuting the positivist assumption that theoretical inquiry can be detached from normative commitments. I have sought to highlight the benefits and problems of understanding as a methodology, and have argued that an explicit moral judgement remains a requirement of theoretical inquiry.

I have also argued that, in order for a theory-as-political-practice to be practical, in its interest of social transformation it must also identify the sources of change. The theory, therefore, must first acknowledge the ethnic process as a realm of moral contestation, not conformity. Importantly, furthermore, the theory must engage with the ethnic process ethically. In other words, the theory must ask what its political purpose should be and whose interests it wants to bring into the analytical foreground. To ask these questions is to ask what politics are morally defensible and indefensible and, how these politics should be endorsed. Thus, the political ends are no longer taken as given and as not worthy of being thematised. Political ends become a central theoretical concern.

Given the aims and methods of normative theory, it should also be clear why normative theory is not concerned with explaining an 'emergence' of ethnicity, what ethnicity really *is*. When conceived normatively, ethnicity as an *historical phenomenon* does not have an essence: there are no 'hard facts' in the ethnic process waiting to be captured and be assigned causal worth; and ethnicity does not have a single function, or a single moral status. As such, there can be no prior grounds, derived from an empirical theory, to regard ethnicity as a 'deplorable' form of consciousness, one that is held in error. For the substance of ethnicity, that is, the particular ethnic identity, can be many things, and can take on morally defensible and indefensible forms. Thus, normative theory views ethnicity as a valid form of identity, on an equal footing with other constructed identities, and is concerned not with what ethnicity is, but with what its moral substance *should be* and how the theory can practically contribute to its realisation.

The Ethics of Explaining Ethnicity

The politics of methodology in the writing of African history have received significant and critical attention.[16] In the study of ethnicity in particular, insights into politico-methodological problems have been offered both by anthropologists and historians. A useful starting point for my purposes consists of the critical reflections offered by Jean and John Comaroff, among anthropologists, and Terence Ranger, among historians.[17] A common disposition in their work has been to view theory as political practice. This is evident in the way which they reveal their own normative commitments and concern themselves with the political implications of ethnographic and historiographical methods. It is in this spirit that the Comaroffs reflect upon the politics of anthropology as a discipline, and ask the existential disciplinary question: is anthropology intrinsically a violation of its object of study, the 'other' which it constructs and assumes? To this they respond that, '[b]y revealing the structures and processes by which some people come to dominate others, it may just as well affirm – indeed, chart the way to – revolutionary consciousness'.[18] It is in this spirit, as well, that Ranger revisits the invention-of-tradition approach and distances himself from it for its positing of colonial subjects as passive and powerless recipients of ethnic consciousness.[19]

While viewing theory as a political practice *is* what normative theory is about, I believe that the work of the Comaroffs and Ranger departs in significant ways from normative theory, in my use of the term, as does the work of other constructivists. In this section, I will demonstrate how constructivist theories, as explanatory and empirical theories, impute a single socio-political function and moral standing to ethnicity – that is, how they essentialise ethnicity as an historical phenomenon. I will review four influential constructivist approaches. These include the 'transactionalist' approach of Fredrik Barth, the 'instrumentalist' approaches of Abner Cohen and Robert Bates, the 'inventionist' approach as presented by Ranger as well as Martin Chanock, and the 'moralist' approach of John Lonsdale and Steven Feierman. To arrive at my central claim about the above theories of ethnicity, I will concern myself with three issues: the way in which each approach selects its privileged agents and institutions; the axis along which moral values are said to be generated; and the political purpose and implications of the theory itself.

Transactionalism

An important early constructivist account of ethnicity consists of the transactionalist approach of Barth.[20] Although Barth incorporated insights that were already in currency among the Manchester School anthropologists – their understandings of ethnicity as situational, relational, and instrumental, for instance, as well as their terminological shift from 'tribe' to 'ethnic group'[21] – I regard Barth's work as innovative insofar as it integrated these insights to produce a new 'ethnicity paradigm'.[22]

According to Barth, the need for a reconceptualisation of the ethnic group was raised by two empirical discoveries: that ethnic groups are formed and persist through interaction, and not isolation, and that ethnic boundaries persist *despite* the flow of personnel across them.[23] Since ethnic groups could no longer be imagined as self-contained cultural islands – as the term 'tribe', in its sociological usage, hitherto connoted – and since ethnic values were evidently exchangeable with the flow of personnel, Barth sought to shift the focus of inquiry to seek out the social, not cultural, function of ethnic groups. He thus came to understand ethnic groups not as culture-bearing units, but as a form of *social* organisation. As a theoretical departure, the new approach had three interconnected parts: the first, emphasising the importance of the subjective understanding of ethnicity, or the 'native model' of ethnicity, held ethnic groups to be categories of ascription and identification by the actors themselves; the second, emphasising social process, viewed ethnic groups as being generated and maintained for social-organisational purposes; and the third, emphasising group boundaries and their maintenance, viewed boundaries as socially effective and meaningful.[24]

These three theoretical emphases – on subjective meanings, social process, and boundary maintenance – constituted, and continue to constitute, a critique of theories of the ethnic group (or 'tribe') which give central importance, in definitional terms, to the sharing of cultural values and symbols. I say that Barth's work continues to constitute an important critique, because similar understandings of ethnicity remain in wide currency thirty years on, as, for example, in the influential work of Anthony D. Smith.[25] One problem that Barth saw in such definitions is that it conflates ethnic identity with culture. This conflation, Barth has argued, obscures the variations in the subjective meanings that are attributed to ethnic symbols and institutions and that could exist regardless of differences in objective culture.[26] Relatedly, the prioritisation of shared culture as a definitional characteristic, according to Barth, 'entails a prejudged view-point both on (1) the nature of continuity in time of such units, and (2) the locus of the factors which determine the form of such units'.[27] In other words, such a definition has a conceptual nationalism built into it, by doing, to put it crudely, what nationalists do: it assumes the continuity of symbolic meanings and the continuity of the ethnic unit. Smith once accused nationalists of being 'guilty of telescoping history' in the way in which they conceived of the nation: '[s]ubjectively...locating the nation', he wrote, 'hinges on a reading of ethnic history, which presupposes links between generations of a community of history and destiny in particular places of the earth'.[28] Barth, in effect, applied the same criticism, to sociological definitions of ethnic groups that assume the ethnic groups and their continuity by defining them by objective cultural symbols. For Barth, the clear conceptual distinction between culture and ethnicity, and the emphasis on ascription as the critical feature of ethnic groups, clarifies the nature of the ethnic unit and its continuity: '[continuity] depends on the [active] *maintenance* of the boundary'.[29] It is thus the ethnic boundary as a *social* boundary that defines the group, and not the 'cultural stuff' it encloses, that becomes the critical focus of investigation:

> [t]he cultural features that signal the boundary may change, and the cultural characteristics of the members may likewise be transformed, indeed, even the organizational form of the group may change – yet the fact of continuing dichotomization between members and outsiders allows us to specify the nature of continuity, and investigate the changing cultural form and content.[30]

I concur with Barth's critique of the approaches that do not adequately problematise 'shared culture', that imagine 'shared culture' to be what an ethnic group is mainly about, and that use 'shared culture' as the starting-point of inquiry. His alternative suggestion, however, to focus on external group boundaries, is also problematic. Barth, not unlike Smith, ultimately imagines the ethnic group as a homogeneous and consensual moral group at any given point in time. This is because Barth's interest in inter-ethnic boundaries inevitably locates the significance of social boundaries in the context of *inter*-group relations of stratification and competition, not *intra*-group ones. Central to his argument, as noted above, is the notion that ethnic distinctions result from social interaction, and are precisely the basis of social relations across boundaries.[31] For Barth, social interaction is the source of ethnic formation and dichotomisation, and not a source, for example, of cultural syncretism or moral boundary contestation within the group. While Barth rejects 'shared culture' as a starting point of inquiry, he returns to locate the 'shared' aspects of the ethnic group not in its culture but in its moral boundaries, thereby reifying the moral homogeneity of the ethnic group. Similarly, as Marcus Banks has pointed out, by focusing on boundaries, 'Barth reifies a correlation between the physical boundaries of a population and the conceptual boundary of its ethnic identity'.[32]

The understanding of the ethnic group as a homogeneous and consensual group seems necessary to Barth's approach in order for his particular concept of the ethnic group as an 'organisational vessel' to hold together. To regard the ethnic group primarily as a socially effective form of organisation one would generally have to imagine the ethnic group as being internally orderly, uncontested, and functional. Indeed, this is the general picture that emerges from Barth's analysis, drawn from his own fieldwork, of the interaction between Pathans and Baluchis. For Barth, the contents of the ethnic group, that is, the overt signs and signals (the diacritical features) and, more importantly, the standards of morality and excellence by which performance is judged (the basic value orientations), change insofar as individuals or households cross ethnic boundaries and choose to adopt the moral standards and political obligations current in the host ethnic group.[33] As such, the ethnic boundaries, as moral boundaries, are not contested and redefined from within the group.[34]

In the absence of such moral contestation, the institutions which Barth singles out as being important in the boundary maintenance of Pathan identity, in particular, acquire a moral legitimacy, as does the power of the patriarchs whose values are realised through these institutions. Specifically, when addressing the intra-group dynamics of Pathan boundary maintenance, Barth focuses on the institutions of hospitality, the council meeting of men, and seclusion (*purdah*). These pertain to the honourable uses of material goods, the honourable pursuit of public affairs, and the honourable organisation of domestic life, respectively. 'These three central institutions', Barth argues, 'combine to provide Pathans with the organizational mechanisms whereby they can realize core Pathan values fairly successfully, given the necessary external circumstances....They also facilitate the maintenance of shared values and identity within an acephalous and poly-segmentary population'.[35] Thus, Barth identifies singular, *core* Pathan values which, furthermore, are shared, accepted, and legitimate. Barth does not treat intra-group stratification and competition as problematic. Most crucially, he treats neither the *enforcement* of moral codes, such as *purdah*, by the patriarchs as problematic, nor the need to *publicly* demonstrate Pathan male virtues – either through the institution of hospitality or the council meeting of men – even though the acts of enforcing moral codes and publicly demonstrating adherence to them imply that moral values are inherently contestable and problematic in the first place.

To not acknowledge moral contestation, to assume the existence of *core* values, and to conflate these with the values of those that enforce them, is not to explain *the* process of ethnic formation, that is, produce a general theory of ethnicity as a historical phenomenon, but to morally endorse and represent only one interpretation of the 'native model' of ethnicity. Furthermore, in so doing, Barth identifies particular agents as being the politically capable ones, as well as the legitimate ones, at the expense of those who become politically and morally passive. In turn, the function of the ethnic group as a social 'organisational vessel' acquires a constant moral standing in its own right, regardless of the values which it carries.

Instrumentalism

Instrumentalist approaches have served as a counterpoint both to primordialist interpretations that regard ethnicity as an 'irrational' and 'innate' force and to the evolutionary tenets of modernisation theory.[36] Instrumentalists have sought to emphasise the 'rationality' of ethnicity in the process of political organisation, in the context of novel social, economic, and political circumstances. By attributing a rationality to ethnicity, they have also sought the means to 'explain' it in a way that morally cleanses it. A comparison of the work of Abner Cohen and Robert Bates will reveal their similarities in this regard. Their differences, however, are also significant. Although the two authors share an instrumentalist approach, their normative differences stem from a more fundamental difference in the way they conceptualise the nature of society, with Cohen writing within a functionalist tradition and Bates within the framework of rational choice.[37]

Cohen and Bates agree on the economically-driven political, as opposed to cultural, function of ethnicity. For Cohen, ethnic groups – and in his particular case study, the Hausa of Ibadan – are 'informal interest groups' that organise themselves through the idiom of custom, share institutions such as kinship and religion, and communicate among themselves relatively easily.[38] Ethnic groups form not by disengaging from each other. In a process which Cohen terms 'retribalisation', ethnic groups form by increasing interaction between them, within the context of new political situations, particularly in urban centres. In this process,

> a group from one ethnic category [that is, a cultural group without a corporate identity], whose members are involved in a struggle for power and privilege with members of a group from another ethnic category, within the framework of a *formal* political system,

manipulate some customs, values, myths, symbols, and ceremonials from their cultural tradition in order to articulate an *informal* political organization which is used as a weapon in that struggle.[39]

Similarly, for Bates, ethnic groups are 'coalitions' whose distinguishing characteristics are a symbolism of collective myths of origin, an assertion of ties of kinship or blood, a mythology expressive of cultural uniqueness or superiority, and a conscious elaboration of language and heritage.[40] The structural reasons for ethnic formation are to be found in the spacial character of modernisation; for Bates, '*where* modernization takes place often largely determines *who* gets modernized'.[41] This spacial factor, furthermore, often coincides with administrative districts, such that 'it is often useful for those engaged in competition for modernity to generate and mobilize the support of ethnic groupings'.[42] The ultimate objective of ethnic formation is, for Cohen, the control over trade, and, for Bates, the competition for the goods of modernisation, particularly for higher income and the resources that create it, such as land, markets, jobs.[43] For both authors, therefore, ethnic formation is not an expression of conservatism – despite the invocation of customs and traditions – but a calculated political response in the pursuit of power, privilege, and wealth. As such, ethnic groups, as political groups, are not substantively different in their motivations than other forms of political organisation. In this regard, moreover, one can infer that ethnic groups are no less legitimate forms of political organisation.

Although both authors are primarily concerned with inter-ethnic relations, Cohen places larger emphasis than Bates, as well as Barth, on intra-ethnic politics.[44] For Cohen, intra-ethnic discipline *is* problematic. 'Politics', he argues, 'refers to the processes involved in the distribution and exercise of, and struggle for, power within a social unit. Power is the control by men over the behaviour of other men and is thus an aspect of all social relationships'.[45] While in all political systems, he continues, use is made of a combination of physical coercion, economic reward and punishment, and moral and ritual obligation, the latter is especially important in informal organisations. In such organisations, authority relies greatly on moral and ritual mechanisms to apply pressure to individuals to fulfil their obligations to the collective interests, as well as to maintain mechanisms for political communication, for the formulation of problems, deliberation, decision-making, and coordination of action. Authority itself derives its legitimacy from custom – manipulated though this might be.[46] In contrast to Barth, intra-group politics, and the political/disciplinary use of moral codes, becomes an important aspect of ethnic formation and maintenance. As such, Cohen locates the significance of moral codes not only in the context of inter-ethnic relations but also in intra-ethnic ones. Moral codes, as social boundaries, are not maintained only for the purpose of distinguishing one 'organisational vessel' from another, but also for maintaining internal order, authority, and loyalty.

Despite Cohen's emphasis on intra-ethnic politics, however, the ethnic group retains an organic quality, with an in-built logic of collective survival. On the one hand, Cohen's concept of the ethnic group does not have the 'morally consensual' quality that is inherent in Barth's concept. On the other hand, Cohen interprets the application of moral sanctions as being applied by persons of authority in order to maintain group solidarity which, in turn, is generally viewed as serving the interests of the group as a whole. This is evident, for example, in the way in which he conceptualises the role of women in the economy of the group. Whether as 'housewives' in seclusion, or as 'prostitutes' with more independence, their roles in each status are deemed to be functional to the survival of the group.[47] It should be noted, furthermore, that Cohen, not unlike Barth, does not interpret the particularly strict interpretation and enforcement of *purdah* in the Hausa Quarter as an indication of a moral code that is contestable.[48] Similarly, political conflict between landlords is not theorised as a process of moral contestation. While customs and the moral order are indeed interpreted as being redefineable within the group – illustrated by his analysis of the establishment of the Tijanyya religious order, interpreted as a means to reinforce moral and ritual distinctiveness and group solidarity – they are done so in the interests of the political *order* and, hence, the group as a whole.[49] Ultimately, Cohen conceives of a set of superordinate, homogeneous interests that apply to the whole group. These interests, furthermore, are voiced by those who he regards as being in the realm of politics: the chief, the landlords, and the *malams* (the teachers and interpreters of the principles of Islam). Thus, Cohen, like Barth, identifies the values of his capable political actors with the values of the ethnic group as a whole. In so doing, he also lends legitimacy to these actors, as well as to the ethnic group as a community with a general purpose and logic.

Bates's rational-choice instrumentalism differs from the functionalist one of Cohen. In his theory of ethnicity, Bates does not share an 'organic' understanding of society, despite the fact that he places less emphasis on intra-ethnic competition and politics. Ethnic groups, for Bates, represent a coalescence of preferences with respect to allocational decisions, due mainly to corresponding spacial and administrative factors in modernisation. No internal contest – at least, one that is relevant to ethnicity – is implied here. The primary political actors in Bates's model of the ethnic group are the 'modern' elements within ethnic groups, comprising politicians, clerks, cash croppers, traders, and the formally educated. Given the corresponding spacial and administrative boundaries of ethnic groups, Bates observes that 'it has been in the interests of the most modern elements to sponsor the growth of "traditional" consciousness in Africa', so as to gather political support in the competition for the benefits of modernisation.[50] While the moderns are the main actors, Bates does include, it should be noted, the 'less advantaged' as political actors, insofar as they activate the sense of 'ethnic obligation' on the part of the more advantaged ones to gain higher social status and access to the modern sector.[51] The less advantaged are not viewed as contesting the values of the ethnic group; they simply use the sense of ethnic obligation, as they perceive that their individual progress is closely determined by the collective standing of their group.

The moral standing of Bates's concept of the ethnic group as a form of political expression gains legitimacy, as mentioned earlier, insofar as its economic logic does not differ from that of other political groupings. As much may be said of the moral standing of each individual political agent – even though, in Bates's actual method, some agents regarded as being more involved in the realm of politics, some are deemed to be more responsible than others for the growth of ethnic consciousness, and all, in the ethno-spatial context, are presumed to have homogeneous interests upon which they act as one undifferentiated whole.[52] If one were to assess Bates's normativity on the basis of his stated methodological individualism, one would infer that the political claims of the political agents, since they are uniformly rational, can only be of equal moral worth as well, regardless of whether they express the 'moderns' or 'traditionals', the 'more advantaged' or 'less advantaged'.

Yet, there is an added ethical nuance – in fact, a contradictory one – in Bates' work that needs to be brought out. Bates departs from the moral relativism inherent in the functionalism of both Cohen and Barth by making policy recommendations with a view to encourage the formation of non-ethnic political organisations. 'The appropriate response', he argues, 'is one of institutional design. Efforts should be devoted to creating institutional environments which alter incentives so that persons organize coalitions of a different nature when in pursuit of their interests. Attempts should focus on exploiting the very nature of ethnic competition so as to channel and diffuse it'.[53] This policy appeal creates a moral energy which is problematic for two reasons. First, by claiming what a more appropriate institutional environment *should be* for the collectivity, Bates contests the rationality of the collective outcome, as he is well aware. However, he does not view this contestation as being a contestation of the political order as well. He assumes that the attainment of the political end of 'modernisation', as he understands it, does not entail a restructuring of the political order – that is, that his recommended institutional design does not challenge the political order. This assumption follows from his belief in the concept of 'instrumental rationality', which itself assumes that ends are given and unproblematic, and which is only able to concern itself with the means, the technical solutions, towards the given end. The ethical contradiction lies herein. By contesting the political order, as he is, in fact, doing, Bates contests its legitimacy, even though his use of methodological individualism legitimates the individual claims that lead to it.

The second, and related, problem is that Bates' recommendation is addressed to an unnamed political agent, who, nonetheless, is regarded as responsible for the implementation of the 'institutional design'. One is left to assume that the responsible agent for the implementation of his recommended political order is the state or the political class that runs it. That which is left untheorised here is, first, why politicians should act against their own interests, their own concept of what the political order should be, and, second, how Bates theorises himself as a political actor who is capable of appealing to the state or the politicians. Bates' theory of ethnic groups and politics thus makes claims for a more appropriate political end without viewing political ends as inherently contestable, and makes policy recommendations to political actors who have political ends of their own, without theorising what access he has to them.

The two instrumentalist approaches reviewed above attribute a similar, and singular, socio-political function to ethnic groups. For both, ethnicity has an economically-driven political function. Both also lend legitimacy to the ethnic group as a form of political organisation insofar as the ethnic group does not differ in its goals and motivations from other political organisations. The ethnic group itself is ultimately not regarded as being capable of having a variable moral standing since it does not entail a competition of diverse moral principles; it is regarded either as an organic whole, in Cohen's case, or as a coalescence of preferences, in the case of Bates. In this regard, Cohen conflates the dominant values of the group with the values of the group as a whole, in a fashion similar to Barth's, and further legitimates the ethnic group by interpreting its values as contributing to the functioning and survival of the group as a whole. By contrast, Bates, by virtue of his methodological individualism, attributes equal moral worth to the rational choices of individuals, even though he ultimately contests the legitimacy of the political order which results.

Inventionism

The approach which has sought unequivocally to denounce ethnicity as a form of political organisation has been the 'inventionist' one. Most influential exponents of this approach have been Eric Hobsbawm and Terence Ranger.[54] They have sought to 'unmask' ethnic ideology, establish its historical novelty and fictitiousness, and lay bare the social hierarchies which it conceals. In this respect, the work of Martin Chanock has been similar.[55] Ranger has specifically located the era of inventions in the colonial period, interpreting invented traditions as the ideological instruments of colonial administration and social control.[56] More recently, he has distanced himself from this approach, as mentioned earlier, for reasons that have to do just as much with the normative problems of inventionism as with the empirical evidence on which Ranger largely relies. Nonetheless, it is worth reviewing this approach once more from a normative perspective, not least because many of its assumptions remain in wide currency.

In contrast to the transactionalist and instrumentalist approaches, the inventionist one gives central importance to social hierarchy in the production of traditions, customs, and ethnic consciousness. Here, traditions are not interpreted as serving a 'collective political survival'; and the ethnic group is not interpreted as 'a socially effective form of organisation', or 'a coalition of preferences'. For Ranger, traditions have served to justify a hierarchical social order. Locating their production in the colonial period, Ranger observes that traditions were used in multiple ways. This was due not only to the demands of governing subject societies which were rapidly changing, but of governing them 'indirectly'. The shared ideology of 'Imperial Monarchy', for example, and the rituals associated with it, served to 'embrace whites and blacks alike, to dignify the practicalities of collaboration, and to justify white rule'.[57] Traditions defined the relationship between the rulers and the ruled. Thus, the 'regimental tradition' defined the role of officers and men; the 'great-house' tradition of rural gentility defined the roles of both masters and servants; and the 'public school' tradition defined the roles of prefects and fags. In Ranger's words, '[a]ll this might be made use of to create a clearly defined hierarchical society in which Europeans commanded and Africans accepted commands, but both within a shared framework of pride and loyalty'.[58] Despite their modernising intentions and appearance, such invented traditions of governance helped to produce a 'feudal-patriarchal' ethic, rather than a 'capitalist-transformative' one.[59]

Ethnic consciousness is seen as a corollary of the invention of tradition, as well as a product of missionary work. Ranger argues that, along with the above inventions, colonial administrators set out to define clearly and formalise social, political, and judicial institutions. The rationale for the choice of institutions was provided by a European concept of what was 'customary' and 'traditional' in Africa. This process of the formalisation of social relationships, political authority, and law during colonial rule has been described extensively by Chanock in a similar vein. He argues that colonial administrators, equipped with a functionalist and consensual understanding of African societies – the influence of which, as I have shown, remains noticeable in the much later work of Barth and Cohen – conceived of the 'traditional African community', in the form of 'the tribe', with a traditional political authority, in the form of 'the chief', and with a 'customary law' which they regarded as an 'amorphous batch of mutable equitable principles which were more or less suited to African social conditions'. Customary law was not regarded as being subject to historical process; instead, it was seen as having an 'essence' which needed to be restored from the pre-colonial order, purified, and applied systematically to the colonial order. It was in this context, Chanock argues, that the previously ill-defined role of the chief, the tribe, and custom were reified and institutionalised; as such, 'the package of tribe, chief, custom and judgement was largely a colonial creation'.[60]

Alongside the reification of tribe and custom by colonial administrators, missionaries functioned as 'unofficial' agents of ethnic consciousness. Ranger gives an account of their role in the invention of Manyika identity in colonial Southern Rhodesia.[61] In their efforts to understand the spoken vernacular and to develop it into written form, he argues, missionary linguists transformed unbounded dialect zones into discrete ones, by emphasising particular variations and standardising them into written form. Different missions, whether working together or separately, thus produced several different named languages. These, in turn, went a long way in building a common sense of identity, which itself was activated in competition between the created ethno-linguistic groups, and was heightened among labour migrants in their diaspora.

In the above accounts of both the production of neo-traditions and ethno-linguistic consciousness, African participation and agency is accorded a place. The Manyika identity, Ranger observes, was a product of both church and local entrepreneurial elites, and was reinforced, furthermore, by protests in its name, against the failing political economy of the region.[62] Customs, similarly, were extensively manipulated by Africans themselves. Elders, men, paramount chiefs, and ruling aristocracies all appealed to custom as a means of maintaining and extending their control over youth, women, and labour; and in an inter-ethnic context, indigenous populations appealed to custom to ensure that migrants who settled among them did not achieve political and economic rights.[63] For Chanock, central to all such appeals is the struggle for control over labour, and it is here where he locates agency. In the rapidly changing political economy of the colonial period, he notes, conflicts about what sorts of social institutions were or were not customary intensified. Class conflicts, generational conflicts, and gender conflicts expressed themselves through claims about custom and sought legitimation in its name; above all, customary law served not as a system of rules, but as a method of legitimation.[64] Chanock stresses that customary law should not be seen merely as a creation of the British: '[w]hat they had done was unknowingly to create opportunities which were seized upon by some Africans'.[65]

Yet, both Ranger and Chanock agree that there occurred a 'freezing' of moral status and contestation, and a diminution of agency, with the advent of colonial rule. Whereas custom in pre-colonial Africa was 'loosely defined and infinitely flexible', and whereas African societies were previously competitive, fluid, and dynamic, Ranger claims that the invention of customary law, customary land rights, and customary political structure henceforth rendered social relations inflexible.[66] '[T]he dogmas of customary security and immutably fixed relationships', he remarks, 'grew up in the same societies, which came to have an appearance of *ujamaa* style solidarity'.[67] Chanock concurs that '[l]egalization led to a freezing of moral status and stratification, henceforth defined and not negotiated. Custom became a resource of the instruments of government, rather than a resource of the people'.[68]

The above inventionist interpretation has constituted an important departure from previous interpretations of ethnicity which have not been inclined to emphasise the conflicts entailed in the articulation of ethnic identity. Nonetheless, significant problems remain. In revisiting the inventionist approach a decade after the publication of *The Invention of Tradition*, Ranger has taken issue with both the concepts of 'invention' and 'tradition'.[69] Built into the inventionist approach and the terms which it employs is an imaginary dichotomy between a 'pre-colonial' and a 'colonial' world: a pre-colonial world in which custom is more contested and dynamic, less hegemonic, and more 'authentic' and legitimate; and a colonial world in which customary law and tradition are more uncontested and static, more hierarchical, and less 'authentic' and legitimate. 'Tradition' embodies all of the latter judgements, conceiving, as it does, a transformation of a dynamic society into an inertial one. 'Invention', just as well, implies the imposition of an identity resolutely; it implies a too one-sided and once-and-for-all event.[70]

The moral judgements unavoidably extend to the particular agents associated with either custom or tradition. The African agents of tradition and ethnicity are the 'reactionary' forces, which are pitted against the 'positive' ones of custom: chiefs against commoners, fathers against sons, patriarchs against wives and daughters.[71] Political agency, however, is of a diluted sort in a thoroughly 'traditionalised' and 'ethnified' colonial order. In the way in which it is theorised, agency is preponderantly associated with the reactionary forces that have recast African societies on the basis of a moral order which henceforth has become immutable and uncontestable. In this light, wherever agency is considered, it is most likely to be interpreted as 'collaboration', not contestation. Indeed, as Ranger points out, the agency of the positive forces effectively is theorised out of the inventionist model; the positive forces become, instead, passive recipients of ethnic consciousness.

In so doing, the internal sources of change are effaced as well. In an uncontested political order, there are no internal sources of change, as the actors to whom the inventionist theory is addressed are not theorised as politically capable. In fact, they are not even theorised as having an 'appropriate' political consciousness – that is, one that is in accordance with that of the theorist. Nonetheless, the theorist would claim to represent their true interests, if only the falsity of the current political order could be revealed. Even in this act of unmasking the political order, however, the theorist would be required to theorise himself or herself explicitly as a capable political actor, to demonstrate his or her influence over those to whom the theory is addressed, in order for the theory to make sense.

The illegitimacy attributed to the political order also raises the question of responsibility for political action and social change. While the political order is assumed to be uncontested and, hence, legitimate in the eyes of the relevant actors, it is nonetheless contested and judged as illegitimate by the author himself. This generates an energy of responsibility which is not addressed directly, but which may be partly inferred. Since the most capable political actors are also those whose political claims are morally indefensible, the responsibility for political action must be located elsewhere. Where exactly, remains unspecified. However, in order to avoid a paternalistic, save-the-victim approach to political action, one would need to theorise the addressees of the theory not as incapable and politically unaware *objects* of political action, but as actors capable of knowing what their needs are and capable of contesting their political order, whether explicitly or less so.[72]

Inventionism not only fails to locate the sources of change internally, but thus justifies external political intervention. This is mainly because 'tradition' is associated, first, with reactionary forces and, second, with immutability. It is also for this reason that ethnicity cannot be entertained as a defensible form of politics. There is only one type of ethnicity, only one type of claim made in the name of tradition. Inventionism privileges this, at the expense of other competing claims. Inventionism then extrapolates from this to produce a general theory of ethnicity, with a single socio-political function, with a constant moral standing, with an historical essence, and with all the trappings of empirical theory.

Moral Ethnicity

The conceptual problems inherent in inventionism are addressed by the 'moral ethnicity' approach, most closely associated with John Lonsdale, but which also shares an affinity with the work of Steven Feierman.[73] Both Lonsdale and Feierman have sought to demonstrate the political contestations that are voiced in the language of tradition and ethnicity. They have thereby re-opened a space for viewing such political claims under a favourable light. Integral to this moralist reconceptualisation has also been an indictment of deep-seeded conceptual dichotomies, those of the colonial/pre-colonial, modern/pre-modern, and ethnicity/nationality, that have severely constrained our inquiry.

In light of the foregoing discussion, it should be clear why the ethnic group should not be considered as a 'pre-political' form of organisation, one that awaits the ideas of 'the enlightenment' and 'modernity' for its politicisation.[74] Whereas inventionists have emphasised the moral-political contests entailed by their understanding of pre-colonial custom – contests which 'freeze' when transformed into tradition and become 'ethnified' – moral ethnicity theorists emphasise the continuation of moral contestation and politics in the name of tradition and ethnicity. For Lonsdale, ethnicity is precisely about moral debate; it is a debate about political community, about rights and obligations, about 'ethnic citizenship'. 'Tribes', he argues, 'like nations – and they are like nations in most respects other than their lack of a state – are changing moral arenas of political debate'.[75] He views ethnic groups as plural communities, and 'ethnic identity as the reverse of what is often said to be, unthinking conformity'; referring to the case of the Kikuyu, '[a] common ethnicity was the arena for the sharpest social and political division'.[76] In this light, he disputes the view that the Mau Mau was a process of 'cultural renewal' – perhaps, what Smith would classify as an ethnicist movement – but interprets it as a process of 'historical contestation'. Indeed, as Lonsdale indicates, interpreting such a movement as cultural renewal would suggest that there was an unproblematic culture to renew.[77] The non-homogeneity of small-scale, and specifically peasant, societies is addressed by Feierman in a similar manner when he sets out to demonstrate that long-term continuities in political language, in the idioms of tradition, are the outcome of radical social change and of struggle within peasant society. He disputes the assumption that the whole of society shares a single body of practice. He notes that, '[a] single local culture, superficially homogeneous, includes many streams of discourse each located in the differentiated organization of intellectuals. The intellectuals can be understood, for their part, with reference to their social position and their interests'.[78] 'Intellectuals' here are conceived not in the sense of a formally educated stratum of society, but in a quasi-Gramscian sense, which departs from Gramsci's conception insofar as it is applied to peasants for their capacity to act as historical agents themselves by engaging in organisational, directive, educative, or expressive activities.[79]

Moreover, the ethnic group, or local culture, is not isolated but is capable of syncretising diverse political languages. In disputing assumptions about the ethnographic objects as being bounded in space and time, Feierman stresses the ability of peasant intellectuals to reinterpret inherited vocabulary and symbols by actively responding to, and investing with meaning, the new political language and boundaries introduced by a new political order.[80] In this manner, 'local society and the larger society', he argues, 'merge and interpenetrate at many levels, to the point where we cannot say what is local and what is larger'.[81] Elevating to the analytical foreground this far from passive act of investing changing political discourse with meaning is where Feierman's interpretation contrasts that of inventionism. It is here, too, where the authentic/inauthentic, imported/autochthonous, and imposed/non-imposed dichotomies relating to identities break down. For an identity cannot be 'inauthentic' if it is made meaningful, and cannot be 'stripped away' for the restoration of a more 'essential' identity. From this, it follows that competing political claims made in the name of tradition and ethnicity cannot be judged on the basis of a 'cultural authenticity'. Competing political claims are equally meaningful, even as 'one appeal to past identity', in Lonsdale's words, 'may defend traditional hierarchy, another demand the equally traditional – or invented – rights of all free-born fellow countrymen'.[82]

The ethnic group becomes, above all, a moral community. In a critique of modernisation theory, Lonsdale argues that 'ethnic thought had long addressed issues of civic rights and duties, inseparable from those of gender, with more passion than the extramural class of territorial nationalism could ever have had before independence'.[83] The moral economy of ethnicity – that is, the local conceptions of justice, liberty, equality, and moral rights and obligations – is given central importance, as this constitutes a meaningful moral framework and a source of political thought. In times of political and economic transformation, whether during or prior to colonial rule, this moral framework became subject to fervent contestation. Resulting political claims made in the name of tradition and ethnicity were claims about how the community should be ordered, who 'we' are and who 'we' are not, and what is 'the proper' way of doing things. Entailed in all such claims is a contestation of moral knowledge and a process of moral exclusion. Lonsdale describes the dynamics of this process with reference to the Kikuyu:

> [a]fter British conquest [rival leaders] had to thrash out again the old issues raised by their society's unequal moral economy, at a time when its distribution of wealth, honour and power was being subverted by external pressure for change. Some tried to subject the new forces to their existing sway, to enlarge old wealth and power. Their rivals had first to persuade themselves, and then their kin, that their novel beliefs and forms of wealth gave authority for new power. Later, yet other, with scant prospect of wealth, tried instead to throw new forms of organization into the competition for honour. To debate civic virtue was to define ethnic identity.[84]

The moral ethnicity reconceptualisation goes a long way towards meeting many of the preconditions for a normative approach to ethnicity set out in the first part of this chapter. First, it conceives of ethnicity as a moral community, whose traditions, moreover, are subject to ongoing contestation. In this manner, it identifies the sources of change internally. Second, it allows the possibility of bringing diverse actors into the analytical foreground, and of not privileging and then reifying a singular axis of social relationships along which moral values are generated. By virtue of its non-exclusionary inner workings, the moral ethnicity approach thus has the capacity to 'empower' theoretically those social actors who are contesting social and political exclusion as they perceive it. The transactionalist, instrumentalist (with the potential exception of the rational choice variant), and the inventionist approaches, as we have seen, do not allow this possibility. Third, the moral ethnicity approach allows the possibility of regarding ethnicity as having a variable socio-political function and a variable moral standing, steering our inquiry away from imputing an essence to ethnicity as an historical phenomenon.

Regardless of the respective normative projects that underlie their analyses, however, what is clear is that they resort to validating their theoretical choices – that is, not their ultimate theoretical statements on ethnicity and tradition, but their prior angle of vision – on the basis of empirical observation. It is here that normative theory begins to diverge from the moral ethnicity approach as presented above. Both Lonsdale and Feierman strive to 'capture' a 'reality', and, as such, remain true to empirical theory. Feierman, for example, states that 'we…need an approach to understanding the *actual* historical actors'.[85] His proposed shifting of the angle of vision to peasant intellectuals is deemed necessary not because their political claims are judged as morally right on the basis of a well-explicated normative framework, but because they are the 'objectively' true historical actors. Associating these particular actors in an essential way with the construction of ethnicity risks essentialising their particular understanding of ethnicity, at the exclusion of competing understandings of ethnicity held by other social actors, and risks essentialising ethnicity as an historical phenomenon in its entirety. As I will explain in the next section, the 'hard fact' approach to choosing which social actors to emphasise forecloses on ethical debate, on who *should be* brought into the analytical foreground. It also lends itself to writing of micro-histories of struggles for recognition which are not interpreted within an over-arching concept of social change with normative meaning.[86]

A second, and related, reason for which the moral ethnicity approach diverges from normative theory is that the authors do not explicitly theorise themselves as political actors in the act of doing ethnography. An advantage of the moral ethnicity approach is that, by contrast to the inventionist one, it does not seek to 'awaken' the actors to which it is addressed. To use Feierman's case again, the peasant intellectuals are already treated as competent moral agents, aware of their political needs, and capable of contesting their political order. However, it remains unclear what the political purpose of their theoretical project is, and how, practically, it contributes to the political project of those actors whom it brings into the analytical foreground. Without addressing this issue, the theory risks gaining the characteristics of a general theory of ethnicity which, like empirical theory, detaches itself from the political process, and assumes that the knowledge it produces is of general utility, of use to anyone, as if political ends are homogeneous, uncontested, and given.

Towards a Normative Theory of Ethnicity

At the crux of normative theory, as I have noted, is that there are no hard facts about ethnicity as a general historical phenomenon – facts that can be observed without being given value in the act of their selection. It is therefore futile to rely on facts to make a moral judgement about ethnicity as a general historical phenomenon. Our inquiry, I argue, should start elsewhere. We need first to be explicit about our normative projects *vis-a-vis* such questions, for example, as exclusion, inclusion, and citizenship. To ask these questions, however, does not mean that we cannot pursue empirical questions, that we cannot do ethnography in the interest of the politics that we wish to endorse. Empirical inquiry can be combined with normative theory in this manner, as long as we recognise that the empirical inquiry is of a secondary order and, as such, is not equipped, in itself, to provide answers to ethical questions.

I have set out the preconditions for a normative theory of ethnicity in the first section of this chapter, and I have subsequently argued that only the moral ethnicity approach comes close to meeting them. To recapitulate, a normative approach to ethnicity requires that the ethnic group is conceptualised as a moral community; that it is regarded as a realm of moral debate about rights and obligations, and about inclusion in and exclusion from the political processes of the community. This means that the ethnic group is not a homogeneous body of political practice; it is a contested community, inherent in which are sources of change. Such a reconceptualisation seeks to bring into the analytical foreground social actors whose political claims have long been excluded from theories of ethnicity, and who have thereby been assumed to be incapable of contesting the political order of which they are a part and on which they rely for the fulfilment of their material and non-material needs. To not theorise the social actors who are contesting the political order is to privilege the political order and objectives of the actors who are brought into the analytical foreground. As I have argued in the cases of the transactionalist, instrumentalist, and inventionist approaches, such a privileging has moral and political implications that cannot go unattended. They create a moral energy by addressing themselves to particular agents who, by implication, are assumed to be the legitimate and responsible ones for political action – often in spite of their own political objectives and conceptions of what the political order should be. Shifting the angle of vision to privilege political claims that are deemed legitimate has an 'empowering' capacity, in the sense that it does not take a political order as given, and it does not assume that the relevant social actors are unaware of their political needs, that they speak the language of a meaningless and inauthentic consciousness, that they are incapable of contesting their political order, and that they are to be treated as objects of political action. Shifting the angle of vision to claims that are deemed legitimate also entails an acknowledgement that ethnicity may have a variable socio-political function and moral standing.

The moral ethnicity approach does allow us to recognise the competing claims. However, it does not explicitly begin its inquiry by setting out how to think about exclusion and citizenship. Instead, the moral ethnicity approach, as empirical theory seeking to capture a 'reality', resorts to an empiricist epistemology to establish the validity of its angle of vision. In so doing, it forecloses on ethical debate, without providing a moral framework with which to distinguish between the competing claims. As such, one is left to assume that any political claim against the political order is equally valid. The claim of any social actor who fulfills, for example, the criteria of a 'peasant intellectual' – that is, that he or she engages in 'socially recognised organisational, directive, educative, or expressive activities' – is assumed to be legitimate, regardless of the substance of the particular claim. The same, of course, would appply to a methodological individualist approach, which does have the capacity to bear out the agencies competing against a political order, but which does not discriminate between the diverse claims of the agents on ethical grounds. Nor would the framework of an inventionist approach be adequate, by judging competing claims on the basis of an 'authentic' ideal.

Our inquiry, as I have argued, should begin by locating itself within an explicit normative framework that is concerned with distinguishing between the progressive and the reactionary and with coming to terms with what constitutes social and political exclusion. A normative framework is an equally necessary precondition for doing ethnographic research. It is only when one is equipped with an explicit normative framework that one's angle of vision may be shifted in favour of the particular politics that one seeks to endorse. It is also through this type of inquiry that ethnography and historiography gain an 'advocative' character, concerned, as they are, with defensible, contemporary, and relevant politics. Although ethnography has long been criticised for having a presentist preoccupation which has excluded historical inquiry, I would argue for a presentism of a different sort. Not a presentism which excludes historical account, but one which makes historical and ethnographic accounts relevant to the political present. After all, our presentist lenses, that is, the ways in which we conceive of society and the reasons for conceiving it, cannot be shed.

Finally, what does all this make of our concept of ethnicity, or nationality for that matter? Thomas Hylland Eriksen, in calling for a reconceptualisation of ethnicity and nationality in terms of a 'life-world' approach, has remarked that '[c]oncepts can serve as both intellectual tools of liberation and as straightjackets. Their only claim to legitimacy lies in their ability to help us conceptualise the outside world more accurately; when they cease to do that job, they are ready for replacement'.[87] I concur with the former statement on the liberating or constraining nature of concepts of ethnicity. Predictably, however, I differ in my reasons for abandoning them. Concepts of ethnicity need to be, first and foremost, *personally* and *politically* useful. It is on the basis of their political utility that concepts should stand or fall. It follows also that, as long as we conceive of ethnicity normatively, as long as we acknowledge that our political ends differ, our concepts of ethnicity will differ as well. As such, it is impossible to have *one* concept of ethnicity. We can only have competing ones, reflecting our competing political projects.

NOTES

I am grateful to a number of friends and colleagues for their critical comments and advice on various versions of this chapter. They include Erica Benner, Molly Cochran, Thomas Hylland Eriksen, Dominique Jacquin-Berdal, João Marques De Almeida, James Mayall, Henrietta Moore, Sarah Owen, Lothar Rast, and Susanne Zistel. Versions of this chapter have also been presented at the Africa Workshop and the International Political Theory Workshop of the Department of International Reltions at the LSE, as well as at the Contemporary Research in International Political Theory panel of the British International Studies Association Annual Conference, Leeds, December 1997. I also thank the participants in these sessions.

1. See the introduction to this volume for an account of constructivism in the study of ethnicity and nationalism in Africa and for a range of authors who have come to be known as constructivists.
2. See Charles Taylor, *Sources of The Self* (Cambridge: Cambridge University Press, 1989).
3. For a discussion and critique of empirical and normative theories, see Richard J. Bernstein, *The Restructuring of Social and Political Theory* (London: Methuen and Co., 1979). I am adopting here the definitions of the terms 'empirical' and 'normative' as provided by Bernstein.
4. Isaiah Berlin, 'Does Political Theory Still Exist?', in Peter Laslett and W.G. Runciman (eds.), *Philosophy, Politics and Society, Second Series* (Oxford: Basil Blackwell, 1964), p. 8.
5. An empirical theory is not necessarily incapable of conceiving of more than one type of ethnicity. For two such exceptions, see Thomas Hylland Eriksen, *Us and Them in Modern Societies: Ethnicity and Nationalism in Mauritius, Trinidad and Beyond* (Oslo: Scandinavian University Press, 1992), Chapter 1, and more recently, Jan Nederveen Pietrse, 'Deconstructing/Reconstructing Ethnicity', *Nations and Nationalism* (Vol. 3, No. 3, 1997), pp. 365–95. This way of thinking in the study of ethnicity begins to compare with developments in the study of nationalism in which one does find a much longer lineage of thinking along typological lines, from Hans Kohn's 'Eastern' versus 'Western' nationalisms, to Anthony D. Smith's 'ethnic' versus 'civic' ones, and to David Miller's pursuit of a morally defensible basis for nationality. See Hans Kohn, *The Idea of Nationalism: A Study in its Origins and Background* (New York, NY: The Macmillan Company, 1946); Anthony D. Smith,

National Identity (London: Penguin Books, 1991), Chapter 1; and David Miller, *On Nationality* (Oxford: Clarendon Press, 1995).
6. Charles Taylor, 'Neutrality in Political Science', in Charles Taylor, *Philosophy and the Human Sciences: Philosophical Papers II* (Cambridge: Cambridge University Press, 1985), p. 81.
7. Charles Taylor, 'Social Theory as Practice', in Taylor, *op. cit.*, in note 6, p. 107.
8. See, for example, Clifford Geertz, 'Thick Description: Toward an Interpretive Theory of Culture', in Clifford Geertz, *The Interpretation of Cultures: Selected Essays* (New York, NY: Basic Books, 1973), Chapter 1.
9. See also Charles Taylor, 'Understanding and Ethnocentricity', in Taylor, *op. cit.*, in note 6, Chapter 4.
10. *Ibid.* Such imagery of cultures as distinct and autonomous also finds its way into Taylor's *Sources of the Self*, *op.cit.*, in note 1, in which he interprets the making not only of a modern identity but also of the 'West'. Similarly, in his article on 'The Politics of Recognition', in Amy Gutman (ed.), *Multiculturalism: Examining the Politics of Recognition* (Princeton, NJ: Princeton University Press, 1992), he makes similar claims about 'our' civilisation, as well as about Québécois culture; for such a critique, see William E. Connolly, 'Pluralism, Multiculturalism and the Nation-state: Rethinking the Connections', *Journal of Political Ideologies* (Vol. 1, No. 1, 1996), pp. 53–73.
11. *Ibid.*, pp. 125–6.
12. See also Mervyn Frost's critique of understanding in which he makes the similar point that even understanding as a methodology cannot avoid the requirement of value judgements precisely at the moment that inquiry begins. Mervyn Frost, *Ethics in International Relations: A Constitutive Theory* (Cambridge: Cambridge University Press, 1996), pp. 23–30.
13. Charles Taylor, 'Interpretation and the Sciences of Man', in Taylor, *op. cit.*, in note 6, pp. 37–9.
14. Jürgen Habermas offers a similar criticism of understanding when he argues that it does not necessarily entail an acknowledgement of the interest-based character of knowledge, and, as such, does not contemplate an emancipatory pursuit in the sense that Critical Theory does. See Habermas, trans. J.J. Shapiro, *Knowledge and Human Interests* (Cambridge: Polity Press, 1987), pp. 309–10.
15. Here, I am employing specifically the earlier definition of 'critical' theory as provided by Max Horkheimer, for this can be said to have a closer affinity to the project of the 'invention-of-tradition' theorists of ethnicity who are concerned with 'unmasking' assumptions that are deemed to be held in error. See Max Horkheimer, 'Traditional and Critical Theory', in Max Horkheimer, trans. M.J. O'Connell, *Critical Theory: Selected Essays* (New York, NY: The Continuum Publishing Company, 1995).
16. See, for example, the compendium of articles by eminent Africanists in Bogumil Jewsiewicki and David Newbury (eds.), *African Historiographies: What History for Which Africa?* (Beverly Hills, CA, London, and New Delhi: Sage Publications, 1986).
17. See Jean and John Comaroff, *Of Revelation and Revolution: Christianity, Colonialism, and Consciousness in South Africa, Volume I* (Chicago, IL, and London: The University of Chicago Press, 1991), especially the Preface and Introduction; John and Jean Comaroff, 'Ethnography and the Historical Imagination', in John and Jean Comaroff, *Ethnography and the Historical Imagination* (Boulder, CO, San Francisco,

CA, and Oxford: Westview Press, 1992), pp. 3–48; and Terence Ranger, 'The Invention of Tradition Revisited: The Case of Colonial Africa', in Terence Ranger and Olufemi Vaughan (eds.), *Legitimacy and the State in Twentieth-Century Africa* (Basingstoke: Macmillan, in association with St. Antony's College, Oxford, 1993), pp. 62–111.
18. Comaroff, *Of Revelation and Revolution, op. cit.* in note 17, p. xiii.
19. Ranger, 'The Invention of Tradition Revisited', *op. cit.*, in note 17.
20. See Fredrik Barth, 'Introduction', in Fredrik Barth (ed.), *Ethnic Groups and Boundaries: The Social Organization of Culture Difference* (Oslo: Universitetsforlaget, 1969), pp. 9–38.
21. For a discussion of the contributions of the Manchester School which preceded Barth's work, see Marcus Banks, *Ethnicity: Anthropological Constructions* (London and New York, NY: Routledge, 1996), pp. 25–9.
22. See Richard Jenkins, 'Social Anthropological Models of Inter-Ethnic Relations', in John Rex and David Mason (ed.), *Theories of Race and Ethnic Relations* (Cambridge: Cambridge University Press, 1986).
23. Fredrik Barth, 'Introduction', in Barth (ed.), *op. cit.*, in note 20, pp. 9–10.
24. *Ibid.*, pp. 10–14.
25. For Smith, the dimensions of an 'ethnie' are a collective name, a common myth of descent, a shared history, a distinctive shared culture, an association with a specific territory, and a sense of solidarity. See Anthony D. Smith, *The Ethnic Origins of Nations* (Oxford and New York, NY: Basil Blackwell, 1986), pp. 22–30, and, more recently, John Hutchinson and Anthony D. Smith, 'Introduction', in John Hutchinson and Anthony D. Smith (eds.), *Ethnicity* (Oxford: Oxford University Press, 1996), especially pp. 5–7.
26. Barth, *op. cit.*, in note 23, pp. 14 and 32–33. It should be noted that Smith has sought to 'subjectivise' our understanding of ethnicity. However, he treats the referents of 'myth of descent', 'history', 'distinctive culture', and 'specific territory' singularly, abstractly, and, hence, objectively, as not having simultaneously contested meanings.
27. *Ibid.*, p. 12.
28. Smith, *op. cit.*, in note 5, pp. 69–70.
29. Barth, *op. cit.*, in note 23, pp. 14–15, emphasis added.
30. *Ibid.*
31. *Ibid.*, pp. 9–10.
32. Banks, *op. cit.*, in note 21.
33. Barth, 'Pathan Identity and its Maintenance', in Barth (ed.), *op. cit.*, in note 23, pp. 124–7.
34. In this way, Barth generally restricts identity choice to the *swapping* of ethnic identities. Nonetheless, in his discussion of the Pathans and Baluchis, he notes an exception: 'the identity retains its character because *many* change their ethnic label [upon entry into the host ethnic group], and only *few* are in a position where they cling to it under adverse circumstances. Only when the many choose to maintain the claim despite their [moral/social] failure – as where no alternative identity is possible – or where the failure is a common and very costly one...do the basic contents or characteristics of the identity start being modified'. *Ibid.*, pp. 133–4, emphasis in original. The theoretical implications of the dynamics of identity contestation, however, are not explored further and are not integrated into the thrust of his general framework. It should also be noted that other authors have criticised Barth's

conceptualisation of identity choice, for different reasons. Abner Cohen and Marcus Banks, for example, have criticised Barth for conceptually restricting identity choice to the particular contents of the ethnic group, thereby not allowing for the possibility of opting out of ethnic thinking altogether. Such a limiting understanding of identity choice has earned Barth the label of a 'primordialist'. See Abner Cohen, 'Introduction: The Lesson of Ethnicity', in Abner Cohen (ed.), *Urban Ethnicity* (London: Tavistock Publications, 1974), p. xii, and Banks, *op. cit.*, in note 21, p. 13.

35. Barth, *op. cit.*, in note 33, p. 123.

36. For an influential primordialist account, see Clifford Geertz, 'The Integrative Revolution: Primordial Sentiment and Civil Politics in the New States', in Clifford Geertz (ed.) *Old Societies and New States: The Quest for Modernity in Asia and Africa* (New York, NY: The Free Press, 1963), pp. 105–57. Primordialists and modernisation theorists, of course, did not agree with each other either. Geertz's account itself constituted a critique of modernisation theory, insofar as it gave central importance to primordial (and 'irrational') sentiments as bases for political mobilisation in new states: 'it is the very process of the formation of a sovereign civil state that, among other things, stimulates sentiments of parochialism, communalism, racialism, and so on, because it introduces into a society a valuable new prize over which to fight and a frightening new force [ideas of citizenship, self-rule, and popular participation] with which to contend' (p. 120).

37. I will be focusing mainly on two works, Abner Cohen, *Custom and Politics in Urban Africa: A Study of Hausa Migrants in Yoruba Towns* (London: Routledge and Kegan Paul, 1969), and Robert Bates, 'Modernization, Ethnic Competition, and the Rationality of Politics in Africa', in Donald Rothchild and Victor A. Olorunsula (eds.), *State Versus Ethnic Claims: African Policy Dilemmas* (Boulder, CO: Westview Press, 1983), pp. 152–71.

38. Cohen, *op. cit.*, in note 37, p. 4.

39. *Ibid.*, p. 2.

40. Bates, *op. cit.*, in note 37, p. 153.

41. *Ibid.*, p. 156, emphasis in original.

42. *Ibid.*

43. Cohen, *op. cit.*, in note 37, p. ix, and Bates, *op. cit.*, in note 37, p. 153.

44. Bates refers to the existence of intra-group divisiveness, which, as he notes, should not be ignored, though he qualifies this by stating that '[t]he fact of internal division and conflict should…not be taken as evidence of the absence of effective ethnic collectivities'. Bates, *op. cit.*, in note 37, p. 153, n. 2. Despite the reference, the existence of intra-group competition is not important to his theory of ethnicity.

45. Cohen, *op. cit.*, in note 37, p. 5.

46. *Ibid.*, p. 161.

47. Thus, Cohen interprets prostitution – which, as he makes clear, does not carry the sort of stigma current in Western societies, but simply indicates that a woman is a former housewife – as 'an institution which frees women from the ties of their natal homes and renders them mobile within the network [of Hausa communities]. The significance of this institution is not that it has supplied migrant men with sexual pleasures in foreign lands, but that it has been perhaps the most important channel for mobilizing potential housewives for the pioneering communities'. *Purdah*, similarly, is important to the functioning of the network of Hausa communities, as these require that 'women should be completely settled in order to perform the many domestic,

7. Concluding Comments

Terence Ranger

My own work on ethnicity in Africa has fallen into the category described by the contributors to this book as 'constructivist' or 'inventionist'. I think, then, that my closing comment should respond to some of the criticisms made here of constructivism.

It is not necessary for me to rehearse my second thoughts on the 'invention of tradition' in Africa. These have already been fully set out.[1] What I want to do here is to voice some preliminary third thoughts. When I revisited the idea of the invention of tradition I did so because it had become necessary to carry the story forward from the moment of colonial definition of ethnicity. The concept of invention, I thought, was still a useful one since it drew attention to a key moment of paradigm shift in Africa. Nineteenth-century European ideas of race, nation, and tribe, together with missionary language work, colonial administrative requirements, and the ethnographic labours of African catechists and evangelists had combined in many cases literally to invent ethnic identities. However, the subsequent development of such identities and the debate about their meaning was a much more internal process of African imagining.

Third thoughts need to move in the opposite direction, not forwards but backwards from colonial invention. They need to respond to Ronald Atkinson's challenge to take fully into account 'pre-colonial collective identities', and to Thomas Hylland Eriksen's reflection that, if humans have an innate propensity to distinguish outsiders from insiders, then ethnicity may be as universal as age and gender. My good friend Adrian Hastings in his latest book has posed the challenge particularly starkly. For Hastings, ethnicity *is* a universal and the stuff of all small-scale human societies. To deny ethnicity to Africans is to deny them humanity:

> While purportedly anti-colonial in its critical edge [constructionism] is very much a South African academic view of the impact of the West upon Africa because – like so much of traditional white South African culture – its thrust is to deny any significant identity to pre-colonial Africa. Every identity must be found to have been somehow given by Europeans, even ethnic identity....It was surprising to find Terence Ranger, who has spent his academic life defending African initiative, appearing to succumb to a theory which wished to deny Africans even

the ability to provide themselves with the sort of ethnic identity which every people possesses in Europe.[2]

Such a view, says Hastings, is 'shallow and anti-African, an odd mix of Marxism and white racism'.[3]

This is certainly fighting talk. It becomes clear that those who like myself still insist on colonial inventions of ethnicity now have to explore above all the question of pre-colonial identity. To begin with, it seems necessary to spell out something which one might have hoped would be taken for granted. Even under the momentary spell of Marxism and racism I could never have intended to suggest that pre-colonial Africans had no 'collective identities'. That would be manifestly absurd. I have always agreed with Atkinson's contention that historians should not ignore such 'pre-colonial identities'. The question, however, is whether they were *ethnic*.

One of the great strengths of ethnicity as ideology is that once it has been invented and imagined it becomes virtually impossible to imagine any other basis of human association. Ethnicity seems so closely associated with such fundamentals as kinship and language as to appear primordial. Yet, in the history of Europe there are many early examples of collective identities which were manifestly not ethnic. Neal Ascherson's marvellous study of the Black Sea, for example, is in some ways an account of the tragic triumph of ethnic and national identities over earlier, more open and inclusive principles of association and incorporation.[4] Black Sea peoples were members of states and empires and cults and, above all, of cities. Writing to Ascherson to say how much I admired his work, I remarked that what we needed now was a book called *Red Sea*, which brought together in a similar way the flows of migration, religions, and trade between continents and across the sea. Such a book would, for example, provide a secure background to John Markakis' work on nationalism and ethnicity in the Horn of Africa.

To turn Hastings' polemic in upon itself, one might well ask why Africans should be denied the identities of citizen, subject, townsman, believer, *etc.*, which so many people possessed in Europe. Why should Africans be allocated only, or essentially, ethnic identities? And with this question one comes close to the polemical intention of the constructivist or inventionist approach. Its motive was not to deny identity to Africans but to liberate them from the assumption that African identities always have been and still are 'tribal'.[5]

However, even if one looks at pre-colonial Africa with no polemic intention, one can certainly see operating there all the identities which Ascherson describes for the Black Sea zone. There were cities, whose principles of incorporation overrode original kin and 'mother-tongue', and overrode ideas of race and even realities of class. The inhabitants of Mombasa or Lamu, for instance, competed with each other in moieties which grouped together the richest merchant and the poorest slave. The Islamic cities of the East African coast, like the Christian cities of early modern Europe, expressed their identity through the contestations and contradictions of carnival. It was only in the twentieth century that categories like 'Swahili' became ethnic rather than cultural categories.

Rather differently, the major collective identities of pre-colonial 'Yorubaland' were also civic. Whatever similarities of language, religion, and culture might exist over a wide region, the identities of one 'Yoruba' town were asserted primarily against other 'Yoruba' towns. In this, they were similar to Italian city states. And as in Italy, it was only in the nineteenth and twentieth centuries that the idea of an overarching ethno-national identity – 'Italian' or 'Yoruba' – asserted itself.

In Africa, too, people possessed and articulated political identities as members of chieftainships, kingships, or empires. In pre-colonial Zimbabwe, for instance, there existed a broad zone of similar language and cultural and religious practice which today we have come to call 'Shona'. (By doing so, incidentally, we have ironed out the very significant variations and contradictions within this zone). But no-one thought of themselves as Shona. Identities were asserted by one 'Shona' chieftainship against another. Such chieftainships were not communities of kin. There was a constant flow between them of political exiles, skilled warriors or hunters, well-known herbalists or diviners – men who were welcomed as immigrants and bound into the political identity of the polity.

At various moments in pre-colonial Zimbabwean history, moreover, systems of over-rule emerged which historians have come to call 'empires'. Such empires were based on formidable military organisation, wealth in cattle, and the profits of trade. Their culture – forms of religion, language, ceramics, residence, *etc.* – came to exercise a prestige which made other groups want to associate themselves with the imperial identity. Thus, in pre-colonial Zimbabwe words such as 'Karanga' or 'Rozwi' implied self-identification with the empires of Mwene Mutapa or of the Mambo rather than membership of an ethnicity. This often makes it difficult to interpret archaeological findings, since stone-walling and quasi-urban settlement may either imply outlying units of the imperial state or cultural and political emulation, rather as 'Roman' remains in England are often really 'British' remains.

All this was even truer of the triumphant Ndebele state of nineteenth-century western Zimbabwe, where many conquered peoples adopted – or were brought into – 'Ndebele' language, dress, and military organisation. As polemicists for some of the submerged identities in Matabeleland have often pointed out in the twentieth century, if 'Ndebele' were a strictly ethnic word, then only a very small minority of the African inhabitants of Matabeleland could claim it. Yet, nineteenth century European travellers and missionaries recorded local admiration for Ndebele style, and especially for the sophistication and oratorical power of Sindebele language. Many members of the subject peoples were among the crowds which applauded Sindebele poetry or public debate.[6]

In the emerging states of what is now Botswana, there was quite open advocacy of state rather than ethnic identities. In the assemblies of the Bamangwato, for example, Tswana was the compulsory language of debate and judgement. This was justified by Khama the Great or by Tshekedi Khama not on the grounds that 'the Tswana' were the dominant ethnicity. It was justified on the opposite grounds, that Tswana was the language of the state and thus overrode all the submerged languages of the Tswana imperium, allowing for the integration of all its members. In the nineteenth century most subject peoples in Bamangwato accepted this, and their ruling houses gloried in a Tswana imperial identity. With the rise of the ethnic imperative in the twentieth century, however, there were 'Kalanga' challenges to Tshekedi and demands for Kalanga language use and Kalanga chiefly independence. Strikingly enough, the outstanding 'Kalanga' resister – John Nswazi – was descended from immigrants from much further south and had no claim by 'blood' to either Kalanga or Tswana ethnicity.

This mode of self-identification with empire remained strong enough in southern Africa for many members of the new literate mission elites to want to associate themselves with a British Imperial identity after European conquest, rather than with the emerging ethnic and tribal identities. While some catechists and teachers were helping to invent and imagine ethnicity, others were demanding freedom from tribal customary law and equality before the justice of the Empire.

And, of course, there were many examples of primarily religious self-identification in pre-colonial Africa. This has been easier to see with the 'historic' religions of Christianity or Islam. Thus Richard Gray has shown how the principality of Soyo manifested its autonomy from the kingdom of the Kongo by its adherence to Catholic teaching and structures.[7] Both in West and East Africa Islamic brotherhoods constituted a dominant form of pre-colonial collective identity – and in West Africa still assert themselves against attempts to impose ethnic boundaries. By contrast, it is often supposed that African traditional religions were by definition small-scale, face-to-face, ethnic. John Mbiti's best-selling *African Religions and Philosophy* has that title because he asserts that every African tribe/ethnicity has its own particular and constituent religion.[8] But I have myself long waged war upon this view which seems to me to be a reflection of twentieth-century rather than pre-colonial realities.

It seems to me that one can identify in pre-colonial Africa many focal points of religious pilgrimage to which came envoys from a wide region, speaking many different dialects and languages, and crossing the political boundaries of states and empires. Belonging to such a cultic system gave, at the least, another layer or level of identity which at particular times asserted itself against political affiliations. In some ways, the whole point of such pilgrimage centres was that they brought together people from many different linguistic zones. 'God is Language', say the priests of Mwali, the High God of western Zimbabwe, to whom came – and still come – speakers of every Shona dialect, of Venda, of Tswana, of Sotho, and of many other southern African languages. The present scholarly debate on whether the Mwali cult is really Venda or Kalanga or Rozwi is more a reflection of twentieth-century preconceptions than of cult realities. In the Zimbabwean north-west is the rain-medium, Nevana, whose forbears may have been Tonga or Shangwe or Rozwi, and who speaks all those languages and more as he interacts with pilgrims from many different cultural and ecological zones. Just as in Europe confessional identities were expressed in different observations of holy days, so too in western Zimbabwe whether one 'belongs' to Mwali or to Nevana can readily be observed by whether one keeps Mwali's Wednesday rest-day or Nevana's Thursday rest-day. (Nowadays, of course, varying Christian adherences and identities in western Zimbabwe are expressed either in Saturday or Sunday sabbath-keeping. This gives at least four different holy rest-days in the north-western Zimbabwean week).

These examples are of what have been called 'territorial' or 'regional' cults – located centres mainly concerned with rain, fertility, and ecology. However, there are other cultic forms of primary collective identity in pre-colonial Africa. One of the most spectacular of these is the Lemba possession cult of the Congo region, whose power to absorb non-kin into a new network of fictive kinship has been described by John Janzen.[9]

It seems to me, then, pre-colonial collective identities in Africa were richly various. One could certainly apply to pre-colonial Africa Eriksen's warning against 'isolating ethnicity as a focus for research', with the result that 'one easily loses everything else from sight'.[10] I think myself that even in the case of the Acholi, which Atkinson has dealt with much more extensively elsewhere, what he is showing is the development of collective identities but not the development of a specifically *ethnic* identity. I would hazard a guess that as with 'the Shona' or 'the Yoruba', his seventy kingdoms were units of competitive collective identity. I would also hazard a guess that the emergence of a perceived 'Acholi' identity is a later development. In this sense I am still inclined to credit Tim Allen's account of the Madi.[11]

There remain two points to make about pre-colonial Africa. The first is that neither language nor kinship are nearly such straightforward indicators as ethnicity theorists often suppose. But the second is that ethnicity *was* one of the possible ways of conceiving collective identity even in pre-colonial Africa. It just was not the main way.

In many parts of pre-colonial Africa, so it seems to me, the concept of 'the mother-tongue' is a very difficult one to apply. We have already seen that regional cults were systems of linguistic interaction and synthesis. And we have already seen with reference to the Ndebele and Tswana polities, how in large states or 'empires' many languages might be spoken beneath the political dominance of the state language.

Another striking example of this is the kingdom of Bulozi, or Barotseland, in the flood-plain of the upper Zambezi. At the end of the nineteenth century its state language did not derive from any of its long-established peoples but was the speech of a small immigrant minority from the south, the Kololo, which had briefly dominated the Lozi state but which had been overthrown and virtually wiped out in a counter-revolution. To participate in state politics, one needed to be able to speak Kololo; to participate in state religion, one needed to be able to speak Luyana; to participate in long-distance trade, one needed to be able to speak one or other of the languages of eastern Angola; to participate in divination or witch-finding, one needed to be able to speak Mbunda; to make music for the king, one needed to be able to sing in all the languages or dialects of the area over which he ruled. The missionaries and their catechists came speaking Sotho, which was for a time the language of the new Christian identity. To participate in international diplomacy, King Lewanika had to acquire the rudiments of English. The great public ceremonies of the Lozi state drew on all these languages and identities. It was all very different from the current Zambian notion that each 'tribe' – including the subject groups of the Lozi kingdom – has its own language and its own annual festival.

It might be argued that such multi-lingual states were the exceptions in pre-colonial Africa. Yet, bi- or multi-linguism was a feature of 'stateless' systems too. To the north of the Lozi state the peoples of north-western Zambia and eastern Angola constituted a set of inter-related, mobile, and fluid societies. Their members were continually on the move – as traders, as hunters, as miners of salt or copper, as participants in cults, as immigrants to favourable environments. Scattered strongholds of predatory 'nobles' represented a loose political domination, which came to be called 'Lunda'. However, until the twentieth century, identities were diffuse, multiple, unbounded. Only with the classifying influence of missionary language work and colonial administrative necessity did clear-cut identities – and languages – like 'the Luvale' emerge. Nor can one sensibly see the societies of this zone as pre-political, essentially face-to-face, and small scale. The region was a loosely articulated system – and one much more favourable to exchange and production than the bounded tribal units of the colonial political economy. These colonial structures were designed not to make the most of regional economic possibilities but rather to provide a flow of migrant labour for white-controlled enterprises to the south, while at the same time 'maintaining' rural stability. The extraordinary linguistic capacity of the labour-migrants and their command of several different African languages, however, was a legacy of the older and more open system of identities.

As for the idea of kinship, one has to grasp that this was such an important organisational *notion* in pre-colonial Africa that it did not simply represent any sort of primordial reality. Anthropologists have long revealed the extraordinarily varied and socially constructed nature of African kinship systems. More recently, historians have shown the dynamism of these systems and their capacity to change.[12] They have also shown the predominance of 'fictive' kinship.

Kinship was an idea of assimilation rather than a reflection of descent. Igbo or Kalibari 'Houses', made up of African masters and dependent slaves, brought to the coast from many different places in the interior, expressed these relations of seniority and juniority in kinship terms; European observers were astonished at the 'clannish' loyalty of slaves to their 'fathers'. In the West African interior, as Joseph Miller has shown for eastern Angola, 'families' were radically reconstructed during the slaving era.[13] Lords and elders sold young males and bought slave women, surrounding themselves with the loyal children of these alliances. The villages of central Angola – filled with women and children, and with young wives surrounding male elders – clearly were not expressions of the primordial operation of kinship, nor were they bases, as Miller has demonstrated, for the stereotyped ethnic and 'tribal' labels that are in currency in twentieth-century Africa.[14] Long ago, Wyatt MacGaffey showed how in the Lower Kongo family heads claimed a 'traditional' descent from the founding clans of the Kongo kingdom.[15] He also showed that they were very well aware of 'history' rather than 'tradition', and that history was a matter of slave incoporation and descent.

So neither 'mother-tongue' – and what was the mother-tongue with mothers of such varying origins in the West African coastal Houses or in the villages of Central Angola? – nor kin descent operated to give simple ethnic collective identities. Moreover, important as kinship ideology was in pre-colonial Africa, it did not prevent the expression of collective identities which had little to do with ideas of family and descent – those memberships of states and cities and cults which I have already described.

Yet, amidst all this, ethnic identity *was* a pre-colonial possibility. This took two forms: fully developed ethnicity and what might be called latent ethnicity. In my second thoughts, I wrote at some length about the ethnic basis of the pre-colonial Zulu state. I do not need to repeat this here, save to spell out more clearly why the Zulu state can be called 'ethnic' and the Ndebele state not. Ethnicity, it seems to me, is not a given primordial identity but an ideologically asserted one. It depends on the ideological assertion of the centrality of language, and of the superiority of one language, or dialect, to another. This does not merely mean insistence on a language of state – as in the Ndebele, Tswana, and Lozi examples. It means insistence on language as a criterion of membership of the collectivity and on dialect as a criterion of hierarchies of prestige. This was the case in the Zulu state. Ethnicity also depends on the ideological assertion that not only the ruling lineage but also all the people are linked by 'blood'. This was manifestly not true of the Ndebele state, but it was claimed for 'the Zulu'.

So, far from being the most accessible and natural collective identity, asserted ethnicity requires the existence of a powerful ideological elite. Caroline Hamilton and John Wright, for instance, have shown the systematic linguistic and dialectical manipulations of the Shakan state.[16] Hamilton has also shown the role of Zulu oral poetry, as well as of white myth-makers in creating the stereotype of Shaka as superhuman culture hero. And here, I may as well address the criticism that, in my own work on ethnicity in Zimbabwe, I focus too much on elites and not enough on popular culture. The full expression of collective identities, it seems to me, always depends on their articulation by elites and this is just as true of pre-colonial as of colonial Africa.[17]

Fully fledged ethnicity, such as was demonstrated in the Zulu state, required various conditions to develop, the most important being competition for dominance in a system of unequal production and exchange. However, what one might call latent ethnicity could exist in a wide variety of circumstances.

Latent ethnicity is really a retrospective category. I deploy it in order to meet the objection often made against the constructivists that identities cannot just be invented out of nothing. This is a variation of Hastings' indignant repudiation of the notion that Europeans can just come along and invent identities for Africans. Plainly, the idea of ethnicity must have had plausibility, not only for African elites who saw it as a way of creating larger units of self-rule, but also for African populations as a whole. What one can still call the colonial invention of ethnicity was a matter of selecting from among the elements of identity in a situation, and then privileging the elements selected at the expense of others.

Thus, in many African situations very different from that of early nineteenth-century Zululand some elements of later ethnic definition certainly did exist. Many African groupings, for example, were known to themselves and to others by collective names. Often these names were not in any sense ethnic, and related neither to language nor kinship. Many – like Ndebele or Shona – were in fact descriptive (and often insulting) terms imposed by others. Many were indicative of the nature of the territory in which groups lived or of their geographical location – 'mountaineers', 'lowlanders', 'forest-dwellers', 'northerners', *etc.* Others were derived from political identities and came to be applied more generally to asserted cultural collectivities. These

Concluding Comments 141

names were both available to colonial classifiers, who tended to select some names and to discard others, and carried meaning to the people classified.

Similarly, colonial codifiers of African languages did not invent new ones. They selected from among the many languages with which people were familiar. Once selected, given an orthography and used for school and church texts, that particular language became enormously privileged and powerful. People who had once made an almost equal use of a number of languages or dialects now focused on the privileged language of state, school, and church. It was not difficult in such circumstances for the European idea that language in itself determined cultural identity to find parallels in African attachment to the new dominant 'tongue'.

In the same sort of way, even where Africans over a very wide area had been members of a regional cult, there had also existed much more local centres of ecological and ancestral religion. Colonialism, which wanted defined and bounded entities and feared communication over large zones, privileged the small-scale religious forms and sought to repress the regional ones. Some Africans struggled to continue regional observances, but all were familiar with privileged local religion. The same processes operated where African 'empires' failed to get colonial recognition and were replaced by 'tribes'. In Matabeleland, for example, the Rhodesian state refused to allow a paramount or king; it ruled through salaried *indunas*, whose basis of authority was very different from pre-colonial times, but who retained enough in common with regimental commanders and local governors to be recognisable to their people. Everywhere it was a process of transformation by selection.

A situation of pre-colonial latent ethnicity particularly favourable to the later making of tribes was that in which collective identity was largely given by a particular environment. In a recent chapter entitled 'People into Places', Maurice Bloch has described the perceived identity of the Zafimaniry of eastern Madagasgar.[18] The Zafimaniry were defined as people of the forests; negatively, they could not grow rice and sugar cane, like the so-called Betsileo. But the Zafimaniry now have rice fields, as the forests retreat. Bloch writes:

> The Zafimaniry primarily interpret this process of change in ethnic terms. For them, people who live *an patrana* – that is, in the treeless land where irrigated rice cultivation is possible – are Betsileo; and because their own land is becoming *an patrana*, they say that they too are becoming Betsileo. This might seem strange to those unused to Malagasy notions of ethnicity...[which depend] much more on the type of life one leads than on who one's parents were....The Zafimaniry do not seem to mind this de-ethnization, though they find

the process very interesting and are continually talking about it. They neither regret it nor attempt to resist it.[19]

Yet, Malagasy ideas of ethnicity are not so peculiar as all that. Many African 'ethnic' identities originated as collective representations of a 'type of life' rather than of descent. A recent study calls the Meru 'The Mountain People'. In a similar way the Kikuyu were 'Forest Cultivators', the Dorobo were 'Forest Hunters', the Maasai were 'Cattle herders of the Plains' – and individual identities could change as people changed from one of these environments and activities to another. In the nineteenth century, the Kikuyu were not a consciously conceived ethnicity. The multiple origins of those who had come to clear the forests were too recent; the triumph of cultivators over hunters was not yet fully achieved. Yet, their identification with place and type of life made the Kikuyu tribal identity, once it had been adumbrated, one of the easiest to identify with. And the ideas of virtue and power which derived from forest settlement and labour became the ideological inheritance of 'the Kikuyu'.

The colonial invention, in other words, built on much of what was already there. Nevertheless, it *did* represent a profound paradigmatic shift from a situation in which ethnic collective identification existed in rare cases to one in which ethnicities and tribes became the *necessary* form of African identity expression. Thereafter, the imagination of African organic intellectuals gave moral weight to ethnicity.

This book ends with emphasis on the normative function of ideas about ethnicity. Perhaps it is as well for me to spell out in conclusion the normative implications of these third thoughts.

When I first wrote about the colonial invention of tribes the moral that I drew was that Africans did not need to be tribesmen but could construct and participate in other identities, and particularly that of the nation. My second thoughts emphasised the investment of African imagination in ethnicity. The moral drawn was that the most desirable contemporary situation was one in which an open and inclusive ethnicity interacted with a pluralist nation state. The normative moral of these third thoughts is different again.

It seems to me that, just as one can see ethnicity as latent in pre-colonial Africa, so one can see other identities as latent in colonial and post-colonial Africa. In particular, one can see identification with polities, cities, and religions – those great pre-colonial collective realities – as latent and indeed as beginning once again to develop. This is partly a matter of the dogged continuance of such identities under colonialism, and partly a matter of their congruity with post-colonial realities.

Contemporary South Africa can be analysed in many different ways. It can be seen as the 'Rainbow Nation', asserting a civic identity over cultural or linguistic ones. Or emphasis can be placed on the revival of ethnic discourse and of 'traditional' political authorities. But there is yet a third way of looking at South African realities. Some scholars insist that South Africa is essentially made up of great cities – Cape Town, Durban, Johannesburg – and their hinterlands. And indeed such a model can be advanced for many parts of post-colonial Africa where ethnic and territorial boundaries become increasingly irrelevant and rural zones are drawn into the sphere of the often criminal economies of cities.

Rather differently, as Africa becomes more and more urbanised there seems a need for scholarship to move away from studies of rural ethnicity to studies of urban identities. Among other things, this seems likely to give emphasis to the new pentecostal churches, which liberate people from their ancestors and 'traditional' cultures and make them part of a trans-ethnic Christian family.

In many parts of Africa one can see religious affiliation becoming more important than ethnic. In Nigeria, for example, the existence of antagonistic Islamic and Christian blocs is under-studied by comparison to the question of ethnic tension.

In short, it is as dangerous with reference to contemporary Africa as with reference to pre-colonial to focus on ethnicity to the exclusion of all other collective identities. At a time when ethnic conflict seems predominant, other identities, some of them with deep historical roots, may be emerging.

NOTES

1. Terence Ranger, 'The Invention of Tradition Revisisted', in Terence Ranger and Olufemi Vaughan (eds.), *Legitimacy and the State in Twentieth Century Africa* (Basingstoke: St. Antony's/Macmillan, 1993).
2. Adrian Hastings, *The Construction of Nationhood: Ethnicity, Religion and Nationalism* (Cambridge: Cambridge University Press, 1997), pp. 148–9.
3. *Ibid.*, p. 149. Hastings is kind enough to say that I have now repented and 'largely repudiated the claim that African ethnicities were a colonial invention' (p. 149). In fact, such a repudiation is not exactly what my second thoughts are about.
4. Neal Ascherson, *Black Sea* (London: Jonathan Cape, 1995).
5. That this is necessary is evidenced, for example, by Eric Hobsbawm's treatment of Africa in his *Age of Extremes: The Short Twentieth Century, 1914–1991* (London: Michael Joseph, 1994). Nationalism, says Hobsbawm, was an impossibility in Africa since Africans are essentially tribal. One does not have to be an apologist for African nationalism to find this a very odd judgement.
6. Sindebele was itself a 'new' language, a mixture of Nguni and the words and idioms of many conquered peoples. Cultural nationalists in the twentieth century maintained that it bore the same relationship to Zulu which Afrikaans did to Dutch. But administrators, missionaries, and educators tried to bring the Ndebele 'back' to Zulu, as an expression of that particular and prestigious identity.
7. Richard Gray, *Black Christians and White Missionaries* (New Haven, CT: Yale University Press, 1990).

8. John S. Mbiti, *African Religions and Philosophy* (London: Heinemann, 1969).
9. John Janzen, *Lemba, 1650-1930: A Drum of Affliction in Africa and the New World* (New York, NY: Garland Publishers, 1982).
10. Thomas Hylland Eriksen, 'A Non-ethnic State for Africa? A Life-world Approach to the Imagining of Communities', in this volume, p. 46.
11. Tim Allen, 'Ethnicity and Tribalism on the Sudan-Uganda Border', in Katsuyoshi Fukui and John Markakis (eds.), *Ethnicity and Conflict in the Horn of Africa* (London: James Currey/Athens, OH: Ohio University Press, 1994).
12. Gray, for example, has shown how kinship patterns changed in Christian Soyo. See Gray, *op. cit.*, in note 7.
13. Joseph C. Miller, *Way of Death: Merchant Capitalism and the Angolan Slave Trade, 1730–1830* (Madison, WI: University of Wisconsin, 1988).
14. *Ibid.*, pp. 99, 163–7.
15. Wyatt MacGaffey, *Custom and Government in the Lower Congo* (Berkeley and Los Angeles, CA, and London: University of California Press, 1970).
16. John Wright and Caroline Hamilton, 'The Making of the Amalala: Ethnicity, Ideology and Relations of Subordination in a Precolonial Context', *South African Historical Journal* (Vol. 22, November 1990).
17. An excellent demonstration of the role of pre-colonial ideological elites in the articulation of collective identities can be found in the work of Tom McCaskie on the Asante state. See Tom McCaskie, *State and Society in Pre-colonial Asante* (Cambridge: Cambridge University Press, 1995). Obviously, non-ethnic collective identities, such as membership of states, empires, cities, and cults also require articulation by ideological elites.
18. Maurice Bloch, 'People into Places', in Eric Hirsch and Michael O'Hanlon (eds.), *The Anthropology of Landscape* (Oxford: Oxford University Press, 1995), pp. 63–77.
19. *Ibid.*, p. 64.

cultic 136–7
imperial 135–6
political 135
state 136
'type of life' 142
primordialism 3, 22, 83–4, 87
Ranger, T. 4–5, 9–10, 24, 26–7, 32, 117–21
Sharp, J. 18–19
Smith, A.D. 66, 72, 111
Somalia
  nationalist movements 67–8
South Africa
  Afrikaner identity 86, 90
  coloured identity 87–8
Sudan
  nationalist movements 67–8
Taylor, C. 82–3, 87, 105–7
theory
  empirical 102–4
  normative 102–9
transactionalism 110–13
Trapido, S. 24
tribe
  concept of 17–19
Vail, L. 3–5, 20–1, 24–5
van Binsbergen, W. 26
Waller, R. 26
White, L. 26
Wright, J. 25–6
Young, C. 3–6, 21–5

Index

Ahmed, S. 89–90
Allen, T. 33
Ambler, C. 26
Anderson, B. 2–3, 47
Appiah, K.A. 95
Ascherson, N. 134
Atkinson, R. 4–5, 9–10
Banks, M. 112
Barth, F. 6, 18–19, 110–13
Bates, R. 113–17
Berlin, I. 103
Bhabha, H. 81–2, 88–91
Breuilly, J. 66
Butler, J. 85–6
Chanock, M. 117–21
Cohen, A. 17, 113–17
Comaroff, J. 6
Connolly, W. 93
constructivism 1–15, 23, 84–5
Derrida, J. 91
democracy
 multi-national 77–9
 pluriculturalist 52–3
 radical pluralist 92–5
 supra-ethnic 52–3
Eriksen, T.H. 2–3, 10–11
essentialism 59–61
Eritrea
 nationalism and sectarianism 70–1
Ethiopia
 OLF 73
 multi-nationalism and citizenship 77–9
 nation- and state-building 69–70
 TPLF 73–5, 77–9
ethnic conflict
 concept of 76
Fanon, F. 67
Fardon, R. 27
Feierman, S. 121–5
Gellner, E. 66

Gray, R. 136
Hamilton, C. 26
Harries, P. 26
Hastings, A. 133–4
hybridity 88–91
 intentional 90, 92
 organic 90
identification
 process of 84–6
 situational and relational 55–9
Iliffe, J. 24
imagined community 2–4, 47
instrumentalism 3, 5–6, 21–2, 83–4 87, 113–17
inventionism 117–21
life-world 45
Kenya
 nationalist movements 68
Lonsdale, J. 121–5
Markakis, J. 6, 11
Marks, S. 25
Mauritius 50–5
Mbiti, J. 136
methodology
 advocative 108, 126
 interpretive and evaluative 104–8
 positivist 102–4
moral ethnicity 121–5
Newbury, C. 26
Norval, A. 7, 12
O'Brien, J. 27
Papastergiades, N. 81, 90
Papstein, R. 26
pluralisation
 and democracy 92–4
 and hybridity 92–4
pre-colonial identities
 and kinship 137–9
 and language 137–9
 ethnic 28–34, 137–42
 civic 135